ISBN 978-1-934655-32-0

06-018 • COPYRIGHT © 1983 **World Evangelism Press**®
P.O. Box 262550 • Baton Rouge, Louisiana 70826-2550
Website: www.jsm.org • Email: info@jsm.org • (225) 768-7000
13 14 15 16 17 18 19 20 21 22 23 24 25 26 27 28 29 / RRD / 20 19 18 17 16 15 14 13 12 11 10 9 8 7 6 5 4
All rights reserved. Printed and bound in U.S.A.
No part of this publication may be reproduced in any form or by any means
without the publisher's prior written permission.

TABLE OF CONTENTS

CHAPTER   **PAGE**

    INTRODUCTION 7
1. CHAPTER 1 – The Holy Spirit In The Godhead 9
2. CHAPTER 2 – The Holy Spirit In Creation 35
3. CHAPTER 3 – The Holy Spirit In The Old Testament 43
4. CHAPTER 4 – The Holy Spirit In The Life Of Christ 61
5. CHAPTER 5 – The Holy Spirit In The Early Church 75
6. CHAPTER 6 – The Holy Spirit In The Believer 97
7. CHAPTER 7 – The Gifts Of The Spirit 121
8. APPENDIX 'A' – Bible References Pertaining To The Baptism With The Holy Spirit 173
9. APPENDIX 'B' – How To Receive The Baptism With The Holy Spirit 175

The Holy Spirit
From Genesis To Revelation

The Cross Of Christ Series

THE HOLY SPIRIT – *From Genesis To Revelation*

INTRODUCTION

The greatest thing in life is to know God. Knowing Him can be joy unspeakable and glory beyond expression. We know God through Jesus Christ, our Lord and Redeemer. The Holy Spirit (the Comforter Whom Jesus sent) is the One Who convicts of sin and gently leads us to our Lord and reveals Him.

To know and understand more about God (our Father), Jesus Christ (His Son and our Lord), and the Holy Spirit (the Comforter) is life's most precious pursuit. There is so much that God through His great Love and Grace has provided for us. Those who hunger and thirst for the things of God will truly receive.

Many books have been written on the Holy Spirit. The subject is one of vital significance for every Believer. This study on the Holy Spirit is designed to help you understand more fully what His Work is and how you can have a fuller, more wonderful, and victorious life in Christ. Great things are available to us from God. We need to desire and receive all that He has for us.

Chapter 1

The Holy Spirit In The Godhead

SUBJECT	PAGE
BASIC CONCEPTS	11
TERMINOLOGY	13
CHARACTERISTICS AND ATTRIBUTES	14
NAMES OF THE HOLY SPIRIT	18
SYMBOLS OF THE HOLY SPIRIT	27
CONCLUSION	34

CHAPTER ONE

THE HOLY SPIRIT IN THE GODHEAD

"But God has revealed them unto us by His Spirit: for the Spirit searches all things, yes, the deep things of God" (I Cor. 2:10).

"Where shall I go from Your Spirit? Or where shall I flee from Your Presence?" (Ps. 139:7).

BASIC CONCEPTS

The Holy Spirit is talked about as much as any member of the Godhead today, yet the question must be raised — just exactly Who (or what) is the Holy Spirit? A proper understanding of the *Person* of the Holy Spirit is absolutely essential if we are to be the kind of Christians we should be. Unfortunately, there is much confusion at best, and downright error at worst, concerning the exact definition of this third Person of the *"Trinity,"* the *"Triune God,"* or the *"Godhead."* (All three terms will be discussed a little further on.)

It might be well to begin with, to state first what the Holy Spirit is *not*. The Holy Spirit is not a *"thing"* or an *"it."* He is neither a material nor ethereal *substance*, nor an impersonal force, or energy (such as electricity, radiation, or magnetism). He is not a *quality* (of goodness, love, morality, or something of this nature). The Holy Spirit is not a fuzzy, *abstract* idea. He is not a *"universal mind"* nor some kind of vague *"life-giving force."*

And since He is none of these things, just Who and what *is* the Holy Spirit?

First, the Holy Spirit is a *Person*, a real Being Who thinks, acts, wills, feels, loves, and speaks. The Holy Spirit exhibits all the responses that identify one as a *"person."* He cannot be seen by the natural eye, but His actions fulfill all the requirements of a Personality.

In Acts 13:2 it says, *"The Holy Spirit said, Separate **Me** Barnabas and Saul for the work whereunto **I** have called them."*

As the Holy Spirit referred to Himself here, He used the pronouns *"I"* and *"me."* These words identify a Person and not some abstract idea.

The Holy Spirit is a Person, but *He is also a Deity!* He is the Third Person of the Godhead — the Trinity. This does not mean that the Holy Spirit is one-third God, nor one-third *of* God. God cannot be divided.

Neither does this mean that He is one of *three* Gods. God is One God (Deut. 6:4), yet He is eternally self-existing in three distinct Persons: the Father, the Son, and the Holy Spirit. Each of these Persons is fully God,

SELF-HELP STUDY NOTES

SELF-HELP STUDY NOTES

yet each is an individual Person within Himself. Jesus is God, the Father is God, and the Holy Spirit is God.

Because we are working with our *human* minds, it is extremely difficult for us to try to picture three individuals in perfect agreement and harmony. If any three of us (humans) tried to accomplish something, we would be a *committee*. We would argue and debate and finally vote on matters, with the majority ruling — or all three compromising on some middle ground. The Godhead doesn't work this way.

Because all three members of the Godhead are *God*, which infers infinite knowledge, infinite love, infinite mercy, and infinite justice, all three are always and eternally in complete agreement on *everything*. There is always one *perfect* solution to anything — whether or not we (as humans) can see this perfect solution. But God is Omniscient (all-knowing) and thus always knows this perfect way for anything. It is therefore possible for all three Beings to be in *perfect* unity at *all* times — if those three persons all have infinite (unrestricted and unending) knowledge.

This then is why it is possible to have *"three members in one,"* which is what the words *"Triune," "Trinity,"* and *"Godhead"* describe. It is *three individual Persons* — each with His own Personality, Awareness, and Mission — occupying the *position* of God.

The closest analogy we might make in today's social structures (and it is admittedly a *poor* analogy) would be the *"juntas"* which rule some countries. These are *groups* of men (often military men) who jointly act as the *leadership* of those countries. The *junta* rules the nation, although there is more than one *co-equal* person comprising the junta. Now corrupt, flawed, inadequate politicians or generals are a poor parallel to the Triune God. They argue and bicker and often plot the overthrow of one another — and in so doing, demonstrate the difference between men and God.

The three Persons of the Godhead, on the other hand, never argue or debate. Each One *knows*, at all times — even before things happen — what *should* be done and what *will* be done. They, therefore, don't even have to *discuss* matters. Each knows — before, during, and after — what should and what will happen. The *final* result, as we know, will be *"God's will."* Everything happens for good to those who love the Lord (Rom. 8:28), and thus the three Persons who constitute God agree together *always* — never debating, never voting, and never disagreeing.

All three members of the Trinity are equal in omniscience (knowledge of *everything*) and thus have three Minds that act as One. They are a *unity*. And the Holy Spirit possesses all the attributes that both God the Father and God the Son possesses.

The story of Ananias and Sapphira is told in Acts 5:3-4. *"But Peter said, Ananias, why has Satan filled your heart to lie to the Holy Spirit?"* And then just a sentence or two later he states, *"You have not lied unto men, but unto God."* This confirms that the Holy Spirit is God because Scripture here states that when Ananias lied to the Holy Spirit, he was simultaneously lying to God.

Numerous Scriptures could be cited to demonstrate that the Holy Spirit is a *Person* of the Godhead. In Matthew 28:19, Jesus said, *"Go ye therefore, and teach all nations, baptizing them in the Name of the Father, and of the Son, and of the Holy Spirit."*

In John 4:24 it is written, *"God is a Spirit: and they who worship Him must worship Him in spirit and in truth."*

Another Scripture linking the Spirit with God is to be found in II Corinthians 3:17. *"Now the Lord is that Spirit: and where the Spirit of the Lord is, there is Liberty."*

Many times the Bible will state in one place that God said certain things, and then in another place it will say that it was the Holy Spirit Who said them. This is neither incorrect nor a contradiction. It is completely correct because the Holy Spirit *is* God.

For example, Exodus 17:7 says that Israel tempted the Lord. (The word translated *"Lord"* here is Jehovah, or God.) This is referred to again in Hebrews 3:9 where Paul states that they tempted the *Holy Spirit*.

Again, in Jeremiah 31:33, it says that Jehovah gave a promise concerning the New Covenant. The writer to the Hebrews referred back to this and said that it was the Holy Spirit Who spoke this promise (Heb. 10:15). So it is apparent within Scripture that the Holy Spirit is God — a member of the Godhead. There are several different incidents in the Bible which could be mentioned to further reinforce this conclusion.

TERMINOLOGY

It is a bit confusing to some people to hear the term *"Holy Spirit"* used, while at other times the term is *"Holy Ghost."* There is really no difference. *"Holy Spirit"* and *"Holy Ghost"* mean exactly the same thing.

In Saint John 7:37-38 we read, *"Jesus stood and cried, saying, If any man thirst, let him come unto Me, and drink. He who believes on Me, as the Scripture has said, out of his belly shall flow rivers of Living Water."*

Then the Thirty-ninth Verse goes on to explain, *"(But this spoke He of the Spirit, which they who believe on Him should receive: for the Holy Spirit was not yet given; because that Jesus was not yet glorified.)"*

In this Scripture, both *"Spirit"* and *"Ghost"* are used — with both referring to the same Divine Person. In the original manuscript, the Greek

SELF-HELP STUDY NOTES

SELF-HELP STUDY NOTES

word used for *"Spirit"* and *"Ghost"* was *pneuma*, which literally means *"breath"* or *"breeze,"* but which *came* to be used for a *"spirit"* or *"ghost"* which *could* make a candle flame flutter, or leaves rustle.

What it boils down to is that the third Person of the Trinity was referred to by the Apostles as *"God's Pneuma"* which *could* be translated as *"the Breath of God," "The Essence of God," "God's Spirit,"* or the Holy Spirit or Holy Ghost. We (because the King James translators chose to use the two terms *"Holy Spirit"* and *"Holy Ghost"*) are most familiar with these two terms. They can be used interchangeably.

The expression *"ghost"* is an old English word, and its meaning has changed a bit since King James ordered his great translation. Today when one says *"ghost,"* one usually thinks of haunted houses and disembodied spirits floating around causing terror. Today ghosts are invariably evil. Originally, however, the word *"ghost"* did not have this meaning or connotation. The term *"Holy Ghost"* was perfectly in keeping with the beautiful poetic language of the King James Version. In modern usage, the word or term most commonly preferred is *"Holy Spirit,"* and this is always proper. *Either* term is correct and acceptable, however, for they are both found in God's Word.

CHARACTERISTICS AND ATTRIBUTES

INDIVISIBLE — The Holy Spirit is God indivisible. In Ephesians 4:4-6 it says, *"There is one body, and one Spirit, even as you are called in one hope of your calling; One Lord, one Faith, one Baptism, One God and Father of all, Who is above all, and through all, and in you all."* However, John, in Revelation, relating his vision, speaks of *seven* Spirits of God (Rev. 1:4; 3:1; 4:5, and 5:6).

John was caught up in a vision and saw Heaven, the Throne, God, Jesus Christ, and the Holy Spirit. John also saw the Elders, the Angels, and events that were to take place in the future. And during all this, he refers to the *seven* Spirits.

The word *"Spirits"* is capitalized, meaning the Holy Spirit. Of course, in the original Greek manuscript inspired by the Holy Spirit and written by John, this word would not have been capitalized because capital letters were not used until centuries later. Capitalization of certain words, punctuation, and division of Scripture into Chapter and Verse were all additions made by men translating the original documents for King James. These were all done to make study of the Bible easier for ordinary men and women so everyone could read God's Word directly.

The number seven, however, need not be confusing. In Bible terminology and typology the word *"seven"* means completion or perfection.

Seven is said to be *"God's number."* Therefore, this does not necessarily mean that John saw seven Holy Spirits, but rather a total, complete, and perfect Spirit.

We read in Revelation 5:6, *"And I beheld, and, lo . . . in the midst of the Elders, stood a Lamb as it had been slain, having seven horns and seven eyes, which are the Seven Spirits of God sent forth into all the Earth."*

Jesus is, naturally, the Lamb in this Scripture, and the Spirit of God is there with (or upon) the Lord Jesus Christ. The Holy Spirit aided Jesus Christ in all the Work which He did. Of course, the Holy Spirit *is* God, Jesus is God, and God the Father is God.

UNITED BUT DISTINCT — They are all of one purpose, one design, and one desire. They are one in fulfillment of the duties pertaining to the Godhead, yet there are certain statements that can be made for *each* that don't apply for *all*. Jesus is the Son of the Father. He is not the Father of the Son, so you cannot say that Jesus is the Father, while you *can* say that Jesus is the Son. Conversely, the Father is not the Son, but Jesus *is* the Son. The Holy Spirit proceeds from both the Father and the Son, while neither the Father nor the Son proceed from the Holy Spirit.

In referring to the Holy Spirit, Jesus Himself said that if you say a word against Him it will not be forgiven. Jesus pointed out that you could say something against the Heavenly Father, or even the Lord Himself, and it could be forgiven (if one asks for forgiveness). But He stressed that blasphemous utterances against the Holy Spirit would *not* be forgiven. So there is a difference even in what can be said to each, or about each.

Jesus was on Earth when He came to redeem man. God the Father did not come to Earth to redeem man, (sending Jesus to accomplish this task), and the Holy Spirit was not present on Earth at that time. The Holy Spirit was only sent to be man's Comforter *after* Jesus departed to sit at the Right Hand of the Father.

The Holy Spirit is now present upon this Earth, while God the Father and Jesus are in Heaven. Jesus sits at the Right Hand of the Father — and the Father does not, of course, sit at the Right Hand of Jesus. We know that there is an omnipresent factor in the locations of the three members of the Trinity, but still these specific differences should be noted. While there are differences in description, the Holy Spirit is, nevertheless, totally God.

ETERNAL — The Holy Spirit is eternal, just as God is eternal. This means that He always was, is now, and ever shall be. He had no beginnings and He will have no end. In Hebrews 9:14 it states, *"Christ, Who through the **Eternal Spirit** offered Himself"* which confirms that the Holy Spirit is eternal.

SELF-HELP STUDY NOTES

SELF-HELP STUDY NOTES

OMNIPRESENT — The Holy Spirit is omnipresent (just *one* of the "omni" attributes of the Godhead). This means that He is present everywhere at once. The Holy Spirit has *all* the omni-attributes of the Godhead. The Psalmist declares in Psalms 139:7-10, *"Where shall I go from Your Spirit? Or where shall I flee from Your Presence? If I ascend up into Heaven, You are there: If I take the wings of the morning, and dwell in the uttermost parts of the sea; Even there shall Your Hand lead me, and Your Right Hand shall hold me."*

It is impossible to escape the Presence of the Spirit of God for He is everywhere. A sinner under conviction might move from the community in which he was first touched by the Spirit of God, thinking he can escape Him. But even changing a particular environment, a set of circumstances, a church, or preacher, he will be unable to rid his heart of the feeling of conviction. Wherever that person flees, he will not escape the Holy Spirit. Wherever the sinner goes, the Holy Spirit will be there awaiting his arrival, faithfully reproving of sin and pointing the soul toward Jesus Christ.

OMNISCIENT — Another of the omni-attributes is omniscience, which means that the Holy Spirit is all-knowing and all-wise. His wisdom cannot be increased because He already knows *all* things. A question asked in Isaiah 40:13-14: *"Who has directed the Spirit of the Lord, or being His counselor has taught Him? With whom took He counsel, and who instructed Him, and taught Him in the path of Judgment, and taught Him in Knowledge, and showed to Him the Way of Understanding?"* Of course, the answer to all these questions is obvious. *Nobody* directs, counsels, or teaches the Holy Spirit.

The Holy Spirit is the Teacher. As God, He is perfect in Knowledge and Understanding. A declaration is made in I Corinthians 2:10-11 that the deep things of God are always open to the Holy Spirit. He knows everything that God the Father knows. *"The Spirit searches all things, yes, the deep things of God."* The deepest limits of knowledge are an open book to the Holy Spirit.

OMNIPOTENT — Not only is the Holy Spirit omnipresent and omniscient, He is also omnipotent — or all-powerful. It is impossible for Him to be more powerful. Another question is asked, in Micah 2:7: *"Is the Spirit of the Lord straitened?"* Now this word *"straitened"* (in the King James Version) means *"narrowed."* It suggests being limited or restricted. The text literally asks, *"Is the Spirit of the Lord restricted?"* The answer, of course, is *"no."* The Holy Spirit can *not* be restricted, He is all-powerful. His Power is seen both in the Creation, and in His Work in the world today.

Someone might then ask, *"Well, why doesn't He do something about the problems existing in the world?"*

He *could* do anything He wanted, of course, but there is the factor of mercy here — mercy mixed with compassion and love. You see, when the Holy Spirit *does* finally intrude to bring forth God's Righteous Kingdom on Earth, all problems *will* be Divinely removed. But at that moment, everyone's *"second chance"* will have been lost. The mercy involved in this means that judgment is currently being withheld. Compassion and love enter in because the sinner is being given the opportunity for Salvation and Redemption from sin *before* God finally intervenes.

There is a time when judgment *will* come, evil *will* be punished, and the orders of God the Father eternally established *throughout* Creation. Then the orders of God *will* be carried out (His Will be done) — with eternal punishment for those who have not responded to God's Mercy and Love. The Great Tribulation is coming when the Holy Spirit will resolutely carry out the orders of God the Father, and God's Wrath will be poured out upon this Earth.

Even evil isn't immediately stopped and punished (and the power of the Holy Spirit immediately demonstrated), the Holy Spirit *is* omnipotent. He is referred to as *"the Power of the Highest"* in Luke 1:35. In other words, He is power personified. He is fully God — and through Him the Power of the entire Godhead is fully expressed. It is God's desire that every Believer be *"tapped in"* to this power. This precious promise is presented in Acts 1:8: *"But you shall receive power, after that the Holy Spirit is come upon you: and you shall be witnesses unto Me both in Jerusalem, and in all Judea, and in Samaria, and unto the uttermost part of the Earth."*

Enduement with power by the Holy Spirit in the life of the Christian is very important. Immersion (baptism) in the Holy Spirit *gives* one power. It is not to *"get one ready for Heaven"*; because, as we know, a person is saved by *Grace*, through Faith in Christ — with the Holy Spirit bringing conviction. But one of the main purposes — one of the primary reasons for the Holy Spirit's very existence — is to give Christians the *power* to live Godly lives. Holy Spirit Power is the actual *essence* of Christian living.

The promise in Acts 1:8 says we *shall* receive power (the Greek word is *dunamis* — the word from which we derive our word *"dynamite."* He gives dynamic, *dynamite* to the Christian for victorious living.

It is actually impossible for the Christian to be *fully* empowered by God without being baptized with the Holy Spirit. It is impossible for a church to have the Spiritual Growth it should without the Power of the Holy Spirit. And it is impossible for a preacher to be what *he* might be without the infusion of Holy Spirit Power.

The Power of the Holy Spirit is *essential* for dynamic Christian living.

SELF-HELP STUDY NOTES

SELF-HELP STUDY NOTES

NAMES OF THE HOLY SPIRIT

DESCRIBING HIS PERSON — Names are important. As a matter of fact, in Biblical times, a person's name had a special and unique meaning. Reference is made to *"The Spirit"* in I Corinthians 2:10. He is not a unit, quality, or entity — but a Person, a Personality, an Individual. He is *pneuma*, or Spirit. He is called the Holy Spirit in Luke 11:13: *"If you then, being evil, know how to give good gifts unto your children: how much more shall your Heavenly Father give the Holy Spirit to them who ask Him?"*

He is the one and only Holy Spirit who sanctifies and purifies. Holiness is a characteristic of God, and we are to be holy also. The Holy Spirit is also referred to as the Eternal Spirit in Hebrews 9:14. He has been with the Father *always* — from even before the dimmest beginnings of time.

THE SPIRIT OF GOD — Several names reveal this relationship to God. He is called the Spirit of God. I Corinthians 3:16 asks, *"Know you not that you are the Temple of God, and that the **Spirit of God** dwells in you?"*

In Isaiah 61, the Holy Spirit is referred to as the Spirit of the *"Lord Jehovah"* (Jehovah refers to the *covenant-keeping* God).

Another name used to demonstrate the Spirit's relationship to Deity is the *Spirit of the Living God* used in II Corinthians 3:3. Here Paul was writing to the people of Corinth which housed over twenty temples dedicated to various pagan gods. Paul was pointing out that our God is *alive*, in contrast to the pagan gods of those temples.

THE SPIRIT OF HIS SON — The relationship of the Spirit to Jesus Christ is shown by a number of expressions. First there is the term *"Spirit of Christ"* as used in Romans 8:9. We are not in the flesh but in the Spirit, which is sent *"in the Name of"* Christ. That is, the Spirit sent *by* Christ.

The Holy Spirit's activity in no way contradicts or conflicts with the Message or Mission of Christ. Every act of the Spirit in the Church is to *glorify* Christ. One's activities *must* glorify Christ or they are *not* in the Spirit.

He is further referred to as the *Spirit of His Son* in Galatians 4:6 and as the *Spirit of Jesus* in Philippians 1:19. There are many Scriptures which refer to the Spirit of Jesus Christ. Certain ones of that era accepted Jesus, and others accepted Christ, but some did not accept *both*. Jesus means *"Saviour"* and Christ means *"Anointed One."* Of course, Jesus is *both* the Saviour *and* the Anointed One.

THE SPIRIT OF JUDGMENT — The Holy Spirit is referred to by many names and expressions, among them The Spirit of Judgment and also The Spirit of Burning. Of course, the Holy Spirit is intimately involved in the matter of justice, law, and order. He also works in the area of purging, consuming, and purifying — all results of burning within a fire.

Hence the more or less parallel terms *"Spirit of Burning"* and *"Spirit of Judgment."*

The Holy Spirit will not tolerate sin, for He is naturally Holy. It may be said that He is *"the moral policeman of the universe."* He is chief agent of the *"Justice Department"* of God's Kingdom. He is eternally committed to exposing sin and evil wherever they exist. He reproves sin and does His best to turn people from it. The Word of God tells us, in Isaiah 4:4, *"When the Lord shall have washed away the filth of the daughters of Zion, and shall have purged the blood of Jerusalem from the midst thereof by the Spirit of Judgment, and by the Spirit of Burning."*

It is also stated, in Isaiah 28:5-6, *"In that day shall the Lord of Hosts be for a crown of glory, and for a diadem of beauty, unto the residue of His people. And for a Spirit of Judgment to him that sits in judgment, and for strength to them who turn the battle to the gate."* So, two of the names or terms used with reference to the Holy Spirit are the Spirit of Judgment and the Spirit of Burning.

The reference of burning reminds us of the words of John the Baptist who spoke concerning Jesus saying, *"He shall Baptize you with the Holy Spirit, and with fire"* (Mat. 3:11). The Holy Spirit burns out the dross in a person's life. Impurities are revealed and removed as the Holy Spirit brings conviction and judgment. A person responds and is cleansed by the Blood of Jesus Christ. The Spirit of God works to convict individuals of sin, righteousness, and judgment.

SPIRIT OF GRACE AND OF SUPPLICATIONS — The Spirit of God is also called the Spirit of Grace and of Supplications. He is God's Communications Officer, carrying to the soul of man the Divine Invitation to come. The Word of God tells us in Revelation 22:17, *"And the Spirit and the bride say, Come . . . And let him that is athirst come. And whosoever will, let him take the Water of Life freely."*

The Holy Spirit is indeed the Spirit of Grace and of Supplications. In Zechariah 12:10 we read, *"And I will pour upon the house of David, and upon the inhabitants of Jerusalem, the Spirit of Grace and of Supplications."*

It is stated, in the warning in Hebrews 10:29, *"Of how much sorer punishment, suppose ye, shall he be thought worthy, who has trodden under foot the Son of God, and has counted the Blood of the Covenant, wherewith he was Sanctified, an unholy thing, and has done despite unto the Spirit of Grace?"*

Grace is the unmerited, the undeserved, Love and Favor of God. We do not *deserve* the things of God, but because of Grace we can be recipients of His Blessings. The Spirit of Grace brings us the Love, the Mercy, and the Grace of the Lord Jesus Christ.

SELF-HELP STUDY NOTES

SELF-HELP STUDY NOTES

How marvelous and precious is the Grace of God! I remember years ago preaching a church meeting in one of our eastern states. We stayed there for several weeks and God gave us a great moving of the Holy Spirit. Hundreds of people filled the auditorium night after night.

I noticed one particular lady in the services. She was a senior citizen, a very stately and dignified woman — and very lovely for her age. She was obviously one of the Godliest women I had ever met. My spirit instantly bore witness with her spirit. I never had the opportunity to talk with her very much, but I couldn't help but notice her demeanor — the way she entered into the service. The way she participated in the worship was a blessing to behold.

There was something that just poured out of her in the realm of the Spirit. She was a real support for me as I preached, sang, and ministered to the people.

This particular church was a real *"praying"* church, and she never missed a prayer meeting. One day as I was talking with the pastor, she was standing some distance away. The pastor said to me, *"I guess you've noticed that lady."*

I answered, *"Yes, I have."*

He said, *"She is one of the Godliest people I have ever had the privilege of knowing."* I nodded in agreement.

"I wish," he said, *"that I had a thousand more just like her. She is a prayer warrior. She is the kind who has a beautiful spirit. She never sinks to faultfinding. She is always constructive — never destructive."*

As he spoke of her sweet spirit and help, I told the pastor that she was also a great help to me as I preached each night. She hadn't commented on the message or said anything particular, but her spirit could be felt there, encouraging and strengthening me.

Then the pastor told me about this beautiful lady who was the epitome of holiness and perfection in the Lord Jesus Christ. He told me she had once been a prostitute. In fact, she had *run* a house of ill fame with other prostitutes working for her. She had been mired in a sordid life that can hardly be *imagined* by the average Christian. But there she stood now, characterized by the pastor as one of the greatest Christians he knew. Only the Grace of God could have accomplished the complete transformation she represented.

Because of the mighty moving of the Spirit of Grace in our meetings across the country, we see drunkards saved, drug addicts delivered, and lives turned from crime to Christ. People are being saved from the vilest, rankest pits of sin — and all because of the Spirit of Grace.

He is the bringer of mercy, delivering the wayward to Christ, drawing them to their Saviour. The Holy Spirit is indeed the Spirit of Grace. My own heart has been touched, moved, and kept by the Spirit of Grace.

SPIRIT OF WISDOM AND KNOWLEDGE — The Holy Spirit is also called the Spirit of Wisdom, in Revelation. He is called the Spirit of Understanding, the Spirit of Counsel and Might, the Spirit of Knowledge, and Fear of the Lord. He reveals, He illuminates, and He gives Spiritual Insights. He also gives direction and awakens reverence in the hearts of men. It says in Exodus 28:3, *"And you shall speak unto all who are wise-hearted, whom I have filled with the Spirit of Wisdom."*

In Deuteronomy 34:9 we read, *"And Joshua the son of Nun was full of the Spirit of Wisdom; for Moses had laid his hands upon him."*

A number of facts about the Spirit of the Lord are revealed in Isaiah 11:2: *"And the Spirit of the Lord shall rest upon Him, the Spirit of Wisdom and Understanding, the Spirit of Counsel and Might, the Spirit of Knowledge and of the Fear of the Lord."*

The promise of Ephesians 1:17 is, *"That the God of our Lord Jesus Christ, the Father of Glory, may give unto you the Spirit of Wisdom and Revelation in the knowledge of Him."*

All knowledge is wrapped up in the Spirit of God — the Holy Spirit — for He is the One who imparts wisdom, and knowledge. The Spirit of God will guide us to Truth, Wisdom, and Knowledge.

A person may go through academic studies in Bible Schools or seminaries without believing much about the Bible, the atoning Work of Jesus Christ, His miraculous Birth, His Life, or His atoning Death. There are many with impressive academic credentials in religious activity who do not believe many of the fundamentals of Spiritual Faith. Such knowledge comes from man, from structured theological thinking, from books written by individuals who are not inspired or led by the Holy Spirit. It is essential to read books only by those who are full of the Holy Spirit, Spirit-filled and Spirit-led. Let the Holy Spirit be your Teacher.

THE SPIRIT OF COUNSEL — The Holy Spirit will guide the earnest seeker of truth into Divine Truth and Understanding. We must be taught by the Spirit and led by the Spirit — by His Wisdom, His Knowledge, His Understanding, and His Counsel. The Holy Spirit is the Spirit of Counsel and Might (Isa. 11:2).

There are very few days that I do not go before the Lord and ask *specifically* for His Counsel. I long ago learned the secret of asking God's Divine Counsel, because the Holy Spirit *is* the Counselor. We have to listen to our heart and spirit as the Holy Spirit speaks to our spirit.

He doesn't speak primarily to our physical senses or to our human mind, but to our spirit. If you will listen with *your* spirit to the *Holy* Spirit, He will guide and lead you, giving you counsel, knowledge, understanding, and guidance in the affairs of your life. The Lord will give you understanding

SELF-HELP STUDY NOTES

SELF-HELP STUDY NOTES

in areas too difficult for you to understand within your own powers. The Holy Spirit is truly the Spirit of Understanding, Counsel, Revelation, Wisdom, Knowledge, and Truth.

SPIRIT OF THE FATHER — He is called the Spirit of the Father. We read in Matthew 10:20, *"For it is not you who speaks, but the Spirit of your Father which speaks in you."* This refers to the Holy Spirit — the member of the Godhead who is referred to as the Spirit of the Father.

SPIRIT OF TRUTH — The Holy Spirit is also the Spirit of Truth, and there is no error in Him. As the Holy Spirit leads and guides into a knowledge of truth, it is never contrary to the Word of God, for there is never any variation between the Spirit and the Word. As previously discussed, the Mind of the Godhead is always in perfect agreement, never in conflict. Ephesians 6:17 states that the Word of God is the *"sword of the Spirit."* Actually, the Holy Spirit is the Divine *Author* of the Bible. The Prophets of old spoke *as they were moved by the Holy Spirit.* II Timothy 3:16 tells us that *all* Scripture is given by the Inspiration of God. So the Holy Spirit will never contradict or deviate from His Own Word. The Bible is always the basis for any leading of the Holy Spirit. Whenever you are led by the Spirit, you will never be led contrary to the Word of God.

There are some major denominations and preachers who disbelieve certain statements made in the Word of God: that Jesus is the Son of God, that the Bible is Holy and infallible, that Jesus was born of the virgin Mary, and that He died and rose again the third day. Many doubt the *miracles* of the Bible, that God can heal the sick, and that He can do wonders in answer to prayer.

Those who have been baptized (or *immersed*) in the Holy Spirit *know* that the Bible is God's Word and that God performs miracles. They know that the sick can be healed, that Jesus was raised from the dead, and that He's coming back for His people. There may be differences on *minor* points, but people who are led by the Spirit of God believe the fundamental Truths of God's Word as the Spirit of Truth (the Holy Spirit) guides them.

It is imperative that we be led by the Spirit of Truth in order to avoid being led astray. Jesus said in John 14:16-17, *"And I will pray the Father, and He shall give you another Comforter, that He may abide with you forever; Even the Spirit of Truth; Whom the world cannot receive, because it sees Him not, neither knows Him: but you know Him; for He dwells with you, and shall be in you."*

You will never be in error when you follow the leading of the Holy Spirit, for He is the Spirit of Truth. He is referred to as *the Comforter, even the Spirit of Truth,* in John 15:26: *"But when the Comforter is come, Whom I will send unto you from the Father, even the Spirit of Truth, which proceeds from the Father, He shall testify of Me."*

SELF-HELP STUDY NOTES

The Holy Spirit, the Spirit of Truth, will guide a person into all Truth: as promised in John 16:13. *"Howbeit when He, the Spirit of Truth, is come, He will guide you into all Truth: for He shall not speak of Himself; but whatsoever He shall hear, that shall He speak: and He will show you things to come."*

Then in I John 4:2 and 6 we read, *"Hereby know ye the Spirit of God: he who knows God hears us; he who is not of God hears not us. Hereby know we the Spirit of Truth, and the spirit of error."* It is the Spirit that bears witness, because the Spirit *is* Truth. One needs to be baptized in the Holy Spirit and in fire, otherwise he will inevitably fall into error. But having the Spirit of Truth operating fully within one's life, one can be confident that he will be guided by Truth.

There is another aspect to the term *"Spirit of Truth."* The Hebrew word for truth is one of activity — correct action. God is identified in the Old Testament as *"the God who did things for Israel."* He brought them out of bondage and led them into the Promise Land. He is the God of Action — the God who acts.

SPIRIT OF HOLINESS — Another name for the Holy Spirit is the Spirit of Holiness. This expression is used in Romans 1:4. *"And declared to be the Son of God with power, according to the Spirit of Holiness, by the Resurrection from the dead."* The word *"holiness"* is significant and beautiful here. God is Holy, and Believers are to be holy (Lev. 19:2.) An emphasis on Holy is vitally important.

There are groups who concentrate on acting as *"holiness movements."* Now there's nothing wrong, fundamentally, in this. But, tragically, some of these movements become overly legalistic. Legalism and a dedication to often-distorted ideas of holiness can lead to a *hindering* of the movement of the Holy Spirit. There is a tendency to *legislate* conformity, particularly in the matter of outward appearance, and a demand for adherence to specific outward aspects. While there are, of course, actions a Christian should avoid, being holy is not primarily a question of what we *aren't*, or what we *don't do*.

Holiness is a *positive* matter, grained as one draws nearer to God. We should be transformed by the Power of the Holy Spirit. Holiness is related to the idea of Sanctification — which involves the separating of an individual unto God. This drawing near to God results in an individual developing an inner beauty — the beauty of holiness — and is a transforming process produced only by the Holy Spirit.

Holiness is not a rigid set of rules or standards to be imposed on individuals or groups. Often, pharisaical attitudes have developed by those who see holiness as a set of restrictions to which they, and all others, must conform as a *demonstration* of holiness. God knows our hearts, and if we

SELF-HELP STUDY NOTES

are developing holiness He is well aware of it *without* any outward display. True biblical holiness gives one a sweet, pleasant spirit and a new liberty and freedom in the Spirit. This stands out in marked contrast to the bitter, faultfinding, critical attitude so often demonstrated as the hallmark of condescending, pharisaical, religious snobbery (II Cor. 3:17).

Holiness produces a beautiful spirit and provides one with the qualities that are truly the *"beauty of holiness."* In this Spirit there is the possibility of true worship — as well as a true and authentic demonstration, and reflection of some of the most significant aspects of one's relationship to God.

THE SPIRIT OF LIFE — The Holy Spirit is the Spirit of Life. In Romans 8:2 it is written, *"For the Law of the Spirit of Life in Christ Jesus has made me free from the Law of Sin and Death."*

The Law of the Spirit of Life is sorely needed today! Nothing is more boring, lifeless, and depressing than a dead church service. Without the Spirit of Life (the Holy Spirit with His life-giving, dynamic Power), a church service can be the ultimate expression of *boredom!*

Spiritual matters are exciting! Want to discuss something exciting? What about Redemption, the Christian life, Heaven! Heaven is phenomenal. It is awesome, tremendous, and indescribable — the eternal abode of every Child of God. We are talking about an eternal future that is going to be *beautiful!* It is so exciting that it stirs the deepest emotions as one thinks about the sheer splendor of the glory awaiting us.

The Lord Jesus Christ provided for our Redemption at Calvary nearly two thousand years ago. The Gospel is the Good News — the *greatest* news — and it is *exciting!* Church services shouldn't be dead, they should be one of the most pleasant experiences in the life of a Christian. But are they? Unfortunately, not always. Not all churches allow God's Holy Spirit to run their services. The presence of the Holy Spirit should be a part of every church service because He is the Spirit of Life. The Holy Spirit is, in fact, life personified.

SPIRIT OF ADOPTION — Another of the Holy Spirit's Names is the Spirit of Adoption. We are told in Romans 8:15, *"For you have not received the spirit of bondage again to fear; but you have received the Spirit of Adoption, whereby we cry, Abba, Father."* There is great significance in this statement. Jesus is the only begotten Son of God. Through Him (and *only* through Him) can we become God's Sons, as we are adopted into the Family of God.

"For all have sinned, and come short of the Glory of God" (Rom. 3:23). True, but through Christ, provision has been made for the Holy Spirit to reconcile us to God again. Sin separates us *from* God, but Jesus' shed Blood provides forgiveness for our sins and a cleansing for our hearts. The sin barrier is utterly removed and we are reconciled to God. Sin stains

are eradicated by His cleansing Blood. This is another activity of the Holy Spirit — and through the Spirit of Adoption we become children of the King, members of the Family of God.

SPIRIT OF PROMISE — On the Day of Pentecost, the Believers were assembled together, waiting for the promise of the Father, the promise of the Holy Spirit (Acts 2:1-4 and 2:33) as we prophesied in the Old Testament in Joel 2:28. This was a promise that the Spirit should be for all flesh and is a precious promise indeed.

We are told in Ephesians 1:13, *"After that you believed, you were sealed with that Holy Spirit of Promise."* Documents received a stamp, or seal of approval, upon them. Special, important papers have this seal as a certification of their genuineness. In New Testament times, this seal represented ownership. Believers are sealed by the Holy Spirit. Once they are sealed, they no longer belong to the Devil. They become the property of God.

Since we belong to God, once we become God's property (by trusting and accepting Jesus as our Lord and Master) the Holy Spirit bears witness in our spirit that *"we are the children of God"* (Rom. 8:16). Paul goes on to state that if we *are* His Children, then we are *"heirs of God, and joint-heirs with Christ"* (Rom. 8:17).

When a person becomes an heir — it means that someone has died. Christ died for us, and we are saved to become heirs. Even if others might try, they won't convince you that you *aren't* an heir. The Spirit bears witness with your spirit and you *know* what you are.

THE SPIRIT OF HIS MOUTH — This may sound like a strange name or designation for the Holy Spirit. However, in II Thessalonians 2:8 it says, *"And then shall that Wicked be revealed, whom the Lord shall consume with the Spirit of His Mouth."*

The declarations of God are powerful, and what He says is always significant. His Word is likened to the sword of the Spirit of Hebrews 4:12. In the combination of His Word and the Power of the Holy Spirit, we see a consuming force. As God's Word came, the Holy Spirit moved upon the Apostles and Prophets of old to write the Word of God.

Knowledge and Inspiration of Divine Truth and Messages of God are conveyed by the Holy Spirit. What God says is important, and what a Christian says under the Anointing of the Holy Spirit is also important. What one confesses and says is of great significance.

SPIRIT OF FAITH — Faith is basic and absolutely essential to the life of a Christian. Faith is necessary for Salvation, and it is also essential for day-to-day Christian living. *"The just shall live by Faith"* (Rom. 1:17).

Once again, God's moving in the heart of the Believer is through the Holy Spirit, and the Holy Spirit is the Spirit of Faith. According to the

SELF-HELP STUDY NOTES

SELF-HELP STUDY NOTES

words of II Corinthians 4:13, *"We having the same Spirit of Faith, according as it is written, I believed, and therefore have I spoken; we also believe, and therefore speak."*

The Holy Spirit is the Spirit of Faith assuring us of the *certainty* of what we believe. This gives us boldness to confess the Truth with conviction. It is really difficult to exercise faith, to understand faith, or to put faith to work — without the Power of the Holy Spirit. *"So then Faith comes by hearing, and hearing by the Word of God"* (Rom. 10:17).

One builds Faith by reading and studying the Word of God, and by applying it within his life. This comes about through the action of the Holy Spirit. Without the baptism with the Holy Spirit, an individual is limited in his development. He is handicapped in his exercise of faith because the infilling of the Holy Spirit *builds* Faith.

The mere study and memorization of Scripture will not, of itself, ensure faith. It is possible to have the letter without the Spirit. The Bible says, *"The letter kills, but the Spirit gives life"* (II Cor. 3:6). The Holy Spirit enables the individual to put the Word of God to *work*. The Spirit of Faith will move in the life of the Believer, who will then grow in his Knowledge of God's Word. At this point, he will be able to *exercise* genuine Faith and begin to see the Power of God at work.

Faith comes to an individual from God, but it is the Holy Spirit (the third Person of the Godhead) who moves in on the life of the Believer (as the Spirit of Faith) to produce glorious results.

THE SPIRIT OF GLORY AND OF GOD — Yet another name for the Holy Spirit is found in I Peter 4:14: *"If you be reproached for the Name of Christ, happy are you; for the Spirit of Glory and of God rests upon you."*

The Holy Spirit is the Spirit of Glory and the Spirit of God. He is a Part of the Godhead, and He rests upon us and preserves our joy — even when we are reproached (rejected by the world) for the Name of Christ.

Sometimes — especially when Satan works to hinder the Move of God and the Blessings of God in a person's life — there is a flood of God's Glory and Joy that wells up like a river. This is the Holy Spirit moving upon an individual. It is difficult to describe the Presence of God's Glory, but anyone who has experienced it does not require a description. It is that overwhelming joy and serenity that floods us — by the Holy Spirit — in the midst of dire threats, dangers, and difficulties. It is wonderful to experience this feeling of envelopment by the Holy Spirit — the Spirit of Glory and of God.

THE COMFORTER — The Holy Spirit is the Comforter. Jesus made a precious promise to His followers, *"And I will pray the Father, and He shall give you another Comforter"* (Jn. 14:16).

The word translated *"comforter"* is from the Greek word *parakletos*. *Para* means *"alongside of"* and *kaletos* is from *kaleo* which means *"to call."* The basic meaning refers to someone who is summoned — called to one's side. In the broad sense, a paraclete is someone who pleads another's case before a judge. He is a defense counsel, a legal aid, an advocate, a spokesman, an intercessor.

Jesus said He would send the Holy Spirit to be our Comforter; to be with us, to instruct us, and be our source of aid and assistance. We read in John 16:25, *"These things have I spoken unto you in Proverbs: but the time comes, when I shall no more speak unto you in Proverbs, but I shall show you plainly of the Father."*

The Holy Spirit always reveals and promotes Jesus. For the person who is truly baptized with the Holy Spirit, there is greater and more glorious revelation and understanding of God the Father and God the Son. The Holy Spirit also encourages, comforts, strengthens, and helps us.

MANY NAMES — There are other names and expressions used to identify the Holy Spirit which give insight into His Nature and Function. These all relate to the Work of the Holy Spirit as a Part of the Trinity. The Holy Spirit has many names and designations. He is called (in Luke 1:35) the Power of the Highest. In other places: the Holy Spirit, the Spirit of Judgment, the Spirit of Burning, the Spirit of Grace, the Spirit of Understanding, the Spirit of Wisdom and Revelation, the Spirit of Counsel and Might, the Spirit of Knowledge, and the Spirit of Truth. He is called the Spirit of Holiness, the Spirit of Life, the Spirit of Adoption, the Spirit of His Mouth, the Spirit of Faith, and the Spirit of Glory and of God. The Holy Spirit is a Comforter, the one who is our paraclete. He is the Power of the Highest and the Eternal Spirit. These names identify the Holy Spirit and also relate to God, for the Holy Spirit *is* the third Person of the Trinity.

SYMBOLS OF THE HOLY SPIRIT

PURPOSE OF SYMBOLS — There are several symbols used in Scripture for the Holy Spirit. These are important, but it must be remembered that symbols are *not* the Holy Spirit. These are types, suggestions, or representations of the Holy Spirit. They are like a Parable, compared to a clear, concise, *factual* account of something. They are like a logo or a trademark that brings a company to mind. These *are not* the company; they *represent* the company.

Sometimes, for some people, a type or symbol can be a substitute for the real thing. The symbols representing the Holy Spirit are not mystical, nor are they objects of worship. Types and symbols are not intended to become the underpinning of bizarre religious exercises or ritualism. Their

SELF-HELP STUDY NOTES

SELF-HELP STUDY NOTES

purpose is simply to illustrate, to point to something else (namely, the Holy Spirit in this case). Symbols are for the purpose of illuminating and giving new insight and understanding. They are not to obscure, nor to become a substitute, replacing that which they symbolize.

OIL — Oil is a type of the Holy Spirit in Scripture. There are numerous Old Testament uses of oil which relate to the things of God and the Work of the Holy Spirit. When the Israelite priests were consecrated to their office, oil was poured over their heads (Ex. 29:7, 29-30; Lev. 8). We read in Psalm 133:2, *"It is like the precious ointment upon the head, that ran down upon the beard, even Aaron's beard: that went down to the skirts of his garments."* It appears that oil was used so abundantly that it ran down the beard and saturated the priest's robes as they were ordained into the great priestly office.

When a king was chosen in Israel, he was also anointed with oil. After Saul failed God and a new king was to be found, the Spirit of God came to Samuel and sent him to the house of Jesse. The sons of Jesse were assembled — strong, powerful, robust young men — but the Spirit of God revealed to Samuel that none of those present was meant to be king.

Samuel was perplexed and asked Jesse, *Is this all of your sons?*

Jesse informed him that there was one other son, but he was just a lad who tended the sheep. Samuel told him to bring the young man. David came, and the Spirit of God revealed to Samuel that he was the one.

God looks on the heart, for at that time David looked an unlikely prospect. Still, he was God's choice. Samuel took his horn of oil and poured it on David's head, and the oil flowed over his face and garments. Of course, this doesn't mean that today we have to be anointed with a pint or quart of oil in order to have the Presence and Power of the Holy Spirit.

When Jesus completed His Redemptive Work and ascended to the Father, He sent the Holy Spirit, Who came in a new and unique way as He descended on the Believers on the Day of Pentecost. Since that time, people have been able to experience the *baptism* with the Holy Spirit. As the Holy Spirit *immerses* an individual in His Presence, there is something that flows through the heart — just as the oil flowed down over David's head, saturating his hair, face, and garments. We can be *saturated* with God's Love as we are baptized with the Holy Spirit.

In Exodus 27:20, oil is described as the fuel for the lamp in the Holy Place — a lamp that was to burn eternally. The lamp itself, as well as the oil it contained, was also a type of the Holy Spirit. This lamp was never to go out, but due to the failure of the chosen priests (representing all of Israel) it did. Samuel was getting old, and he speaks of the lamp going out because the high priest neglected the duties of the Temple. This actually represented the *spiritual* darkening overtaking the land of Israel.

And there are other references to oil. Mark 6:13 tells us that we are to anoint the sick with oil. And James 5:14 also says to anoint with oil and pray for the sick. This emphasis on oil is intended to teach us that the Holy Spirit is totally involved in the Spiritual Life of the Believer in Christ. We are kings and priests under God, and we are to minister. Oil is a beautiful and appropriate symbol for the Holy Spirit because it penetrates, permeates, saturates, soothes, moistens, protects, and lubricates. Notably, one of the most widely recognized properties of oil is its ability to eliminate friction and abrasion.

Oil also purges and cleanses, and if burned its energy radiates light and warmth. Some kinds of oil are edible and have great nutritional value. The Psalmist spoke of being anointed with oil is Psalm 23:5 *"You anoint My head with oil."* Oil is a type, and a beautiful symbol, of the Holy Spirit.

THE DOVE — Another appropriate symbol of the Holy Spirit is the dove. The account in Luke 3:22 mentions the Spirit descending upon Jesus in the form of a dove. There are several excellent reasons why God would use a dove to represent the Holy Spirit. The Holy Spirit's influence and workings are always gentle — which is a bit in contrast to the methods of God the Son. When Jesus came to die on Calvary, neither sinners, devils, nor all the hordes of Hell could stop Him. He died on Calvary, whether they liked it or not. God the Father determines the workings of this world. The seasons come and go, and many things are determined by God that atheists, devils, and demons cannot alter.

The Work of the Holy Spirit, on the other hand, is often quite different. He is either hindered or helped by our reaction to His Leadings. When antagonistic or negative attitudes exist, the Holy Spirit will not remain. There is no great outburst, no clap of thunder, but the *Presence* of the Holy Spirit is no longer felt. The Holy Spirit is gentle like a dove. One must walk softly and quietly before God the Holy Spirit.

God has spoken this to my own heart and spirit, as He has said to me, *"I want you to walk **softly** before me."* God then went on to impress me that because I am somewhat high spirited, I must concentrate particularly on learning to walk softly before Him.

It is not difficult to feel the pressure of responsibility and to respond in a bombastic manner. Such pressure can cause one to lose one's patience and temper. But we should all learn to walk softly and quietly in the Presence of the Holy Spirit.

In His own sweet, quiet way, the Holy Spirit will gently nudge us when we fail to be restrained — as He desires us to be. The Holy Spirit points out our impatience and other faults that can quench the Spirit. If one's spirit is charged up, overactive or abrasive, it will stop the Holy Spirit from moving on him. The Holy Spirit doesn't react with a physical body or brain, but

SELF-HELP STUDY NOTES

SELF-HELP STUDY NOTES

rather with one's spirit. The Holy Spirit is as gentle as a dove, and this is why God used that beautiful symbol when Jesus was baptized.

LIVING WATER — Jesus likened the fullness of the Spirit in the Believer to *"rivers of living water"* (Jn. 7:37-39). For the individual who is truly filled with the Holy Spirit, Jesus said that out of his innermost being, *"out of his belly shall flow rivers of Living Water."*

In Isaiah 44:3 God said, *"For I will pour water upon him who is thirsty, and floods upon the dry ground: I will pour My Spirit upon your seed, and My blessing upon your offspring."*

It is God's Promise and desire to *"pour out of His Spirit."* As used in Joel 2:28 and Acts 2:17, the term *"pour out of His Spirit"* suggests an outflowing, an overflowing, an inflowing — as of a river breaking loose from its banks. One reason Jesus used water as a symbol of the Holy Spirit is because water brings life. It refreshes, cleans, and purifies.

Water is one of the basic requirements of life. The human body consists of a large percentage of water; we must have it for a healthy physical life. The Holy Spirit is likened to water because just as the body needs water, *our* spirit needs the *Holy* Spirit.

When the fullness of the Holy Spirit is within us, there will be a flow of His Presence out through us, touching and refreshing others. When the Word of God flows in a service, under the Anointing of the Holy Spirit, it can be like a mighty river. What blessings are experienced as the Holy Spirit moves!

There are services where people by the hundreds — without invitation, without urging, without physiological gimmicks — spontaneously get out of their seats weeping, crying, responding to God as the Spirit moves. I have seen this many times when, like a miracle river, the Power and Presence of the Holy Spirit flowed through a service.

In my own spirit, I have watched the Holy Spirit flow like a river. If your church is dry, get the river flowing through it — the river of the Holy Spirit. If your messages are dry, get the river of God flowing through them. People will come where the refreshing waters flow. Some preachers are trying to row a boat in a dry riverbed and then wonder what's wrong.

You *need* a river. Find where the river is and leap in. Where you find the Spirit of God moving, that's where you'll find the divine refreshment flowing. And thus it is that the Holy Spirit is likened to living waters or a flowing river.

It is so tragic that some not only have rejected, but *opposed*, the mighty outpouring of the Holy Spirit. Entering into the reality of this Divine refreshing, one can sing with the writer of the song, *"It's real, it's real, I know it's real. Thank God, the doubts are settled and I know, I know it's real."*

I have known individuals who were thirsty for the living waters, but who were hindered and deterred *before* they came to the refreshing experience of the Holy Spirit — finally being baptized or immersed in Him only after a long and agonizing search. They will tell you that no price is too great if it finally gets you to where you can receive the fullness of God's Blessings through His Holy Spirit.

In our old-fashioned, Holy Spirit, campmeeting services, the Power of God *falls*. And people by the hundreds and even thousands worship God with uplifted hands, tears rolling down their faces, and ecstatic joy filling their hearts. This type of old-fashioned campmeeting is not fanaticism. It is worship of the Lord Jesus Christ in Power and Truth. It's an expression of Holy Spirit Power. And believe me, His Power is real!

A story is told of a man who experienced this wonderful reality. It was many years ago (perhaps well over forty) when this well-educated and dignified gentleman felt a deepening desire to receive the mighty infilling of the Holy Spirit. He wanted this mighty river within him, but he could not seem to receive. His wife and family members received, but doubts continued to thwart his ability to just *"let go and let God."*

He had many questions, and there seemed to be something blocking him. Of course, the *basic* problem was Satan doing everything he could to hinder this man from coming into the fullness of the Holy Spirit experience.

This brother knew, somehow deep inside his heart, that it *was* real, so he would not be deterred. After months of searching, hungry for God, thirsting for the living waters, and with people around him telling him how wonderful it was, he still had not been able to experience it for himself.

He finally heard of some precious black brothers and sisters across town in the eastern city where he lived. And he heard of a couple of black sisters in that church whom God was using in a wonderful way as His instruments in praying people through to the Baptism. He told his mother that he wanted to go there, and they rode a streetcar all the way across town.

They found the little church, walked in, and sat down. Before too long the pastor left the platform and came back to where they were sitting. *"What can we do for you?"* he asked. You see, he didn't really know why they had come, because in those days very few whites sought out the churches of black *"Pentecostals."*

They told the pastor that they had heard of many people being baptized with the Holy Spirit in this small church, and that certain black sisters were known to be instrumental in praying for people to receive the Holy Spirit. The pastor said, *"Well, that's right, and they are here tonight."*

The gentleman who had come to the church said, *"That is why I have come. I am hungry for the Holy Spirit. I want to be filled with the Holy Spirit. Will you pray for me?"* The black preacher said, *"Yes sir,*

SELF-HELP STUDY NOTES

SELF-HELP STUDY NOTES

we will." And pray they did — with uplifted hands, worshiping God, and with tears rolling down their faces.

Time went by and it was getting close to midnight and the last streetcar-run. His mother asked him if he had received yet, but he hadn't. She said, *"If we don't go soon, we will miss the streetcar, and we have a long way to go."*

The man had apparently tried everything. He was dejected, discouraged, and grieving inside but he obviously couldn't stay the night. He had been on his knees at the altar, and he got to his feet and thanked the brothers and sisters involved. They were sorry, too, that he had not received. In fact, they were more than sorry, they were heartbroken.

As he and his mother walked to the trolley stop, he reflected that he had done everything he knew to do. *"I have pleaded, cried, and wept. I have prayed and I don't know what more I can do."* Of course, his mother didn't know what to tell him.

They arrived at the trolley stop, and suddenly, as she looked at him, it was like his face was aglow in the moonlight. The streetcar was approaching and his last words in English, as she started to step onto the trolley were, *"Mama, get on the car and go, but I'm not coming along. I suddenly feel it. Praise God, I feel it coming."*

As she got on the streetcar, leaving him there, those were the last words in English he was to speak that night. Because as the mother departed, her son raised his hands toward the heavens and started speaking in other tongues as the Spirit gave the utterance.

Eventually he walked home, completely across town. It took the better part of the night, and all the way he was speaking in tongues as the joy of the Lord permeated his soul.

Later on he wrote that song I just quoted: *"It's real, it's real, I know it's real. Thank God, the doubts are settled and I know, I know it's real."*

Yes, it *is* real. Thousands of lives have been transformed from the mundane to the miraculous, from being dry and dead to refreshed and resurrected. It is more than a refreshing flow, it is *life restoring*. The Holy Spirit is indeed like a river of Living Waters.

WIND — Another symbol of the Holy Spirit is wind. In Acts 2:2 it is stated, *"And suddenly there came a sound from Heaven as of a rushing mighty wind, and it filled all the house where they were sitting."*

In John 3:8 we read, *"The wind blows where it listeth, and you hear the sound thereof, but cannot tell from where it comes, and whither it goes: so is every one who is born of the Spirit."*

The Holy Spirit — like a wind — can be gentle as it blows, bringing refreshing coolness. We had a crusade once in an outdoor stadium in Florida on a Sunday afternoon in late spring. The sun was baking down at

2:30 P.M. and it was *hot*.

Even in the morning as the men were setting up the equipment they remarked that the heat was rising from the platform and burning their feet through their shoes. We knew it was going to be difficult for the people to sit on the concrete risers without anything covering their heads to dissipate the sun's heat. So we asked the Lord for clouds to cover the sun, and clouds soon appeared to do just that, not too long after the equipment was arranged.

But as I said, even with the cloud cover, it was still hot when the crowd arrived and the service started around 2:30 P.M. So we asked the Lord for a gentle breeze — and very shortly a gentle breeze began. This was an amazing answer to prayer, and our gentle wind refreshed the crowd as it blew across the stadium. It was a beautiful time.

The Lord likened the wind to the Holy Spirit, and used it as a symbol. The wind can be gentle, but it can also be strong — *awesomely* strong. Despite what we just said about the meekness and the gentleness of the Holy Spirit, there are times when the Holy Spirit can move in might and strength as well.

The Holy Spirit *can* do mighty and powerful things on behalf of those who are His. The Holy Spirit can be powerful as well as gentle, so it doesn't pay to oppose Him. Tragic things have occurred to those who have tried to oppose the mighty move of the Spirit of God. In addition to oil, the dove, and water, wind is also a symbol of the Holy Spirit.

FIRE — God's Word presents yet another symbol of the Holy Spirit in Matthew 3:11. Here John the Baptist says, *"He shall baptize you with the Holy Spirit, and with fire."* When the Spirit descended on the Day of Pentecost, there was not only the sound of wind, but also tongues of fire.

It is stated in Acts 2:3, *"And there appeared unto them cloven tongues like as of fire, and it sat upon each of them."* Fire is used to illustrate some of the activity and Power of God. Hebrews 12:29 states, *"For our God is a consuming fire."* So fire is another symbol of the Holy Spirit.

Fire refines and can change materials from one form to another. To make a beautiful piece of machinery or equipment from steel, fire must be used to melt the metal so it can be changed to a usable form. Heat it used to soften it so it can be molded or hammered or pressed into shape. Fire can consume an item — to all intents and purposes removing that item from existence. And it can change the appearance of an object, purify it, warm it, light it, or cleanse it. There are many reasons why fire is an excellent type of the Holy Spirit. Each of the actions mentioned is, in fact, typical of *Holy Spirit* action on people. But always remember, the types of the Holy Spirit are not themselves the Holy Spirit, but illustrations or symbols revealing

SELF-HELP STUDY NOTES

SELF-HELP STUDY NOTES

something of the Nature, Function, Approach, or Activities of the Holy Spirit.

CONCLUSION

The many characteristics, names, and symbols for the Holy Spirit reveal much of His nature and activities. There is an intrinsic relationship to God the Father and God the Son. The Holy Spirit is one member of the Godhead, or the Trinity — the Third Member. The Holy Spirit does the Work of God. Jesus said He would return to the Father and send the Holy Spirit. The Holy Spirit reveals Jesus and the ways of God as He moves in the hearts and lives of Believers. The Holy Spirit moves in mighty and marvelous ways to accomplish the purposes of God.

Chapter 2

The Holy Spirit In Creation

SUBJECT	PAGE
THE EARTH WAS VOID	37
CREATIVE POWER	38
FROM CHAOS TO BEAUTY	39
"LET US"	42

CHAPTER TWO

THE HOLY SPIRIT IN CREATION

"In the beginning God created the Heaven and the Earth. And the Earth was without form, and void; and darkness was upon the face of the deep. And the Spirit of God moved upon the face of the waters" (Gen. 1:1-2).

"You send forth Your Spirit, they are created: and You renew the face of the Earth" (Ps. 104:30).

SELF-HELP STUDY NOTES

THE EARTH WAS VOID

The Bible introduces us to the Holy Spirit at the very beginning of the Bible, in the First Chapter of Genesis. The first sentence states that God created the Heaven and the Earth. The second says that the Earth was without form or void, and with darkness upon the face of the deep. And then the third sentence tells us that the *Spirit of God* moved upon the face of the waters.

Somewhere in the dim eons of the past (whether millions, billions, or even trillions of years), God created the Heaven and the Earth. When God creates something, it is invariably good. The six days of *re*creation are referred to in Genesis 1:31, where it says, *"And God saw every thing that He had made, and, behold, it was very good."* No doubt the *original* Creation, which God also made, was very good too.

A part of God's Creation involved Angels — including the great and mighty archangel, Lucifer. However, this *"super-angel"* was lifted up in his own pride, which caused his fall. And *when* he fell, he drew approximately one-third of the angels with him — which caused great chaos in Heaven and upon the Earth.

Many Bible scholars feel that Lucifer was actually the ruler of this world — in the eons of the past. This, of course, was long before Adam and Eve, and long before the chaotic conditions that subsequently developed. Lucifer was beautiful and righteous, and he carefully followed the Lord. Ezekiel 28:12 tells us that he *"seals up the sum."* This means that nothing more could conceivably be added to enhance his perfection.

He had everything associated with greatness. When describing him, nothing more could be said. He was probably the greatest (and most powerful) archangel ever created by God and the Lord Jesus Christ. But he fell, and *when* he fell, utter chaos ensued.

In the Second Verse of the opening Chapter of Genesis, we see that the

SELF-HELP STUDY NOTES

world was void, covered by water, and a totally desolate place. Between the First and Second Verses of Genesis, the Earth *became* void and without form. Many students of Scripture feel that an immense time-gap exists between these two Verses.

It appears that an entire story is left untold, and little information is given to explain just how this created Universe became *"without form and void."* Certainly God did not create it that way, but it may well have come about due to Satan's fall. The Bible states that darkness was upon the deep (Gen. 1:2), and we know that God is not associated with darkness (I Thess. 5:5). It is Satan who delights in darkness. He is the originator of sin, which destroys, injures, and kills. Sin and darkness dwell together, and one causes the other. Wherever there is one, there is the other. They inevitably coexist.

CREATIVE POWER

Now God had a twofold plan. He decided not only to create man, but to make this world a habitable place for him. He would do this *through* Jesus Christ, *by* the Holy Spirit.

Picture the world in its calamitous condition, with nothing but darkness everywhere. Water covered the entire face of the Planet. It was a dead world, totally without life. There weren't even any fish in the seas; God *later* created the fish (Gen. 1:20).

The Holy Spirit is not simply some *"general power"* surrounding the Earth. Instead of having little power, the very opposite is true. While personally meek, the Holy Spirit knows no bounds when exercising the Power of God. The Holy Spirit is actually dynamo, the generator, the Power Source of the Godhead.

We read in Acts 1:8, *"But you shall receive **power**, after that the Holy Spirit is come upon you."* The Power the Holy Spirit can give us as individuals is limited, of course, for He could never turn over His full Power to the fallible hand of man. The Power of the Holy Spirit is an explosive power, a great and mighty power, while at the same time a gentle power. The Holy Spirit Power is particularly needed today to overcome the powers of darkness — the powers of Hell.

Salvation is brought by Jesus Christ. It was bought and paid for at Calvary when Jesus died — and also as He rose again. He redeems us from the Law of Sin and Death — when we are Born-Again. But the Holy Spirit is the One Who gives *power* for the kind of life we should be living.

The Holy Spirit Power was involved in Creation throughout the creative and *re*creative process. The Holy Spirit moved upon the face of this chaotic world to put into effect the creative Word of God, through Jesus

Christ. He carried out the organizing process — assembling, structuring, and intricately balancing all the elements that composed the oceans. He sorted them out and put them in place, carrying out the directives of the Son of God.

Through the Work of the Holy Spirit, continents and mountains began to appear as the oceans sought their proper places. The waters went to one place and the dry lands came to another. That is power — and that is the Holy Spirit at work.

In Job 26:13 it says, *"By His Spirit He has garnished the Heavens."*

It is stated in Job 33:4, *"The Spirit of God has made me, and the breath of the Almighty has given me life."*

In Psalms 104:30 it states, *"You send forth Your Spirit, they are created: and You renew the face of the Earth."* This refers to what the Holy Spirit did. God gave the orders — and, of course, Jesus Christ is also involved in this ordering. After this, though, it was the Holy Spirit who did the actual *"nuts and bolts"* Work of restoring order to the world and to the Universe.

The Holy Spirit was the *"construction foreman"* on this great Work of redevelopment and recreation. It was no problem for the Holy Spirit — the very Spirit of God — to bring the dry land out of chaos or to cause the waters to recede. He thus made this Earth a fit place of habitation for man. But it is easier to control the elements of nature than to move the stubborn will of man.

Jesus had no trouble whatsoever calming the storm in the Sea of Galilee. He said, *"Peace be still,"* and that was the end of it. But when it came to His Disciples, the Pharisees, or the judges and people of Israel — so *many* with whom He had contact — there was *much* difficulty. The reason man is so difficult to work with is because God had given him a free will. He doesn't *have* to obey God as the natural forces do. God never *forces* His Will upon man. He made man a free moral agent, and He never violates the freedom of will *He* guaranteed.

If a man is to be changed, it must be by Divine persuasion, and then by human response. The Holy Spirit moves on man, encourages him, persuades, and speaks to him — but it is man who must do the deciding. Satan comes with force and pressure and enslaves people, while God *never* works this way. Satan puts people into bondage as he forces, binds, and destroys them. Such action is totally opposite to that of the Holy Spirit.

FROM CHAOS TO BEAUTY

When working on the process of recreating the things of the Earth, the Holy Spirit easily transformed the world to a thing of beauty, wonderfully fit

SELF-HELP STUDY NOTES

SELF-HELP STUDY NOTES

for the habitation of man. The Holy Spirit hovered over the waters as today we might see a tern inspecting his oceanic domain. It is not surprising that one of the symbols of the Holy Spirit, as used in the Word of God, is the dove. The personality of the dove illustrates the gentle ministrations of the Spirit.

Originally, as stated in Genesis 1:1, *"God created the Heaven and the Earth."* They were made perfect and without flaw right from the first. But this refers back to the dateless past, or the *beginning* of the creative ages (Job 38; Ps. 8:3-8; 19:1-6; Prov. 8:22-31; Jn. 1:3; Acts 17:24-26; Col. 1:15-18; Heb. 1:1-2, 10-13; Rev. 4:11). It is important that we realize that the six days of Creation described in Genesis 1:3 through 2:25 are not the *original* Creation of the Heavens and the Earth.

FIRST DAY — As the Spirit of God moved upon the face of the waters, He separated them. *"And God said, Let there be light: and there was light"* (Gen. 1:3).

Undoubtedly, light had once existed upon the Earth, but the consequence of sin is darkness. The Earth, therefore, became enveloped in darkness for some indeterminate period. But God now allowed the light to shine through, and divided the light and the darkness, calling them day and night.

This refers to the evening and morning of the first day, with light coming into existence again. However, the sun and other luminaries are not mentioned until the fourth day. The event described for the first day is basically the restoration of the light to the Earth, as it was when Lucifer ruled it before sin brought total darkness (Gen. 1:2; Jer. 4:23-26).

And now God gave the command, *"Let there be light,"* and there *was* light (Gen. 1:3-5). The word *"let"* is used in the sense of *permitting* light to be present. It is as if one were to say, *"Turn on the light."* This word *"let"* does not primarily denote Creation, but rather indicates that the judgment of God upon the Earth is beginning to cease. Now the sun, moon, and stars will be allowed to shine again on the darkened Planet. This, of course, was God's original creative purpose.

Reference is made to the luminaries on the fourth day, but the light existing on days one, two, and three came from this same source. The fourth day reference marks the permanent *regulation* of the Solar System as related to the restored Earth. Light and darkness were distinctly marked off into evening and morning, the tilt of the Earth's axis was established for seasons, and, in short, the celestial controls on our Earth's meteorological systems were regulated.

SECOND DAY — The work of this day has to do with the restoration of the clouds (here called the firmament) to again hold the waters that had inundated the Earth. This second-day action was not so much a *creation* of clouds, but a restoration of them to their original creative purpose.

THIRD DAY — Vegetation was once again restored to the Earth. It had grown profusely on the Earth before the calamity and flood resulting from the fall of Lucifer. It was no doubt during the first Creation that the awesome amounts of vegetation were laid down and buried deep in the Earth's crust, which today supply the Earth with its oil supplies.

"In the beginning God created the Heaven and the Earth." Some reputable scholars feel this might better be read, *"the Heaven and the dry land."* In Genesis 1:2, it is apparent that the dry land is restored with vegetation growing upon it. This vegetation was to sustain life on the restored Earth. The flood was possibly of extreme duration, and all life forms and seeds had been destroyed. Therefore, this *creation* of vegetation was necessary and was accomplished by the Creative Power of the Spirit of God.

This flood was unquestionably much longer than Noah's flood, which came later when man was again destroyed because of his sinfulness. Only righteous Noah and his family were spared. After the flood of Noah's time, vegetation again sprouted up spontaneously (with no further need for God's creative intervention).

FOURTH DAY — It is stated that the sun, the moon, and the stars were created on this day (Gen. 1:14-19). But *light* had been present for the previous three days, and had even been divided into day and night. Here it is the *order* of the plants and their effects upon the Earth that was arranged. The seasons and the meteorological changes associated with them were determined for the newly restored Earth.

FIFTH DAY — On the fifth day there was the creation and formation of new sea life and fowls. Each of these individual creations was to subsequently bring forth *"after his own kind."* (God's Word does not agree with Darwin's theory that one life form will develop into another.)

SIXTH DAY — On the sixth day, land animals and man were created (Gen. 1:24-31). New land animals (and man) were created to replace the animals and the inhabitants of the first system — which were destroyed in the disastrous fall of Lucifer and the angels. In Chapter Two, Genesis gives a more *detailed* account of the creative activity of the third, fifth, and sixth days.

"And God said, Let Us make man in Our Image, after Our likeness" (Gen. 1:26). Man was made in the Image of God — which definitely separates him from the plants and animals.

The Hebrew noun *ruach* means *"wind"* or *"breath."* The associated word is *ruah*. In Palestine the people are totally dependant on the wind to bring rain. Breathing is related to creating — the giving of life. In Genesis 2:7 we read that God *breathed* into man the Breath of Life.

Every man is kept by God. Your life is in God's Hands (Dan. 5:23).

SELF-HELP STUDY NOTES

**SELF-HELP
STUDY NOTES**

God is the Creator, and He sustains us. The Holy Spirit is involved in sustaining. Throughout the Old Testament, the Holy Spirit was the dynamic Spirit.

"LET US"

Returning to the Scripture quoted just above, Genesis 1:26, *"And God said, **Let Us make man in Our Image**."* This is of particular interest.

The Hebrew word for *"God"* used throughout Genesis is *Elohim*. This is a uniplural word, which means a word that implies a *unit* comprised of more than one. In our language, we have such uniplural words as family, troop, herd, association, flock, and congregation. Each of these is a *single* unit, but made up of a *number* of members. Use of the uniplural word *"Elohim"* for God reinforces the concept of the Trinity. As has been noted, this does not mean three Gods, but a tri-unity or a *Tri*une God: God the Father, God the Son, and God the Holy Spirit.

The Holy Spirit, the Spirit of God empowered by God the Father and God the Son, was intimately involved in Creation. God the Father is the Great Designer, the Master Architect. The Son is (in a manner of speaking) the Contractor. And the Holy Spirit is the Energizer, or the Action. He is the Construction Crew! God is indeed a creative God, and God the Holy Spirit is involved in all creative activity.

Chapter 3

The Holy Spirit In The Old Testament

SUBJECT	PAGE
WITH INDIVIDUALS FOR SPECIAL PURPOSES	45
IN THE TABERNACLE	56
THE BAPTISM WITH THE HOLY SPIRIT IN OLD TESTAMENT TYPES	56
GENERAL PROMINENCE	58

CHAPTER THREE

THE HOLY SPIRIT IN THE OLD TESTAMENT

"And thou shall speak unto all who are wise-hearted, whom I have filled with the Spirit of Wisdom, that they may make Aaron's garments to consecrate him, that he may minister unto Me in the Priest's office" (Ex. 28:3).

"Now these be the last words of David. David the son of Jesse said, and the man was raised up on high, the anointed of the God of Jacob, and the sweet Psalmist of Israel, said, The Spirit of the Lord spoke by me, and His Word was in my tongue" (II Sam. 23:1-2).

WITH INDIVIDUALS FOR SPECIAL PURPOSES

The relationship of the Holy Spirit to individuals, in the Old Testament, was not the same as it was *after* the Day of Pentecost. In the Old Testament, the Holy Spirit came *selectively*, falling upon a few of God's chosen *"instruments"* for very special purposes. Then, just before Jesus ascended He informed His Disciples that He would send the Holy Spirit to abide permanently within them.

When a person is truly baptized with the Holy Spirit, the Holy Spirit thoroughly indwells that individual. In the Old Testament they were not *"baptized"* with the Holy Spirit as such, but the Holy Spirit *"came upon"* people. He was there to guide, direct, and help them in a need, or to accomplish a specific and special purpose.

JOSEPH — Few people are afforded unique opportunities for leadership, but of those who are, Joseph was one who played a special and singular role. The Bible tells us (in Gen. 41:38) *"And Pharaoh said unto his servants, Can we find such a one as this is, a man in whom the Spirit of God is?"*

Joseph had the Spirit of God to guide and lead him. He was given true wisdom. Not only was he able to interpret the Pharaoh's dreams, but he was also able to help the entire nation of Egypt through a time of potential disaster when he saved them from their long famine. The Spirit of God was plainly upon Joseph, and he was wonderfully used of God as an instrument for accomplishing God's Purpose.

In the Old Testament, the Spirit of God came over individuals to use them, to help them, and to give them wisdom. He gave them strength for

SELF-HELP STUDY NOTES

SELF-HELP STUDY NOTES

whatever their need. (Read of Gideon in Judg. 6, 7, and 8.)

The Spirit was not available to the general population as such, but only to selected individuals who then became national leaders or powerful workers for God. Among these were Joseph, Moses, Joshua, Samuel, and a goodly number of other leaders and Prophets.

Long before the Patriarchs, God gave Noah words of knowledge and wisdom to save himself and his family when all other life was to be destroyed by the flood. During the time of the kings, Solomon was given great knowledge and special words of wisdom by God's Spirit. As the years went by, the Prophets received special revelation, insight, and understanding. These words of wisdom, delivered to the Prophets by the Holy Spirit, still declare God's Message to us as we read them today in the Old Testament.

MOSES — According to the prophet Isaiah, the Holy Spirit was with Moses in a special way. We find this in Isaiah 63:11 where it says, *"Then He remembered the days of old, Moses, and His people, saying, Where is He Who brought them up out of the sea with the shepherd of his flock? Where is He Who put his **Holy Spirit** within him?"*

And, in Isaiah 63:14 it says, *"As a beast goes down into the valley, **the Spirit of the Lord** caused him to rest: so did You lead Your people, to make Yourself a glorious name."*

This refers to Moses, who was a great and mighty man of God. It was the Holy Spirit who supplied him the resolution, the power, and the wisdom to accomplish all he did. In the Word of God, we find that Moses complained to God concerning the tremendous load placed upon him by God — leading the rebellious Children of Israel from Egypt into the Promise Land.

A rich lesson can be gained from this example. Moses *recognized* his limits and his needs — and then he *declared* them to God. Of course, Moses was one of the greatest men who ever lived so it is hard to compare him to ordinary men. But it was the Spirit of God who made Moses great. And even *with* that, Moses felt unequal to the tasks set before him and the Spirit of God had to lead him in a practical way to seek assistance in his leadership responsibilities.

The Bible tells us in Numbers 11:16-17, *"And the Lord said unto Moses, Gather unto Me seventy men of the Elders of Israel . . . And I will come down and talk with you there: and I will take of the Spirit which is upon you, and will put it upon them; and they shall bear the burden of the people with you, that you bear it not yourself alone."*

Moses had an overwhelming burden of responsibility. There were some three million people who looked to him for leadership and guidance. He had to stand in judgment almost daily, his energy dissipated by attention to minor details that shouldn't have required his personal attention. The sheer mass of these matters had sapped his strength until he had little left to devote to important matters. While the Holy Spirit does not tire, the human body of flesh *does*. Moses complained to the Lord and said he was neither mentally nor physically capable of bearing this load. God then led him to choose out seventy capable men to assist him.

Some say that God could have just given Moses physical strength to carry on. But God does not break His own laws. Of course, individuals do experience special grace and supernatural strength under unique circumstances of short duration. God can, by His Spirit, provide added strength and power, but natural laws are involved, and God will not repeal the natural laws He Himself established.

Even though the Spirit of God gives an individual new power and a dynamic spirit, we can harm ourselves mentally and physically — even though Spirit-filled. There are many great men of God who have overworked to the point of personal disintegration.

The Lord taught me a *personal* lesson in this area some time ago. When I was younger, I had some physical conditions that caused me real distress. They were sufficiently serious that they were actually interfering with my ability to carry out my work for the Lord. Praise God, I finally realized that as a Child of God I could have victory over this nagging situation, and at that point the Lord rapidly *gave* me victory. And from that point to today I have existed in an *almost* continuous state of blooming health.

But, while the Lord *will* heal us physically, this does not give us license to go beyond the bounds of good sense. Having been healed of my chronic conditions, I decided that I was — supported by the strength of the Holy Spirit — relieved of normal, common sense health requirements. I threw myself into my work with a zeal that went beyond rational limits. I felt I could drive myself beyond the point of physical exhaustion and the Lord would give me the strength to maintain this killing pace.

Well, needless to say, I soon found my strength waning. Before long, I was suffering from an almost constant series of colds that sapped my strength until I could barely maintain a *normal* schedule.

So what did I do? While burdened by a particularly vicious cold, I went before the Lord and cried out one more time for healing — so I could go on with the insane pace I felt I *should* be maintaining. And as I cried out before Him, He suddenly spoke to me — a circumstance I would like to comment on in a moment.

"*Son*," He said, "*I have been trying to teach you something but you refuse to listen. Now I want you to stop telling me how to handle things and start doing what I want you to do.*"

The problem, of course, was my obstinate refusal to admit that I'm no

SELF-HELP STUDY NOTES

SELF-HELP STUDY NOTES

different from anyone else. Sure, *others* would break down from overwork, but it couldn't happen to me. Well, the fact of the matter was, it *was* happening to me, and if I didn't start taking better care of my physical plant, the Lord would have to allow me to suffer more and more problems until He finally got my attention.

Needless to say, I changed my ways. I saw that one's *physical* body can be almost as important as one's spiritual *condition*, and that one inevitably influences the other. And as soon as I began leading a more balanced life, the succession of colds that had been plaguing me stopped. I have had almost *no* physical problems since then.

And now I would like to comment on a statement I just made. I said that as I cried out to the Lord he *"spoke to me."* This is a statement that Spirit-filled Christians often make that can be confusing or disturbing to non-Christians, or to the newer Christian. While the more experienced know exactly what you mean, it can shock the uninitiated when they hear, *"the Lord said"* or *"the Lord told me."*

The Lord did *not* speak to me in an audible voice. He *can* speak in an audible voice, and there are Scriptural accounts of just such incidents (Mat. 3:17; Mk. 9:7; Acts 9:4, and others). But these seemed to be reserved for historic occasions. The Spirit-filled Christian does, however, have access to communication with God, and it is not all uncommon.

When the Christian casually says, *"the Lord said . . . ,"* he *really* means that God has spoken to his heart or his inner ear. It is an experience we all have when we suddenly *know* something we *didn't* know a moment before. Suddenly our inner ear — our consciousness — hears words echoing within us that have *not* been generated by our brain or intellect.

There are two possible *false* sources of these messages. One is our subconscious, and the other is the enemy — Satan or one of his demonic helpers. And how do we sort them out? I pause a second and analyze the *message* I've just received. If it's a logical extension or development of my conscious thoughts on a problem, it's probably from my own mind. If it's something irrational, unsavory, or contrary to Scripture, it's certainly from Satan. But if it's logical, rational, and wholesome (although perhaps contrary to what I might want or *choose* for the situation), I feel it is no doubt God's Will, by way of the Holy Spirit.

I find that communications from God tend to come suddenly, arrive *completely* formed (requiring no further mental effort to *"work them out"*), and leave one with a feeling of, *"Wow! Of course! Why didn't I think of that?"*

God *did* speak to His Children in Biblical times, and he *does* speak to us today. We must, however, tune our Spiritual ears to *receive* His Messages, sharpen our Gift of Discernment (I Cor. 12:10) to reveal the source, and then confidently *act* upon the new course the Holy Spirit has set for us.

And returning to this question of mentally and physically exhausting ourselves, what better example could we find than the Lord and Master. Jesus was anointed by the Holy Spirit and went about healing the sick and all who were oppressed of the Devil (Acts 10:38). Still He said to His Disciples that they needed to separate themselves and rest for a time (Mk. 6:31). The baptism with the Holy Spirit does not give a person license to misuse his body. Neither does it give license to sin or disobey God. We must still use wisdom in practical matters. God gives wisdom and direction in even commonplace matters — if we will seek His Face and follow His Leadings.

Another event concerning Moses is found in Numbers 11:24-26 where Moses *"gathered the seventy men of the Elders of the people, and set them round about the Tabernacle. And the Lord came down in a cloud, and spoke unto him, and took of the Spirit that was upon him, and gave it unto the seventy Elders: and it came to pass, that, when the Spirit rested upon them, they prophesied, and did not cease. But there remained two of the men in the camp . . . and the Spirit rested upon them; and they were of them who were written, but went not out unto the Tabernacle: and they prophesied in the camp."*

When Joshua, Moses' helper and assistant who was himself a great man, discovered the two men prophesying (who weren't of the *"official"* group) he became excited. He went to Moses and said, *"My lord Moses, forbid them"* (Num. 11:28).

Even though Joshua was one of the greatest men who ever lived, he wasn't viewing this situation in the proper perspective. He wanted Moses to issue directions as to who might, and might not, demonstrate the Power of God's Holy Spirit. But Moses gave an interesting answer to Joshua: *"And Moses said unto him, Do you envy for my sake?"* (Num. 11:29).

In other words, Moses was saying, *"Don't you want me to reprimand them simply because I did not designate them, or because they are not among the select seventy, or because I didn't lay hands upon them?"* Then he said, *"would God that all the Lord's people were Prophets, and that the Lord would put his Spirit upon them!"*

Even today, I wish that every person in the world could have the Spirit of God moving mightily in his life. Thank God for leaders like Moses who *want* every person to have the Power and Blessings of God for his life. There was no jealousy or envy with Moses. Thank God for this outpouring of the Spirit.

There are some who have the attitude that if it is *not* their church, *their* Bible class, or a prayer meeting under *their* direction, it shouldn't be allowed to function with liberty — or if it *does*, it can't amount to much. All too many Christians feel that *their* church, where they undoubtedly play a

SELF-HELP STUDY NOTES

SELF-HELP STUDY NOTES

central role, is *uniquely* chosen to reflect God's Glory. Other groups, though? If it isn't *their* group, the rose-colored glasses are tossed aside. *"Reality"* rears its ugly head. *"Those"* groups can be viewed as they *really* are. Every spot, wrinkle, and marginal Christian is fair game for merciless appraisal. Groups other than *our* group are all too often sitting targets for ridicule, criticism, and often outright opposition.

We've all seen it. The Spirit of God begins to move and church leaders resist that move with everything at their command. We should thank God for every revival that is taking place — in our church or any other — and for every person being saved. Many leaders are uncomfortable, (or even jealous?), of circumstances over which they have no control. They should realize that the mighty moving of the Spirit of God is something that individuals cannot manipulate.

Paul faced the problem of those who ridiculed and criticized him — but who were at the same time proclaiming a version of God's Word. So Paul said in the midst of all this that Jesus Christ *is* being preached, and thank God for *that*, despite the fact that it was not *personally* favorable to Paul.

I thank God that the Holy Spirit is being poured out upon *all* flesh in *all* groups, and we should all remember that we don't elevate ourselves in God's Eyes by tearing down someone else.

BEZALEEL AND THE BUILDING OF THE TEMPLE — When God instituted laws and sacraments in Israel, He intended them as object lessons for the ages. Many of these are still valid today as *learning tools* for the Holy Spirit to utilize in teaching *us*. We, no less than early Israel, have to be taught at one point or another in our lives about sin and Salvation. As an example, no one — except the High Priest — could enter the Holy of Holies to sacrifice before God. Even then, he entered this sacred inner area of the Tabernacle only once a year, after being ritually purified *for* his entry. Only then could he place the blood upon the mercy seat. The Bible tells us why in Hebrews 9:8: *"The Holy Spirit this signifying, that the way into the Holiest of all was not yet made manifest, while as the First Tabernacle was yet standing."* In other words, at this point Jesus had not yet died for our sins on Calvary. He had not risen from the dead. No mechanism existed for washing away man's sin. Man could not stand before God in righteousness, without guilt. Consequently, no ordinary mortal could enter the Holy of Holies.

The High Priest (in the sinner's stead) would enter just once a year as a dramatic reminder that man was not worthy of contact with God. But now, of course, the lowliest person can enter the Holy of Holies — into God's Presence in the Spirit — and say, *"Lord Jesus, save my soul; have mercy upon me."*

Of course, there is no *physical* Holy of Holies in existence today, as there is no need for one. When Jesus died on Calvary, the veil (which separated mankind from God's Presence by walling off the Holy of Holies) was rent from top to bottom. Spiritually speaking, we can now enter the Holy of Holies through the Righteousness of Jesus Christ. We can walk boldly into the very Presence of God (wherever we may be) if we ask the Lord Jesus Christ to come into our hearts and lives.

The Shekinah Glory existed only in the Presence of God, within the Holy of Holies. When one is saved, he enters into the Holy of Holies because he enters into the Presence of God's marvelous Grace. And even though it may not be seen, he is enveloped in Shekinah Glory.

Even the garments worn by the High Priests were a matter of concern to the Holy Spirit. Exodus 28:3 says, *"And you shall speak unto all who are wise-hearted, whom I have filled with the **Spirit of Wisdom**, that they may make Aaron's garments to consecrate him, that he may minister unto Me in the Priest's office."*

There is a reason for the rigid specifications the Holy Spirit gave for these garments. Special meaning, significance, and purpose were involved.

When it came to the construction of the Tabernacle itself, God wanted a Spirit-led foreman for the job. He told Moses in Exodus 31:2-5, *"See, I have called by name Bezaleel the son of Uri, the son of Hur, of the tribe of Judah: And I have filled him with the Spirit of God, in wisdom, and in understanding, and in knowledge, and in all manner of workmanship, To devise cunning works, to work in gold, and in silver, and in brass, And in cutting of stones, to set them, and in carving timber, to work in all manner of workmanship."* God's Spirit infused this man, enabling him to build the Tabernacle *precisely* to His specifications, for His Purpose, and for His Glory.

BALAAM — Balaam (Num. 22-24) was an appropriate prototype for many Spirit-filled Christians today. Merely because one is Spirit-filled does not make one perfect. Quite to the contrary, we can all be absolutely certified as *not* being perfect. There was only one *perfect* person in all of history, and that was our Lord Jesus Christ. Of course, the Born-Again, Spirit-filled Christian had perfect *Salvation,* because his Salvation was perfected *by* Jesus, *at* Calvary. But as far as Christian *maturity*, we are never perfected. No mortal person living in this world has ever achieved that state of perfect maturity. Some have evinced great growth, *approaching* a state of true maturity, but no one has ever achieved that state of perfection. We will *never* be perfected in maturity until the day the Lord Jesus Christ comes and we have glorified bodies.

But just because we know we won't be perfected, we have no excuse for drifting along accepting our flawed present condition. Rather, we should eternally press on — striving to mature ever further in the Lord. We must be

SELF-HELP STUDY NOTES

SELF-HELP STUDY NOTES

committed to, and striving toward, maturity. Jesus said, *"Be you therefore perfect, even as your Father which is in Heaven is perfect"* (Mat. 5:48).

The word *"perfect"* as used here basically refers to *maturity*. We are to be mature and complete. Although we know we won't become perfect, we should not remain spiritual infants. We should grow in grace every day, pressing on toward maturity.

Balaam was an individual who could apparently yield readily to the Lord and to the moving of the Holy Spirit. But, unfortunately, he demonstrated much carnality intertwined with his spirituality. He had something of a dual personality in that he could apparently yield just as readily to the powers of darkness. One might say he was what we call today a *"wishy-washy"* type. He could really be *"all together"* and *"with it"* one day and completely *"out of it"* the next. At least this appears to be his relationship with God.

God does have patience with this type of individual and graciously deals with each person. Anytime the heart responds to God, He moves to fill it with His Presence — no matter *what* that person may be about to do the following day. God doesn't analyze people when He saves them nor give them gifts on the basis of what they will do in the future. He deals with them according to their faith at that moment. This is why we see Christians committing all kinds of errors after God has abundantly blessed them. They certainly shouldn't do this nor do they have any excuse for such behavior. It undoubtedly hinders the Work of God, not to mention the individual's relationship to God. Continuing to do so can result in eventual alienation from God.

The Spirit of God *was* upon Balaam, for he was a man who was obviously anointed with God's Power of the Holy Spirit. He had the Gift of Prophecy, and God had dealt with him previously. He had sought God and had received marvelous blessings. Seemingly, he was never able to overcome his problems.

Balaam turned from God, and there is nothing in Scripture to indicate that he died the death of righteousness. He was one of those upon whom the Spirit of God came, but who misused the Spirit. He abused his precious privileges by wandering astray. He listened to the voice of the Devil and ended up disobeying God and misusing the gifts given to him by God.

The Bible tells us that there will be someone who will stand before God and say, *We have cast out devils in Thy Name and healed the sick in Thy Name.* They will declare that they have done many wonderful things in His Name. But what will God say? *Depart from me, I never knew you.*

It is possible for people to have enjoyed the great moving of the Holy Spirit in their lives and yet through neglect, stubbornness, greed, carelessness, or their own will and desires go contrary to God? Unfortunately, it is.

However, the Holy Spirit is extremely patient with individuals and will do everything He can to salvage a soul. But a person can grieve the Holy Spirit and rebel against Him to the point where the direction of his life — by his own free will and choice — is a direction totally unacceptable to God. If an individual persists in going the way of disobedience (as Balaam did), the Spirit will not restrain him against his will. The Spirit of God *will not always strive with man.*

JOSHUA — We read in Numbers 27:18, *"And the Lord said unto Moses, Take thee Joshua the son of Nun, a man in whom is the Spirit, and lay your hand upon him."* This is further confirmed in Deuteronomy 34:9 which says, *"And Joshua the son of Nun was full of the Spirit of Wisdom; for Moses had laid his hands upon him: and the Children of Israel hearkened unto him, and did as the LORD commanded Moses."*

Joshua, one of the greatest men of Israel's history, was led and guided by the Holy Spirit. God gave him supernatural victories that could only have come by intervention of the Holy Spirit. The Spirit of God was the driving force in Joshua's life. But even though Joshua, Moses, Joseph, David, and others saw tremendous examples of the Power of God, the Holy Spirit did not *dwell within* these individuals in the same manner in which he indwells people today.

Jesus Himself said that he would send the Holy Spirit to *"be in us"* and *"without measure."* Today there is no limit to what an individual can have, or do, in Jesus Christ — through the Power of the Holy Spirit. Old Testament figures were used in mighty ways by God, but he used them according to the *specific need of the time.*

SAMSON — The Spirit of God came mightily upon Samson during the time of the Judges (Judg. 13-16). This period was known as the Dark Ages of Hebrew history, although there were many impressive moves of the Spirit during these times.

Samson emerges as a fine example, but also as a *horrible* example. Many today mirror Samson's actions — and *re*actions. Even though the Spirit of the Lord moved upon Samson again and again in awesome power, he is a prime example of what happens to people who desire the *Power* of the Spirit — but not the *Discipline* of the Spirit.

Another example of the Spirit of God moving mightily in the time of the Judges was Gideon — who was used of the Lord in a unique way.

Many people desire the blessings. They relish the miracles, the zeal, the excitement, the thrill, and the exuberance, but they refuse to allow the Holy Spirit to develop the *fruit of the Spirit* in their natures. Like Samson, they chose not to bring *their* spirit under submission to the *Holy* Spirit.

Some think once they are baptized with the Holy Spirit that *"everything automatically takes care of itself."* Of course, this doesn't happen. Even

SELF-HELP STUDY NOTES

SELF-HELP STUDY NOTES

though a person is baptized with the Holy Spirit, he must bring his own spirit under submission. The Holy Spirit will not do this for him! The Holy Spirit will *never* force a person to assume a proper attitude. The response is always up to the individual.

Over the years the Lord has seen fit to use me, and I am so grateful. I never cease to view the Power of God — the Greatness, the Majesty, and Glory of God — with wonder and awe. But there is a price attached to God's great Blessings.

We don't have to, nor *could* we, buy Salvation. Jesus paid it all. Neither can we buy the Gifts of the Holy Spirit. They are free Gifts, with no price attached to them. Simon the sorcerer discovered this in Acts 8:9-24.

In order to aspire to becoming of use to God — and thus to know *true* blessings — one has to first bring his own spirit under submission to the Holy Spirit. That is the price one must pay for true discipleship. Full commitment to the Lord, on the part of the individual, can be costly. In accepting total stewardship of one's life, there may be *great* sacrifice required. While these do not *purchase* Salvation — nor the Gifts of God — they are nevertheless a significant part of Christian living. More often than not, seeking the deepest commitment to God will extract an equal reduction in worldly relationships and a comparable rejection of worldly *"pleasures."*

SAUL — Saul, the first king of Israel, is an example of the individual who experiences the Anointing of God — and then turns his back on the *Spirit* of God. Saul enjoyed the privileges inherent in his position, but he rejected the responsibilities.

The People of Israel, despite God's counsel, insisted upon a king to rule them in order to unify them against the Philistines and other enemies. God acceded to their wishes to demonstrate what would happen when *they* took full control of their lives. He gave them Saul.

When the Prophet Samuel found Saul, Saul was little more than a rancher's son. He was overgrown (unusually tall) and had an inferiority complex. Obviously, God would have to do something for Saul to prepare him for leadership of a nation. Samuel said to Saul, *"And the Spirit of the Lord will come upon you, and you shall prophesy with them, and shall be turned into another man"* (I Sam. 10:6). It certainly appears that Saul's attitude is right with God in the beginning, and that he followed the Lord. The Spirit of God was definitely upon Saul. God chose him, anointed him, and used him.

In I Samuel 10:10, we have an interesting account. *"And when they came thither to the hill, behold, a company of Prophets met him; and the Spirit of God came upon him,* (referring to Saul) *and he prophesied among them."* This doesn't happen to an unsaved person, an apostate, or one who has sold out to evil.

The Bible says that the Spirit of the Lord came upon Saul (1 Sam. 10:6-10). The Holy Spirit *was* upon him. But Saul disobeyed God and became proud, hostile, full of neurotic self-pity — and ended up turning away from the Lord.

The Bible states (in 1 Sam. 16:14), *"But the Spirit of the Lord departed from Saul."* Obviously, Saul *had* the Spirit or the Spirit could not have later departed from him. At one time, he *was* a man of God who followed the Lord, prophesied, worshiped God, and gave evidence of being totally committed to God. But at some point he departed from God, and the Holy Spirit departed from him.

This is one of the most tragic lessons that can be learned by anyone. Saul *grieved* the Holy Spirit away. He presented an environment the Holy Spirit couldn't tolerate. Even after he had become mired in sin — disobeying God with murder in his heart and hunting down David — even after all this, the Spirit of God *tried* to influence him. The Holy Spirit tried to move upon him and stir him to Repentance. It was a futile effort. Saul slammed the door, literally turning his back on God. This man who had once walked with God eventually dabbled in witchcraft and ended his life as a suicide on Mount Gilboa (I Sam. 31:4, 6).

A person can fall away from God. The Bible speaks of apostasy and warns that in the latter days, there will be much apostasy. Apostasy means, simply, falling away from God.

Even if a person falls into sin (and moves away from God), the Holy Spirit will again move upon him, bringing conviction. But if the individual consciously persists, by his own free choice, continuing in a direction opposed to God, tragedy and chaos will be the result.

No one is held against his will. If one is deep in sin, there is only one way out and that is God. By His Grace, He will renew an individual into fellowship. It is God's business to lift one higher and higher, into righteousness. But the individual is the one who makes the decision. *You* can depart form God; He won't force you to live for Him. But you can also choose to come *to* Him. And if you do, you will be welcomed back with open arms.

Even after Saul had desecrated the Name of God, cursed and disobeyed God, the Spirit of God still chose to move upon him one more time. If Saul had yielded, God would have accepted him with open arms, blessed him, helped him, and strengthened him. How marvelous is God's willingness to forgive.

Even Judas, who betrayed Jesus, could have been forgiven. Had he not taken his own life — but fallen instead at the Feet of Jesus — he would have experienced forgiveness and God's Blessing. His betrayal of Jesus was despicable, but it wasn't all that much worse than Peter's cursing and

SELF-HELP STUDY NOTES

SELF-HELP STUDY NOTES

subsequent denial of Jesus. But Peter begged for mercy, while Judas hung himself. If Judas had repented and asked for the Lord's Mercy, I believe Jesus would have accepted him with open arms, saying, *"Welcome home."*

IN THE TABERNACLE

God made man for *His* Glory and for fellowship *with* Him. When Adam and Eve were in the Garden of Eden, they spoke with God. However, this sweet communion was shattered by disobedience to God, which is sin.

Fellowship with God was severed as a result of the fall of man. Because of their disobedience, they were removed from the Garden and separated from God. But God does desire fellowship, and it was for this Purpose that man was created. Conversely, man is never truly happy unless he is in fellowship with God.

God relates to man in a variety of ways. When the People of Israel (God's chosen people) were in the wilderness, they were instructed to build a tent of worship — the Tabernacle — according to Divine specifications. In the heart of the Tabernacle was the Most Holy Place, the Holy of Holies, where God actually resided. Thus the very Presence of God was among His People, dwelling in the Holy of Holies, and known as the *Shekinah*, or *"Glory of God."* *Shekinah* is a word related to the word for skin, and also dwelling. The actual Tabernacle, as designed by God, was covered over with badger skins.

Beautiful truths are typified in many Old Testament representations and practices. Jesus, the Word, became flesh and dwelt among us — as John points out in John 1:14. Actually, the word *"dwelt"* here might better be rendered *"tabernacled."* He was the very Presence of God among men. But Jesus said later that He was going to the Father and would send the Holy Spirit, the Comforter, to assume this duty of bringing God's Presence to men.

God has always associated with man, revealed Himself to man, enjoyed association with man, and offered fellowship to man. It is by and through the Holy Spirit that He comes to us today. The Holy Spirit is the very Presence of God among us and in us. By the Holy Spirit, God now *"tabernacles"* in us. The Old Testament Tabernacle is the type and picture of His marvelous Ways.

THE BAPTISM WITH THE HOLY SPIRIT IN OLD TESTAMENT TYPES

FEASTS OF PASSOVER AND PENTECOST (Lev. 23) — In the beginning, at the establishment of the Feast of Pentecost, its date was placed fifty days after the Passover and the Feast of the Sheaf of the Firstfruits. Without the Passover, there would have been no way of determining the date for the Day of Pentecost.

This is an exact parallel to *our* lives. Here the baptism with the Holy Spirit (Pentecost) cannot occur without the *first* experience — Salvation through the Blood of Jesus Christ. How significant that it is the *Jubilee* (fiftieth) Day that results in the *jubilation* invariably accompanying the Pentecostal experience.

THE BLOOD AND THE OIL (LEV. 14) — In the cleansing of a leper, *blood* was first placed upon the tip of the right ear of the one who was to be cleansed, upon the thumb of his right hand, and upon the great toe of his right foot. Then *oil* was placed where the blood had been applied. The oil upon (or following) the blood, demonstrates that we must have the Blood of Jesus applied to our hearts *before* we can receive the Work (and residence) of the Spirit in our lives.

If this oil represents the Holy Spirit's work at *conversion* (which it doubtless does), the type has even more to teach us. *"And the remnant of the oil that is in the priest's hand, he shall **pour upon** the head of him who is to be cleansed."* This typifies the *Anointing* of the Holy Spirit, which comes at the *baptism* with the Spirit, *after* Salvation.

THE OIL, IN AND UPON THE MEAT OFFERING (LEV. 2:6-7) — *"You shall part it in pieces, and pour oil thereon: it is a Meat Offering. And if your oblation be a Meat Offering baked in the frying pan, it shall be made of fine flour with oil."*

This presence of oil *within* the cake represents the Holy Spirit at Salvation, while the oil poured over it later represents the Holy Spirit immersion at the Baptism.

THE PILLAR OF CLOUD BY DAY AND THE PILLAR OF FIRE BY NIGHT (NUM. 9:15-23) — Paul says in I Corinthians 10:1-2 that *"all our fathers were under the cloud, and all passed through the sea; And were all baptized unto Moses in the cloud and in the sea."*

This was typology for the experience received by the Children of God today. They escaped from Egypt (the world) by virtue of the Passover being sacrificed for them. Christ is our Passover (I Cor. 5:7). They then passed through the waters of baptism (Mk. 16:16) as represented by the waters of the Red Sea. And what does being *"baptized in the cloud"* typify? The baptism with the Holy Spirit! That cloud represents the Shekinah Glory of Almighty God, a cloud by day and a pillar of fire by night. It not only *represented* God, but *was* God in His continuing Presence. *"And the Lord went before them by day in a pillar of a cloud, to lead them the way; and by night in a pillar of fire, to give them light; to go by day and night"* (Ex. 13:21). Note that it does not say that the cloud and the

SELF-HELP STUDY NOTES

SELF-HELP STUDY NOTES

pillar *represented* God or that He *sent* them. It says that He went *in* them, continuously.

God dwelt directly over His People and they literally walked *in* that cloud — being in effect *surrounded* by God Himself. This was the continuing situation throughout the wilderness journey.

This figure of baptism *into* a cloud — which implies a continuation in the element into which one has been baptized — is an appropriate picture of the baptism with the Holy Spirit. We do not go into, and immediately come out of, as in water baptism. We instead go into a *condition in which we remain*, as in a Heavenly Cloud. By this experience, we enter into the Holy Spirit and continue to live and walk with the Shekinah Glory of God surrounding us.

GENERAL PROMINENCE

The Holy Spirit was prominent in the Old Testament and gave the inspiration for Scripture. II Peter 1:21 states, *"For the Prophecy came not in old time by the will of man: but Holy men of God spoke as they were moved by the Holy Spirit."* In II Timothy 3:16 we're told, *"All Scripture is given by Inspiration of God."* By saying *"all Scripture"* this, of course, includes the Old Testament.

The Old Testament Prophets were moved on by the Holy Spirit in a special way. The Prophets were granted great revelations by Divine intervention. Obviously, this was the Work of the Holy Spirit.

The Holy Spirit worked not only through the Prophets who wrote down the revelations of the Old Testament but also with the nation of Israel and its leaders. The Spirit of God also worked with individuals after a measure. However, it is not as people are filled today — without measure. Jesus said that He would send the Holy Spirit and out of one's innermost being would flow rivers of Living Water.

Even though individuals were *saved* in the Old Testament, they were operating in a different dispensation — a different set of conditions. Today, after the completion of the Redemptive Work of Christ on Calvary, a new set of conditions is in operation. Old Testament Believers were protected (saved) by trusting in something promised for the future. It was their Faith in something as yet unseen that was imputed to them for Righteousness (James 2:23). They were looking forward to, and believing in, the provision yet to be made by the Messiah.

In Jesus we have the *New* Covenant. Jesus died at Calvary and rose again. By accepting Him, a person is Born-Again and becomes a new creature in Christ. *"Old things are passed away; behold, all things are become new"* (II Cor. 5:17). A new creature in Christ is a fit habitation for the indwelling of, and baptism in, the Holy Spirit.

Even though Old Testament Believers were not *baptized* with the Holy Spirit (as we use the term today), God's Spirit remained among and operated within the chosen nation of Israel. We read in Haggai 2:5, *"According to the word that I covenanted with you when you came out of Egypt, so My Spirit remains among you: fear you not."*

There were many times when Israel fell away from God, and at these times their enemies were victorious; God *allowed* this to happen. Still God promised that He would not take His Spirit from them. He said in Isaiah 59:21, *"As for Me, this is My Covenant with them, saith the Lord; My Spirit that is upon you, and My Words which I have put in your mouth, shall not depart out of your mouth, nor out of the mouth of your seed, nor out of the mouth of your seed's seed, saith the LORD, from henceforth and forever."*

God the Holy Spirit dealt with the Children of Israel in Old Testament times in a great and wonderful way. They grew disobedient and spiteful and allowed Satan to lead them astray. They rejected God and were no longer blessed by Him. During these periods, God withdrew His aid and refused to protect them from their enemies. These were times when the Holy Spirit, in effect, departed. But God's Spirit continues to move with Israel today, and His desire is, as Paul stated, *for all Israel to be saved* (Rom. 11:26).

The three ways the Holy Spirit manifests Himself in the Old Testament are:

1. The Creative Spirit;
2. The Dynamic Spirit; and,
3. The Regenerative Spirit.

The Holy Spirit (as we discussed in chapter 2) was vitally involved in *Creation*.

The *dynamic* Power of the Holy Spirit can be seen in His influence on the leaders during certain critical periods. Despite moral lapses, when it came time to again *"get Israel back on the tracks,"* God's Holy Spirit would *again* intervene, raise up *proper* leadership, and *again* reestablish proper direction.

The Holy Spirit is a *regenerative* Spirit. David, referred to as *"a man after God's own Heart,"* failed and sinned grievously (II Sam. 11 and Ps. 51). But God's Purposes are always Redemptive, and the move of God's Spirit was upon a repentant David, who asked to be cleansed. He prayed, *"take not Your Holy Spirit from me."*

The Holy Spirit was truly at work in the Old Testament and accomplished God's Purpose of bringing people to Himself to experience the fullness of His Goodness, Grace, and Glory.

SELF-HELP STUDY NOTES

Chapter 4

The Holy Spirit In The Life Of Christ

SUBJECT   **PAGE**

RELATIONSHIP TO THE OLD COVENANT	63
IN THE BIRTH OF JESUS	65
DURING HIS YOUTH	65
AT THE BAPTISM OF JESUS	68
DURING THE TEMPTATIONS	69
IN THE MINISTRY OF JESUS	70
HIS ATONING DEATH	72
IN THE RESURRECTION	72
THE ASCENSION	72

CHAPTER FOUR

THE HOLY SPIRIT IN THE LIFE OF CHRIST

"Then said Mary unto the Angel, How shall this be, seeing I know not a man? And the Angel answered and said unto her, The Holy Spirit shall come upon you, and the power of the Highest shall overshadow you: therefore also that Holy thing which shall be born of you shall be called the Son of God" (Lk. 1:34-35).

"How God anointed Jesus of Nazareth with the Holy Spirit and with Power: who went about doing good, and healing all who were oppressed of the Devil; for God was with Him" (Acts 10:38).

RELATIONSHIP TO THE OLD COVENANT

The four Gospel writers — Matthew, Mark, Luke, and John — are the world's basic authoritative sources on the Life of Christ. They relate details of His Birth and some of the events of His early Life, but the bulk of their accounts center on the last three years — the period of His Ministry. *Greatest* attention is devoted to the last *week* of His Life. It is well to remember while studying the Gospels that Disciples were under the Old Covenant. They received the *introduction* to the New Covenant, but this was at the very beginning of this period. The New Covenant really begins to be seen operating in the Epistles and the other writings which follow the Gospels in the New Testament.

God made a covenant with Israel called the "Old Covenant." The *New* Covenant relates to Redemption through Christ. Instead of being under the Law, we now live in the day of Grace. Jesus Christ ushered in the New Covenant when He shed His Blood for our Redemption at Calvary.

Next He sent the Holy Spirit to fill our hearts and lives and to baptize us with the Holy Spirit. The Holy Spirit has now fully come, bringing Gifts and the Fruits of the Spirit. This is a whole new dimension in Christian living. Even though Matthew, Mark, Luke, and John — as we see them in the Gospels — were living in the first days of the *New* Testament, they were conditioned by living most of their lives under the *Old* Covenant. Some of their reactions were, therefore, not in keeping with their *later* wisdom as revealed in the Epistles.

Of course, there were individuals who experienced the Presence and Power of the Holy Spirit in marvelous ways. The Gospel writers themselves

SELF-HELP STUDY NOTES

SELF-HELP STUDY NOTES

typify this. And Mary, the mother of Jesus, experienced the Presence and Power of the Holy Spirit in a unique way. The Bible says in Luke 1:35, *"And the Angel answered and said unto her, The Holy Spirit shall come upon you, and the power of the Highest shall overshadow you: therefore also that Holy thing which shall be born of you shall be called the Son of God."*

Mary's cousin, Elizabeth, had a similar experience as recorded in Luke 1:41. It is clearly stated that Elizabeth was filled with the Holy Spirit. It was foretold that John the Baptist would be filled with the Holy Spirit from his mother's womb (Lk. 1:15). However, one must remember that these are different fillings — different types of fillings within the matter of *measure*.

When Jesus gave His Promise, prior to His Ascension, He said that the Holy Spirit would be *with* us, and *in* us. A new dimension of the Holy Spirit's activity in the lives of individuals was inaugurated on the Day of Pentecost. At that time, and in subsequent experiences, people were *baptized* with the Holy Spirit — and spoke with other tongues as the Spirit gave the utterance.

When Jesus was filled with the Holy Spirit, He was filled beyond measure. It was not limited, as with previous individuals. This was *without measure*, the way we are filled with the Spirit today and baptized with the Holy Spirit. (And of course, when we say *"baptized,"* we are not talking about water baptism; we are talking about being baptized with the Holy Spirit as recorded in Acts 1:5.)

Though the experience was somewhat different (as we have noted), there are individuals upon whom the Holy Spirit *moved* prior to Pentecost. We are told of a man in Jerusalem whose name was Simeon. *"And the same man was just and devout, waiting for the consolation of Israel: and the Holy Spirit was upon him"* (Lk. 2:25). It had been revealed to him that he would not see death until he had seen the *"Lord's Christ."* This Revelation came to him by the Holy Spirit (Lk. 2:26). When Joseph and Mary brought Jesus to the Temple (according to the *"custom of law"* which required a redemption payment for the firstborn), the Holy Spirit revealed to Simeon that this was indeed the Christ — the Messiah — for whom they were waiting (Lk. 2:27). Simeon took Jesus in his arms and blessed God, saying that he could now die in peace, for his eyes had seen the Salvation which would be available through the Messiah (Lk. 2:28-32).

Simeon went on to give Mary other Prophetic utterances (Lk. 2:34-35). It was the Holy Spirit giving a glimpse into the future through this elderly Saint. Also present in the Temple was an elderly, widowed Prophetess named Anna. She had served God in the Temple, with fasting and prayer, night and day for many years (Lk. 2:36-38). The very fact that

Anna was a Prophetess of God implies that the activity of the Holy Spirit was present in her life. Furthermore, she immediately recognized that Jesus was the Provision for Redemption of Jerusalem and the world.

IN THE BIRTH OF JESUS

The initial stages of the Divine Incarnation were set by the Holy Spirit. When Mary, a virgin, was informed she was to bear a child, she questioned the Angel. The Angel told Mary, *"The Holy Spirit shall come upon you, and the power of the Highest shall overshadow you: therefore also that Holy thing which shall be born of you shall be called the Son of God"* (Lk. 1:34-35). Jesus was conceived by the Holy Spirit and born of the virgin Mary.

Many people question the virgin Birth, and even many church leaders deny this fact. But if we have a real concept of the Power of the Holy Spirit, it is no problem to accept the virgin Birth of Jesus. As we accept *all* Scripture by Faith, we can certainly accept His virgin Birth in the same way. But in addition to this, if one chooses to approach it from a point of logic, an understanding of the Power and potential of the Holy Spirit rapidly eliminates any questions.

One of the Cardinal Tenets of Evangelical Christianity has been that Jesus was born of the virgin Mary — as prophesied in Isaiah and as declared in the Gospels. Belief further states that this miraculous event was brought about by the unique and powerful Working of the Holy Spirit.

Jesus was not born under the stain of sin, for He did not come of man's procreation. If Jesus had been born of His earthly foster-father, Joseph, He would have had the stain of sin and He would have needed, as we all do, Salvation. But He was born of Mary and fathered by the Holy Spirit — a miracle of conception.

The Holy Spirit, not man, was responsible for Mary's conception. This was necessary for sinless perfection. The Holy Spirit was the *agent* at the Birth of Jesus. And because of the sinlessness of Christ, the power of sin was broken and He was able to bear our sins on the Cross (II Cor. 5:21).

DURING HIS YOUTH

When Jesus was born into human form, He had to grow in wisdom and knowledge as other children do. He did, of course, develop tremendously because He never yielded to sin or darkness. His Mind and Spirit were totally open to God the Father. Consequently, He learned very rapidly, and at the age of twelve years He was able to discuss the Law with the high priests and doctors of the Law. He astounded them with His Spirit-anointed

SELF-HELP STUDY NOTES

SELF-HELP STUDY NOTES

answers (Lk. 2:41-52).

In Matthew 12:18, Matthew quotes the Prophecy of Isaiah as recorded in Isaiah 42:1: *"Behold My Servant, Whom I uphold; My Elect, in Whom My soul delights."* This refers, of course, to Jesus.

In Isaiah 11:2 it is stated, *"And the Spirit of the LORD shall rest upon Him, the Spirit of Wisdom and Understanding, the Spirit of Counsel and Might, the Spirit of Knowledge and of the Fear of the LORD."*

Myths have arisen that Jesus, as a child, performed amazing transformations with dirt, mud, or pieces of wood — making ships, lakes, and so forth out of them. These stories persist because certain Gnostic writers (e.g., Eusebius, Athanasius, Epiphanius, Stipulensis,) wrote them down and published them. Reputable scholars agree that they are apocryphal (not written under the Anointing of the Holy Spirit). He was, however, anointed of the Holy Spirit and increased greatly in wisdom (Lk. 2:46-52).

Very little is available concerning Jesus as a child or young person. The Bible states that Herod sought to kill Him by murdering all male children of two years and under. After their reunion to Nazareth (following Herod's death), we have only a glimpse of Jesus' Life until He was thirty years old. This is at twelve years, as previously mentioned, when He was debating the powerful men of letters in the Temple. The Bible states that these scholars were astounded at His Wisdom.

Like all young children of that day, Jesus was taught the Scriptures and obviously had a great desire to know and meditate upon the Word of God. Psalms 119:97 is considered to be a reference to Jesus and the actual expression of the Lord. This says, *"Oh how I love Your Law! It is my meditation all the day."* The word *"Law"* in this context means God's Word. He was interested in the Word of God and meditated on it always. He no doubt occupied Himself with this while other children involved themselves in trivial play.

In many respects, Jesus was an unusual child. He was obviously obedient to His Parents. A problem arose, however, at the time we're discussing when Jesus was twelve and remained behind when the family caravan headed homeward. Mary and Joseph had traveled some distance before they realized Jesus was missing.

His parents had been in Jerusalem for the Feast of the Passover. They were under the impression that he was with relatives in another part of the caravan. When they discovered His absence, they returned immediately to Jerusalem.

After three days, He was found discussing fine theological points with the scholars in the Temple. The lawyers and doctors were astonished at His deep perceptions. Mary questioned Jesus, and He responded by saying that He must be about His Father's business. They did not fully understand, but Jesus, even at that early age, knew He had a mission and destiny and was referring to His responsibility to God the Father.

Jesus knew Scripture in depth. He knew the messages delivered by the Prophets and understood their content more than even the Prophets had when they wrote them down. He meditated day and night, and the Scriptures were unfolded by the Holy Spirit, allowing Him to fully understand the Law and the Prophets.

There are children who sense at an early age the call of God in their lives, and who have a deep and abiding interest in God's Word. As a child of eight, God saved me and baptized me with the mighty Holy Spirit. I recall the deep yearning and desires of my heart and life at that tender age.

I vividly remember, at eight years of age, going to my grandmother's house time and time again. She was a true stalwart of Faith and taught me much of what I know about Faith today. She had been baptized with the Holy Spirit and a radical transformation resulted in her life. Glorious and wonderful changes produced a profound effect on our whole family.

I studied the Word of God with her and asked her over and over again to describe how God had filled her with the Holy Spirit. She repeated the experience time and again, but I would go right on asking her to go *on* telling it.

"Jimmy," she would say, *"there is nothing God cannot do. He's a big God, and He wants to do great things for you. Believe Him and stand on His Promises."* She would smile and then as she pointed her finger at me: *"God can do anything."*

She reminded me that God's Hand was upon me, and she would then state without question that I would preach to thousands. Later on, after I began preaching, I found this Prophecy hard to believe — despite the fact that I knew God could do great things. She never failed to encourage me, though. *"Jimmy,"* she would say, *"you will see the sick healed, blind eyes opened, and lame legs walk, and you are going to witness miracles while you see thousands saved."* As she spoke her eyes would sparkle, and influenced by *her* Faith, I almost found myself believing that all this *could* happen in my life.

As I sat, time after time, listening to the account of her baptism with the Holy Spirit, it created a deep hunger in *my* heart for a personal relationship with the Holy Spirit. I wanted what my grandmother had. She would seat herself, and I would kneel down on the floor next to her chair with my eyes closed, listening. I could hardly stand the suspense of waiting for her to reach the part where God had come into her heart, had baptized her in the Power of the Holy Spirit, and she had begun speaking in tongues.

As she recounted this, the Presence and Power of the Spirit of God would move over her in a marvelous way, and she would raise her hands

SELF-HELP STUDY NOTES

SELF-HELP STUDY NOTES

and start speaking in other tongues, praising God. It would literally flow all through me, causing me to tremble and shake under the Power of God. I returned again and again to hear this story and to experience the Presence of God's Power. I felt His Glory move in my heart at the same time it moved in hers.

This repeated exposure to my grandmother's experience affected me deeply. After God baptized *me* with the Holy Spirit (still at the age of eight), I found I had a deep and lasting love for the Word of God. I relished it and read the Word of God constantly throughout my eighth and ninth years. I meditated on it and shared Spiritual Truths with my parents.

My dad encouraged me, asking me to explain obscure Scriptures. I was just a child, but after I would explain them as I understood them, he would consult our pastor for *his* opinion. He supported my interpretations, and convinced both me and my father that my revelations were indeed arrived at with the help of the Holy Spirit. I am convinced that God gave me insight into Scripture because I meditated on it, I dwelt in it, and I loved it.

It *is* possible for a child to have a deep interest in the Word of God and to grow in it. Of course, no one compares to Jesus, who as a child grew greatly in Wisdom and Knowledge of the things of God. But in other ways, He grew much as other children do. Of course, being very God, there was a brilliance and an intellect vastly beyond the normal.

Jesus did lay aside His Attributes of Deity (even though He retained His *basic* Deity) and did not use His Godly Powers as a man. He had the *authority* to take up these Godly Powers as He chose, but He never did choose to do so. The powers He *did* use are also available to us today when we operate in the *authority* of Jesus Christ and the *Power* of the Holy Spirit.

Jesus grew up as a human child. And as a fully human boy, He became involved in many things. Still, He never fell into sin. He loved the Word of God deeply, and the Holy Spirit guided Him during this development.

AT THE BAPTISM OF JESUS

The Holy Spirit was involved in the Life of Jesus from before His Birth. Then after being guided throughout His Childhood and Youth by the Spirit, some very special incidents occurred at the beginning of His Ministry.

First there was the baptism of Jesus. Why was He baptized by John the Baptist in the River of Jordan? Certainly He was not renouncing His personal sin, for He was sinless. He *was* totally identifying His relationship to God.

This was the time for public approval of Christ by the Father. The Spirit descended in the form of a dove, and a voice from Heaven spoke and said, *"This is My Beloved Son, in Whom I am well pleased"* (Mat. 3:13-17).

The Spirit came *"as"* or *"like"* a dove. This is a simile, a comparison. The Holy Spirit came *gently*. This was a witness for all the Trinity being present at this moment — the Father, the Son, and the Holy Spirit. *Jesus* was baptized, the *Holy Spirit* descended, and the *Father* spoke from Heaven. This is a clear demonstration of the Triune nature of God. The Deity of Christ was also demonstrated here. The Holy Spirit was present. The Holy Spirit was present to anoint Jesus for His Ministry. This was a glorious manifestation of the Spirit.

DURING THE TEMPTATIONS

After Christ was baptized with the Spirit, He was soon *"tempted."* The word translated as *"tempted"* is *peirazo* in the original Greek. A better translation of this word might be *"tested."* The word *"tempt"* implies being confronted with something we have been *wanting* all along, a chance to do something we basically *want* to do (that slice of chocolate cake in the refrigerator). Within this definition it is very questionable that our Lord was *"tempted"* at all, while He certainly was *tested* by His trying encounter with Satan — while weakened from His long fast. After being filled with the Holy Spirit, we are all better able to survive difficult or dangerous times.

Following His Baptism — with the Spirit *"as"* a dove coming upon Him — Jesus was immediately led by the Spirit into the wilderness. There He fasted for forty days and underwent three major temptations (or tests) as described in Matthew 4:1-11; Mark 1:12-13, and Luke 4:1-13.

The first temptation was to turn stones into bread — no doubt an attractive offer after His long fast. But Jesus never used His Power for personal needs. Satan uses this same temptation over and over again on us as he attempts to persuade us to use God's Powers for *personal fulfillment*.

In the second temptation, Satan misapplied God's Word by trying to persuade Jesus to *"go along"* with the crowd and to become the type of Messiah they desired — a political leader of a material kingdom. Satan suggested that Jesus hurl Himself from the pinnacle of the Temple in view of the people. It would have been a spectacular act and would have established His supernatural Powers as the Messiah.

Jesus answered by saying that we shouldn't tempt (again, test) God. In answering Satan He used *"the Sword of the Spirit"* — the Word of God. He, however, made *proper* use of it.

Satan then offered Jesus all the kingdoms of the world as his final temptation. Due to the fall of man, Satan had become the god of this world. Jesus' mission was to redeem man and thus enable him to exercise

SELF-HELP STUDY NOTES

SELF-HELP STUDY NOTES

dominion over Satan. Satan tried to appeal to Jesus' human side by suggesting He take a short cut in His redemptive mission. Jesus, of course, refused and *"went the way of the Cross"* to redeem us. Our Lord used the Word of God each time He was tempted. Not only was Jesus led into the wilderness by the Spirit, but He was also sustained and strengthened throughout His fast and afterward. Thus the *"Sword of the Spirit"* helped make Him victorious.

Even though Jesus was born sinless, He could have sinned at any time as a man. There are many people in the church today who erroneously believe that Jesus Christ was incapable of sin. They believe it was impossible for Him to fail or commit error, because He was God. But we must understand that while He was *"very God"* He was also *"very man."*

It definitely *was* possible for Him to fail and sin. If Jesus weren't vulnerable to sin, and if He could *not* have sinned, the temptations would not have been real, and Jesus' whole Life and performance would have been a sham. If His response to the temptations hadn't been possible, He would not have been human. He would have been a moral and spiritual *"superman"* with no knowledge and understanding of our problems.

We are told in Scripture that He was *"in all points tempted like as we are"* (Heb. 4:15). It is clear from this Scripture and others that He understands our situations perfectly and faced every temptation — with all the *potential* failure inherent in human frailty and weakness. Despite all this, He was *"yet without sin."* He was *victorious* over sin and temptation, and you can't have victory *without being in a battle*. His Victory is what provides us with our way to Redemption and victory.

Jesus, the very God, stripped Himself of Divine Glory and took upon Himself *"the form of a servant, and was made in the likeness of men"* (Phil. 2:7). He was, however, still Deity, still God Emmanuel, God in the flesh, and God with us. But when He faced Satan's onslaughts and temptations, He faced them with the Power of the Holy Spirit strengthening the *human* frailty He had accepted. You and I can call upon this same support to strengthen us in times of trial — if we are saved and baptized with the Holy Spirit.

IN THE MINISTRY OF JESUS

As Jesus moved into His three-year Ministry, it was with the Anointing Power of the Holy Spirit. We read in Acts 10:38, *"How God anointed Jesus of Nazareth with the Holy Spirit and with Power: Who went about doing good, and healing all who were oppressed of the Devil; for God was with Him."*

Jesus was filled with the Holy Spirit beyond measure. The same is true of Believers today. It is stated in John 3:34, *"For He Whom God has sent speaks the Words of God: for God gives not the Spirit by measure unto Him."* This is a clear statement that the Holy Spirit is not given in a *limited* way, but rather without measure. The Spirit of God was upon our Lord in a greater way than He had ever been upon John the Baptist, Solomon, David, Isaiah, or the other Prophets and people of Faith. This same unmeasured anointing is available to those who today seek and accept the mighty baptism with the Holy Spirit.

As we have noted, the Spirit of God was in Jesus in a more complete way than had ever been experienced in the Old Testament. Moses wrote in Numbers 11:29 that he wished that God would put His Spirit on *all* people. He knew the dynamic differences the Holy Spirit could make in a person's life. In the Old Testament, Prophet after Prophet spoke of the coming outpouring of God's Spirit.

When the Holy Spirit descended at Pentecost (to inaugurate this great age), Peter announced that this was that which had been spoken of (previously) by the Prophet Joel. Isaiah declared that the Spirit would be poured out upon us from on high. Isaiah 44:3 says, *"For I will pour water upon him who is thirsty, and floods upon the dry ground: I will pour My Spirit upon your seed, and My blessing upon your offspring."*

We are told in Ezekiel 36:27, *"And I will put My Spirit within you, and cause you to walk in My statutes, and you shall keep My judgments, and do them."*

Jesus lived, moved, and worked miracles by the Power of the Holy Spirit. He stressed the *availability* of this Holy Spirit experience for Believers, and the *power* it would bring. He said in Luke 11:13, *"If you then, being evil, know how to give good gifts unto your children: how much more shall your Heavenly Father give the Holy Spirit to them who ask Him?"*

In Luke 24:49 He said, *"And, behold, I send the Promise of My Father upon you: but tarry ye in the city of Jerusalem, until you be endued **with power** from on high."*

At one of the feasts in Jerusalem referred to in John 7:37-39, Jesus said, *"If any man thirst, let him come unto Me, and drink. He who believes on Me, as the Scripture has said, out of his belly shall flow rivers of Living Water. (But this spoke He of the Spirit, which they who believe on Him should receive: for the Holy Spirit was not yet given; because that Jesus was not yet glorified.)"*

The Life of Jesus had been a demonstration of the dynamic reality of the Power of the Holy Spirit. The Disciples had seen Him perform great and mighty miracles by this power. Jesus was the perfect Spirit-filled person. He was anointed with the Holy Spirit, baptized with the Holy Spirit,

SELF-HELP STUDY NOTES

SELF-HELP STUDY NOTES

and literally *filled* with power. Jesus was identified with both God the Father and the Holy Spirit and was the living example of Their Power. His marvelous and miraculous Ministry was in the *Power* of the Holy Spirit and in the *Will* of the Father.

HIS ATONING DEATH

Jesus offered Himself through the eternal Holy Spirit (Heb. 9:14), and by *His* Blood *we* are cleansed. He did not simply die as a man, but as One who was perfect — and thus a suitable sacrifice for sin. He accomplished it once and for all — through the Holy Spirit.

In Christ we are redeemed, forgiven, and cleansed. If a person is forgiven, it is not necessary to go back into sin. Forgiveness of sin is provided by Jesus — who endured the Cross and despised the shame — *through the Holy Spirit*. The Holy Spirit makes effective the crucifixion.

IN THE RESURRECTION

Jesus arose, triumphant over sin, death, and the grave. The Holy Spirit is the quickening life-giving Agent. It is clearly stated in Romans 8:11, *"But if the Spirit of Him Who raised up Jesus from the dead dwell in you, He Who raised up Christ from the dead shall also quicken your mortal bodies by His Spirit who dwells in you."*

If the Spirit dwells in us, He will quicken our mortal bodies. He is a life-giver. Believers will be fully changed by the Power of the Spirit at the rapture, or when raised from the dead. We shall be changed or resurrected by the Power of the Spirit, just as Jesus was raised from the dead.

THE ASCENSION

When the time arrived for Jesus to leave the world to go be with the Father, a cloud received Him up out of their sight and two men in white appeared, saying that He must go but that He would return in like manner.

Why was it necessary for Jesus to leave? He had sustained the Disciples while He was on the Earth. But He was to become our *Heavenly* Sustainer. Thus the Holy Spirit became our Comforter *on Earth*. It was necessary for Jesus to be at the Right Hand of the Father, so the Holy Spirit took His place on Earth.

As Jesus was getting close to the end of His earthly, human life, He told the Disciples He would go to the Father and the Father would send the Comforter in His Name: *"But the Comforter, which is the Holy Spirit, Whom the Father will send in My Name, He shall teach you all things, and bring all things to your remembrance, whatsoever I have said unto you"* (Jn. 14:26).

He also stated in John 15:26, *"But when the Comforter is come, Whom I will send unto you from the Father, even the Spirit of Truth, which proceeds from the Father, He shall testify of Me."*

As He was approaching death, after His fruitful Ministry, Jesus encouraged His Disciples to see and understand some of the truths relative to the Holy Spirit and His Work. In John 16, Jesus told them it was expedient for Him to leave, because if He did not, the Comforter would not come. The Comforter is the Holy Spirit. Jesus said that if He departed, He would send the Holy Spirit to His Followers (which we are as Believers). The Spirit of God would guide them (and us) into all truths, for He is the Spirit of Truth. Jesus then told the Disciples to wait until they were endued with power and strength. As John the Baptist had prophesied, *"I indeed have baptized you with water: but He shall baptize you with the Holy Spirit"* (Mk. 1:8).

Jesus paid the price at Calvary for our Redemption, and rose from the dead. He spoke at great lengths on the Holy Spirit. He commanded the Disciples to tarry, to wait, before beginning their ministries, until they had received the promise of the Father. This is a totally new dimension in Spiritual Life, experienced first by the Disciples and today by Believers. The promise Jesus gave was, *"But you shall receive power, after that the Holy Spirit is come upon you: and you shall be witnesses unto Me both in Jerusalem, and in all Judea, and in Samaria, and unto the uttermost part of the Earth"* (Acts 1:8).

The *Power* of the Holy Spirit is now available to Believers, without measure, to work in and through Christians as it did in the Life of Christ. In fact, Jesus went on to say that His Followers would do the things He did, and even greater things. *"Verily, verily, I say unto you, He who believes on Me, the Works that I do shall he do also; and greater Works than these shall he do: because I go unto My Father"* (Jn. 14:12).

The reason even greater things could be accomplished was because He would go to the Father and the Holy Spirit would be sent. Huge throngs would be baptized with the Holy Spirit, without measure, experiencing the mighty Holy Spirit Power. The results would be far-reaching. The Holy Spirit would be as much with the Body of Christ as He was with the Apostles, and the results would affect every corner of the world. There would be witnesses in Jerusalem, Judea, in Samaria, and to the uttermost part of the Earth.

Jesus Christ was conceived by the Holy Spirit (Mat. 1:20) and for thirty years was led and taught by this Divine Spirit. Was He not *One* with the Holy Spirit? Certainly. Why then was He anointed? Because it was

SELF-HELP STUDY NOTES

SELF-HELP STUDY NOTES

essential for His human nature to be empowered by the Spirit before He could successfully perform His Ministry. Jesus was anointed at the age of thirty when the Spirit descended on Him like a dove (Jn. 1:32). At a later date, Jesus said, *"The Spirit of the Lord is upon Me, because He has anointed Me to preach"* (Lk. 4:18).

First He was born by the Spirit; then He was baptized with the Spirit; and finally He went forth to work out His Life and Ministry in the *Power* of the Spirit. We too need to be born of the Spirit, baptized with the Spirit, and then go forth to live *His* Life and reproduce *His* Works.

Chapter 5

The Holy Spirit In The Early Church

SUBJECT	**PAGE**
THE PROMISE	77
PENTECOST	77
PROPHECY FULFILLED	82
RELIGIOUS RESISTANCE	82
JERUSALEM AT PENTECOST	83
MANY ADDED TO THE CHURCH	84
ACTS OF THE HOLY SPIRIT	85
PETER AND JOHN	86
ANANIAS AND SAPPHIRA	89
OBEYING GOD	89
A SPIRIT-FILLED DEACON — STEPHEN	90
ANOTHER DEACON — PHILIP	92
SIMON'S REQUEST	93
THE APOSTLE PAUL	94
A MAN NAMED CORNELIUS	94
ANOTHER GROUP SPEAKS IN TONGUES	95
A SPIRIT-EMPOWERED CHURCH	96

CHAPTER FIVE

THE HOLY SPIRIT IN THE EARLY CHURCH

"But you shall receive power, after that the Holy Spirit is come upon you: and you shall be witnesses unto Me both in Jerusalem, and in all of Judea, and in Samaria, and unto the uttermost part of the Earth" (Acts 1:8).

"And they were all filled with the Holy Spirit, and began to speak with other tongues, as the Spirit gave them utterance" (Acts 2:4).

THE PROMISE

The first great outpouring of the Holy Spirit occurred shortly after Jesus ascended into Heaven nearly two thousand years ago. Just prior to His Ascension, Jesus instructed the Disciples and His Followers to *wait* in Jerusalem. He promised them they would be endued with power as they experienced the mighty baptism with the Holy Spirit. They were *"in one accord"* as they waited expectantly for the promise the Lord had given them.

A total of 120 people, including the Disciples, (but without Judas, of course, who was now dead) and Mary, the mother of Jesus, waited together *"in one place."* It is generally assumed that this was the *"Last Supper room"* and the room mentioned in Acts 1:13. It may well be that this was where this notable *"Holy Spirit"* revival took place, but there is no *definite* Scriptural indication that this was so.

In any event, several significant lessons can be learned by observing this group. First, they were willing to wait upon the Lord. All too often, people have a tendency to become impatient and refuse to wait for the *Lord's* timetable for events. Often, failure to be still before God results in missing some of His great Blessings. There are, to be sure, pressing demands and great needs everywhere. But one can more adequately respond to these challenges and needs *after* waiting on God for His Direction and Power.

Second, one might observe regarding this group that they were *in one accord, in one spirit,* as they sought the Lord. There is great strength in unity. Strength lies not basically in numbers, but in unity of Spirit.

PENTECOST

"And when the Day of Pentecost was fully come, they were all

SELF-HELP STUDY NOTES

SELF-HELP STUDY NOTES

with one accord in one place" (Acts 2:1). This account describes the phenomenal events the group of Disciples experienced *with* their baptism with the Holy Spirit. Why did this take place on the Day of Pentecost? Why was it simultaneous with the Hebrew Festival of Harvest? Why not just any day? Let's look at the special significance God placed on the feast days and Sabbaths He had established.

We know that the Feast of the Passover had to have occurred just fifty days prior to this because the Day of Pentecost was, by definition, the fiftieth day after Passover. Passover commemorated the killing of the Paschal Lamb, with its placing of its blood on the doorposts in Egypt. This caused the death angel to *pass over* the children of Israel during the tenth (death) plague. Blood was applied to the doorpost and life was spared. Primarily the Passover celebration renews the thought of lives saved by the sacrifice of the lamb.

It has been no coincidence that Jesus was offered as *our* Paschal Lamb on the commemoration of the original Passover. The killing of the Paschal Lamb was the type — the prophetic foreshadowing — of Jesus' later role as the Paschal Lamb for the world. The Jews today still celebrate the Passover as a *historic* occasion, not realizing its *prophetic* significance in regard to Jesus Christ.

Like the Feast of Passover, the Feast of Pentecost had special significance. It was the Feast of Firstfruits as described in Exodus 23:16. This was the day when the celebrants were to consider God's bountiful blessings as they came from their land. It was rather similar to our Thanksgiving, or the "Harvest Picnics" that used to be commonly held in rural areas when the crops were in. It was a time set aside by God for His Children to think about *harvests.*

This Pentecost Day manifestation of the Holy Spirit baptism was the introduction to the *"last days"* outpouring foretold in Joel 2:28-32, which Peter referred to in Acts 2:16-21. It represented the *"firstfruits"* ingathering, the preliminary *sample* of the abundant harvest that was to follow. This was at the very beginning of the time of the Holy Spirit ministry — the establishment of the Church Age. And, of course, there was an immediate and tremendous harvest of souls right then and there. The Disciples burst from the room, and three thousand souls were immediately converted and committed to Christ (Acts 2:41). Shortly thereafter, five thousand men (plus others) became Believers (Acts 4:4).

And in the days immediately following, the Lord *"added to the Church daily such as should be saved."* The *significance* of God's choice of the Day of Pentecost as the *time* of this initial Holy Spirit outpouring is obvious. As the building echoed to the sound of a mighty wind, as the cloven tongues of flame descended on the Disciples, as they broke out in unknown tongues — God was plucking the firstfruits of a harvest that was to sweep over and change the world. To be sure, its world-changing climax is yet to come, but it is just around the corner. Hallelujah! The harvest is almost complete and *we* are lucky enough to be in on its windup. Doesn't that thrill your soul?

The celebration of Pentecost took place fifty days after Passover. This is referred to in Leviticus 23:15, *"And you shall count unto you from the morrow after the Sabbath, from the day that you brought the sheaf of the Wave Offering; seven Sabbaths shall be complete."*

The Scripture refers to a *"new Meat Offering unto the Lord."* And just as the Heavenly fires fell onto the sacrifice presented on the altar (I Ki. 18:38), so the cloven tongues of flame came down on each person on the Day of Pentecost. This manifestation of fire from Heaven fell upon those who *yielded*. These were *submitted* Believers, offering up themselves as a *living* sacrifice, bound in love and obedience.

God's *acceptance* of them was documented by an outpouring *power* as His Spirit breathed new life into the previously ineffectual group of Believers.

Zechariah 4:6 says, *"This is the word of the Lord . . . saying, Not by might, nor by power,* **but by My Spirit,** *saith the Lord of Hosts."* This prophetic utterance is a promise to the Church in regard to the *power* of Pentecost.

Additionally, the Feast of Pentecost was a memorial to the giving of the Law of Sinai. The Sinai experience was accompanied by God's Presence, His communication with Moses, and supernatural manifestations (fire, smoke, and quaking of the Earth). At Sinai, God's Purpose was to administer justice through the Law. At Pentecost, God's Purpose was to administer mercy through Grace.

At Pentecost, God manifested Himself to Israel (and the rest of the world) in the Person of the Holy Spirit. All that was *concealed* at Sinai and in the Old Testament and Covenant, was *revealed* through the Spirit at Pentecost.

Up until that moment, God had spent almost four thousand years projecting the *shadow* of what was to come. All earlier Spiritual Ceremonies (the wave offering, blood sacrifice, circumcision) were *hints* of what was eventually to be demonstrated in *fullness*. And it was this *"latter day rain"* — the release finally of God's Grace in the Person of the Holy Spirit — that brought mankind, at last, *"face to face"* with God. And like Moses — who had to wear a veil to diffuse the glow when he came down from the mountain — man *glows* when he has a personal encounter with God.

Another significant aspect of the *original* Feast of Pentecost was that it was an *all-inclusive* celebration. This was not a case of the solitary priest entering the veil to offer sacrifice to God. *Everyone* could participate: sons,

SELF-HELP STUDY NOTES

SELF-HELP STUDY NOTES

daughters, priests, and strangers were all invited. God was thus announcing to Israel that the blessings of Pentecost were for *all*. This was prophesied by Joel in the Scriptures mentioned (Joel 2:28-32 and Acts 2:16-21).

The Spirit of God was promised for *all flesh*. Obviously God chose this particular occasion for the great initial outpouring of His Spirit to make Israel aware that the benefits were available to all.

And finally we should repeat for emphasis what we noted before: The Feast of Pentecost came *after* the Passover. The baptism with the Holy Spirit comes *after* the conversion. Of course, no specific period is required *between* Salvation and the baptism with the Holy Spirit. For some it comes within moments, while others may wait years. This is often due to lack of knowledge or for other reasons, but the baptism with the Holy Spirit always *follows* one's new birth in Christ — just as Pentecost follows Passover.

The three great feasts of the people of Israel were: Passover, Pentecost, and Tabernacles. The last great Feast is Tabernacles, which many see as foretelling the Return of Christ for His Millennial Reign. Each of these great feasts (together with four other feasts which are related) contain deep meaning and hidden significance.

It was on the Day of Pentecost that the Holy Spirit descended with power on the little group of Disciples. This was the realization of Jesus' Promise of the Comforter who was to come. The world shattering results of this event are still being felt today. The Disciples were well rewarded for their ten-day wait and their trust in the Lord. Who knows *how* much more might be accomplished today if *we* would all follow their example and wait patiently on the Lord.

The Pentecostal outpouring of the Holy Spirit was truly a *phenomenal* event. There were *several* phenomena associated with it. There *was* first the sound of a mighty rushing wind. *Second*, there were tongues of fire upon the heads of those present. And *third*, they spoke with other tongues (and prophesied).

This great outpouring of the Holy Spirit was certainly a dramatic event. Joy permeated the atmosphere, what with 120 people being filled with the Holy Spirit simultaneously! All who have experienced the baptism will almost invariably describe joy as one of the emotions experienced. And the unrestrained expressions of the Disciples' joy drew the attention of passersby. They were even accused of being *"drunk."*

When the Holy Spirit is allowed free reign in a church, joy and excitement are inevitably present. But this is not a run away display of uncontrolled emotion. There are no activities that will embarrass anyone, nor is it ever displeasing to God. There is a definite difference between the joy and excitement of the Spirit-anointing and plain old noise and confusion.

When the joy of the Lord is present, people do not sit idly by with frozen expressions, in the silence of a morgue. There is instead the lifting of hands (as Paul described in I Timothy 2:8). Additionally, there are almost always expressions of joy and exclamations such as *"Hallelujah"* or *"Praise the Lord."* When the Glory of God fills a place — people can't restrain themselves from joining in the worship of the Lord.

Some people are reluctant to allow the Holy Spirit to move in a congregation. Some view the Book of Acts negatively and dislike any emphasis placed on the mighty moving of the Holy Spirit — especially manifestations of the *Gifts* of the Spirit (I Cor. 12:8-10).

The Early Church experienced the Power of the Holy Spirit. As the Spirit descended upon the waiting group, it was with the sound of a rushing wind and with tongues of fire. This was certainly a dramatic introduction of Holy Spirit Power to the Church.

Subsequent to this, people were baptized with the Holy Spirit as described in Acts and throughout the history of the New Testament Church. No further incidents of the rushing wind or tongues of fire are described, however. Why were these manifestations confined only to that *first* dramatic time? Just because, I suspect, it *was* the first time!

Wind is associated with the Spirit of God in John 3:8 (*The wind blows where it listeth*) and fire is associated with the Spirit in Matthew 3:11 (*baptize you with the Holy Spirit, and with fire*). It is therefore logical to conclude that these two phenomena accompanied the *original* visitation to *document* its prophetic legitimacy.

It was an unusual and dramatic event. Nothing like it had ever happened before. The first reaction of those who hadn't experienced the baptism was that the participants were *"drunk with new wine."* God therefore included the wind and the fire to document that this was indeed the phenomenon that had been prophesied. And once established the wind and fire were no longer necessary.

The other new experience was that they were baptized with the Holy Spirit was speaking in tongues — which is the *initial evidence* of the mighty baptism with the Holy Spirit. As later Believers experienced the baptism with the Holy Spirit, they *still* spoke in tongues — but the phenomena of the mighty wind and tongues of fire were absent, because they signaled the *arrival* of the Spirit, just as Jesus had promised.

The Disciples acted in an unusual manner as they experienced the outpouring of the baptism with the Holy Spirit. As mentioned, observers thought they were drunk. It is not unusual to see Believers actually stagger under the impact of the Holy Spirit. When my own mother was filled with the Holy Spirit, she did so. She staggered half a day as if she were drunk. She was in the Spirit, and many recognize this experience because they too have reeled under the Power of God. Others, of course, may not have so

SELF-HELP STUDY NOTES

SELF-HELP STUDY NOTES

unusual an initial encounter with the Holy Spirit, but many *are* overwhelmed and have the appearance of drunkenness.

In crusades across this nation, we see thousands of people worshipping God as His Glory fills the auditoriums. Sometime ago, I saw a distinguished looking gentleman fall under the Power of the Holy Spirit as he was baptized and immersed with the Spirit. As the Power of the Spirit came upon him, he fell to the floor, laughing as he tried to raise himself. There was a steady outpouring from his heart and from his life in the form of a delighted laugh. He struggled time after time to rise from the floor. After the auditorium had emptied, he was *still* trying to rise, laughing in the Holy Spirit, and experiencing the Power of the Almighty God. Now some might call this *"religious fanaticism,"* but it is really the Power of God at work changing lives. God always meets our needs according to His Word.

When the original 120 were baptized, as recorded in Acts, it seems to suggest that scores of people came to mock and accuse them of drunkenness. But Simon Peter (the *new* Simon Peter, bold in the Lord) stood and declared, *"For these are not drunken, as you suppose, seeing it is but the third hour of the day"* (Acts 2:15). This was rather early in the morning — about nine o'clock — and they were not drunk with wine, but rather filled with the Spirit.

PROPHECY FULFILLED

In the next breath Peter told them that this was the fulfillment of a Prophecy by Joel. This Prophetic Promise was: *"And it shall come to pass afterward, that I will pour out my Spirit upon all flesh; and your sons and your daughters shall prophesy, your old men shall dream dreams, your young men shall see visions"* (Joel 2:28). As this promise was fulfilled and the Spirit of God was uniquely manifested in the early Believers, people questioned the experience, mocked them, and claimed they were drunk.

RELIGIOUS RESISTANCE

Jesus was opposed by the religious leaders of His day. Undoubtedly, religious people were involved in mocking the early Believers when they were baptized with the Holy Spirit. Much of the Church world still mocks those who enter into the Pentecostal experience. They fortify their position by saying they are not mocking the Bible but only *"religious fanaticism."* They particularly object to the baptism with the Holy Spirit, *with the evidence of speaking in tongues!*

This criticism comes not from ungodly sinners — but rather from those who identify themselves with the Church of the Lord Jesus Christ. As in the days of the Early Church, there is a religious hierarchy that objects to many things of the Spirit. In some churches today individuals can commit virtually any imaginable sin and remain in good standing. But if they are baptized with the Holy Spirit and speak in tongues, they will not be tolerated in the fellowship.

We have, more than once, heard of church leaders who have stated that they would prefer to see their pastor involved with a woman or involved in theft from the church fund than have him become interested in Charismatic, or Pentecostal, philosophy. This animosity extends *particularly* to the baptism with the Holy Spirit with the evidence of speaking in tongues.

Religious prejudices are always strong, and many fail to study the results (or the *fruit*) of their prejudices. Countless individuals, after the baptism, have experienced new release in their spirit, new joy in their Christian life, new appreciation for God's Word, and new insight and understanding of (and love for) the Lord Jesus Christ. All this is accompanied by a newly empowered witness for the Lord.

There are all too many who faithfully attend church but refuse to open their hearts to the Move of the Holy Spirit. On the other hand, there are multitudes moving into the dynamic power and rich blessings that accompany the baptism with the Holy Spirit.

As in the days of the New Testament Church, as reported in the Book of Acts, people by the thousands are having a similar experience today. And as in the Early Church, this experience often results in churches filled beyond capacity, souls added to the Kingdom, and the Blessings of God flowing forth. The events recorded in the Second Chapter of Acts resulted in momentous events two thousand years ago, and are still making dramatic changes today.

JERUSALEM AT PENTECOST

There were devout men from every nation dwelling in Jerusalem, which was the commercial center of the Middle East. Some were simply on business, while others were present for the religious feast day. As the Disciples erupted out onto the street, word spread rapidly and a crowd gathered because: *"every man heard them speak in his own language"* (Acts 2:6).

"And they were all amazed and marveled, saying one to another, Behold, are not all these which speak Galileans? And how hear we every man in our own tongue, wherein we were born? Parthians, and Medes, and Elamites, and the dwellers in Mesopotamia, and in Judea,

SELF-HELP STUDY NOTES

SELF-HELP STUDY NOTES

and Cappadocia, in Pontus, and Asia, Phrygia, and Pamphylia, in Egypt, and in the parts of Libya about Cyrene, and strangers of Rome, Jews and proselytes, Cretes and Arabians, we do hear them speak in our tongues the wonderful Works of God. And they were all amazed, and were in doubt, saying one to another, What does this mean? Others mocking said, These men are full of new wine" (Acts 2:7-13).

Those in Jerusalem were dumbfounded as they heard and saw the effects of the baptism with the Holy Spirit. The Disciples spoke with other tongues — which is to say, in other languages. These were languages that the Disciples and the 120 had never learned, but which flowed forth from them under the Anointing and Unction of the Holy Spirit. It was the manifestation and evidence of the baptism with the Holy Spirit.

The people present were from a number of different nations and heard them speaking in the individual languages of their native lands. Many times when someone speaks in another tongue or language, there is no one present who happens to understand that particular language. It is then a devotional expression for the individual in his communion with the Lord.

It is both a language that *could be* understood somewhere in the world — *and* an expression of the individual's innermost being or spirit.

This speaking in tongues (or different languages) is not normally for the purpose of evangelizing the lost; it is generally an expression of praise. There are, however, numerous accounts of individuals speaking in an unknown language while someone *is* present who understands the language. Some of these incidents have involved languages used in remote areas which were recognized and understood by a missionary who had worked in these areas. Invariably the message is an expression of praise to the Lord.

MANY ADDED TO THE CHURCH

With the curious crowd of skeptics gathered around the Disciples, Peter seized the opportunity and preached to them. He preached in his own language, which would have been Hebrew or Aramaic. He was not, therefore, speaking in tongues at that moment, but he *was* speaking under the *Anointing* of the Holy Spirit.

Peter declared to them the Promise of God and the Salvation of the Lord. He also told how Joel prophesied this very outpouring of the Spirit of God. He then went on to inform them of some events which would take place just prior to the Great Tribulation, which would immediately precede the Millennium. His primary emphasis concerned the Redemptive Work of Jesus Christ, whom they had rejected.

Peter preached Christ to them under the Anointing and Power of the Holy Spirit, and three thousand souls were added to the Church that day.

Obviously the Power of the Holy Spirit wasn't confined to the *room* where the Disciples had been filled. While Peter gave a fine sermon, by itself it could hardly account for the three thousand spontaneous conversions. There is no question that the convicting Power of the Holy Spirit was heavily on this crowd and that Peter's sermon was only the spark that ignited the Holy Spirit Fire in them.

There have been attempts to explain away speaking in tongues. Many have claimed this experience was an *initial* manifestation of the Holy Spirit's coming, who with no *subsequent* experiences of this type. Still, it had become a *common* experience, with multiplied thousands being immersed, or baptized, with the Holy Spirit with speaking in an unknown language an accompanying phenomenon.

The precise events of the Second Chapter of Acts are being repeated today, and they mark the ushering in of the great Pentecostal, or Charismatic, Age. It is an enduement of power from on high. We are living in an age when the Holy Spirit is presently at work in mighty ways. God is *still* pouring out His Spirit upon all flesh, or at least upon all who come to Him *seeking* this great blessing.

ACTS OF THE HOLY SPIRIT

The Book of the Acts of the Apostles might also be called "The Acts of the Holy Spirit." It recounts the early moving of the Holy Spirit in the lives of the individuals and churches. Marvelous things took place in the Early Church that present-day churches could well profit by emulating. However, some people seem to prefer *not* to be reminded of the events occurring in the Book of Acts, especially those relating to the Work of the Holy Spirit.

A man came to me at one time in great agitation. His son-in-law who had just been baptized with the Holy Spirit was pastor of a church that didn't believe with the Holy Spirit baptism. This young minister's father-in-law wanted him to repudiate what he had just experienced. He said he had to come to *talk* to me, but it really seemed he had come more to *argue*. The Spirit of God told me to just *"love him,"* and that was what I did. This seemed to unnerve him, and he grew more and more uncertain and defensive. I finally decided to share Acts 2, 8, 9, 10, and 19 with him, which describe over and over again the baptism with the Holy Spirit *and* speaking in tongues.

This man shouted, *"No, no, no! That Book of Acts, I don't like it! Why must you always go to the Book of Acts?"*

I was, naturally, surprised. What was *wrong* with going to the Book of Acts? Shouldn't that be our example?

I once heard a preacher on the radio say that we should not use the

SELF-HELP STUDY NOTES

SELF-HELP STUDY NOTES

Book of Acts as our guide. I could only think, *"If we aren't going to use the Book of Acts, what's to be done with it? Should we tear it out?"* But there are other Scriptures, so with this man (whose son-in-law had received the Holy Spirit baptism) I turned to Isaiah and read Chapter 28, Verses 11-13.

"For with stammering lips and another tongue will He speak to this people. To whom he said, This is the rest wherewith you may cause the weary to rest; and this is the refreshing: yet they would not hear. But the Word of the LORD was unto them precept upon precept, precept upon precept; line upon line, line upon line; here a little, and there a little; that they might go, and fall backward, and be broken, and snared, and taken."

The man just sat there and finally said, quietly, *"I didn't know that was there."*

Why do so many persist in fighting against God and His Word? Gamaliel, a great teacher and exponent of Mosaic Law (and who was also Paul's teacher), once said (in so many words), *"Gentlemen, if this is not of God it will come to nought. But if it **is** of God, we will be putting ourselves in the position of **fighting against God!** No man has ever won doing that"* (Acts 5:38-39).

Do not set *yourself* against God. Rather, seek His Truth. In the process of coming to understand the Word of God, *do not neglect the Book of Acts.* It is our definitive account of the Holy Spirit and of circumstances concerning the Early Church.

PETER AND JOHN

Soon after experiencing the baptism with the Holy Spirit, Peter and John were going to the Temple at the hour of prayer. At the gate of the Temple, they encountered a lame man who had been afflicted from the time of his birth. He was begging alms from the people entering the Temple, as is described in Acts 3:1-10.

Spying Peter and John, he begged alms. Peter looked at him and said, *"Silver and gold have I none; but such as I have give I thee: in the Name of Jesus Christ of Nazareth **rise up and walk.**"*

Peter then took the man by the hand and lifted him to his feet. Immediately the man's ankles received strength and he began to walk. Then, overjoyed by what had happened, he began to leap and praise God. Seeing this arresting demonstration of God's Power, the people were amazed at the miracle of healing they had just observed. They came running to Peter to question him, and he used this occasion to preach his second great sermon.

Signs and wonders followed the Believers, just as promised in God's

Word. But the main focus of Peter's preaching was Jesus — whom they had crucified. He was the One who died to save them. And as the Word of God went forth in power and might, still *more* people were saved until they numbered at least five thousand.

The Holy Spirit puts power into preaching: hearts and lives are touched and transformed and thousands are added to the Church. Miracles are performed by the Power of the Holy Spirit. This attracts the attention of the people who respond to the anointed Message of the Gospel.

The religious leaders were amazed, as uneducated men (such as Peter and John) declared great Truths under the Anointing of God. Not knowing how to handle such as these, the religious leaders *"called them, and commanded them not to speak at all nor teach in the Name of Jesus"* (Acts 4:18).

Peter and John, however, declared that they must proclaim the things they had experienced.

From time to time, the early Disciples and Believers were threatened, beaten, imprisoned, and told not to talk about Jesus nor demonstrate the mighty Power of the Holy Spirit. Despite this persecution, the Disciples continued to minister. And thus it is today. From time to time, there has been intense persecution of Believers baptized with the Holy Spirit — and most often by religious *"leaders"* who wield power in the establishment churches.

Peter was preaching with boldness and power, and he was regularly seeing miracles following his ministry. This same Peter had only recently denied Jesus three separate times on the night He was betrayed. On that night, when individuals had asked Peter about his relationship to Christ, Peter denied Him. When questioned by a young maiden in the Temple court, he denied having ever known Jesus.

Peter had been with the Lord Jesus over three years, from the very beginning of His Ministry. He was a part of the *"inner circle"* which was closest to the Lord. Still he denied the Lord Jesus Christ in His time of crisis.

Peter denied the Lord when the Master was crucified. He failed miserably. When Peter was with the Lord, he had seen miracles and had even been involved in them. The Disciples had prayed for the sick, had seen great miracles take place, had cast out devils, and had done mighty things. But what happened as soon as the Lord had departed from them? They fell apart. They became wishy-washy. They were *"up"* one day and *"down"* the next.

There were many things the Disciples didn't understand during Jesus' Ministry. They often blurted out statements or questions that revealed their complete ignorance of what He was trying to teach. On more than one occasion, the Lord actually had to rebuke them. These men were *saved*, but they obviously had no aptitude or talent for ministering to the public.

SELF-HELP STUDY NOTES

SELF-HELP STUDY NOTES

They had no aptitude, that is, *until* they underwent their life-changing experience on the Day of Pentecost. Then Peter and the others — who had been weak, unsure, and incapable — were suddenly transformed into whirlwinds of Faith. And this was no *gradual transformation* that took place; it was a sudden, *explosive* change. It was the reason Jesus had told them to tarry in Jerusalem until they had been endued with power from on high.

Jesus promised to send the Holy Spirit, who would revolutionize their lives. He also told them to *remain* in Jerusalem until they had received the Holy Spirit, and only *then* should they begin their ministries of healing the sick and preaching the Gospel.

The difference in Simon Peter was dramatic; but John, James, Nathaniel, and all the other Disciples were similarly changed. They had new priorities and a new boldness. *Everything* was changed. The Lord had promised that they would have *power*. He had promised in John 16:13 that the Holy Spirit would lead them into all Truth. The Holy Spirit gives insight and understanding and reveals Truth. And He always reveals Jesus — the Way, the Truth, and the Life.

With Peter and John preaching with the Power and Anointing of the Holy Spirit, it wasn't long before they found themselves in trouble and even arrested. How tragic it is that religious leaders don't speak out strongly when church members become involved in the sins of the world — but react violently when someone becomes filled with the Holy Spirit with the evidence of speaking in other tongues.

A person's life is changed, God's Presence and Plan is seen with greater clarity, and they become zealous for saving souls. They suddenly find they love Jesus more deeply than ever before. They are filled with joy and turn from sin while worldly pleasures lose their attraction. All too often, they find themselves alienated from the main Body of the Church. It is not all that uncommon to see people *"expelled"* from their churches. Why? Not because they are mired in sin (as they *may* have been before), but *simply because they were baptized with the Holy Spirit!*

It was God's intention that churches should be patterned after those in the Book of Acts. But if the great Apostle Paul were to return today, what kind of churches would he find? The majority of today's churches are all too often dead, dry, legalistic, stagnant, and totally lacking in life. The Church that appeared in the Book of Acts was alive with power and enthusiasm. The difference? The New Testament Church was totally committed to *"freedom in the Spirit."* The Holy Spirit directed their services — and their lives!

Today, of course, preachers say we are not to go to the Book of Acts. But if that's true, what *should* we use? The Book of Acts is an *extremely* important part of the Bible. The *whole* Bible should be used as the guide to our Spiritual Lives and all church activities.

ANANIAS AND SAPPHIRA

The significance of personal commitment and the seriousness of sin are apparent in the experience of the Early Church as related in the account of Ananias and Sapphira in Acts 5:1-11. There were organizational difficulties and great personal needs in the Early Church. It was common for church members to donate *everything they owned* to the local body. Ananias and Sapphira, perhaps in the effort to be *"accepted"* in the affections of their local church, sold a certain possession to give proceeds to the Church. They were in no way *forced* to do this, nor were they expected to give the entire sale price to the Church. Rather, it was theirs to do with as they wished.

But Ananias and Sapphira came forward and announced that they were giving the entire price of the possession to the Church. When Ananias brought it to the Disciples and laid it before them, declaring it to be the entire amount, Peter stared at him coldly and asked *"Why has Satan filled your heart to lie to the Holy Spirit?"* (Acts 5:3).

Ananias had lied, not unto men but unto God. And at that instant Ananias fell dead at Peter's feet. A group of the young men present carried him out and buried him.

About three hours later, his wife, not knowing what had transpired, came to Peter. Peter asked her if the land had been sold for so much — the same amount Ananias had falsely presented — and she said that, yes, it was the total amount. Peter then asked her why she had agreed with her husband to tempt the Spirit of the Lord. Sapphira also died on the spot, and those who had just buried her husband carried her out also.

On first reading this account, it may seem a severe punishment for their action. Today many assumed Christians seem to do much worse without being blasted on the spot. But this dramatic demonstration of the consequences of sin was necessary at that moment. The Holy Spirit was moving in great power. He was organizing the Church that was going to carry on the Ministry of our Lord. Sin could not be allowed to enter and corrupt the embryonic Church. Great fear came upon all in the Church, and upon as many as heard of the incident (Acts 5:11).

The Holy Spirit *convicts* of sin, righteousness, and judgment. When the Spirit of God is present in power, unusual things can happen.

OBEYING GOD

Not only was sin dealt with swiftly and intently in the New Testament Church, but in another area Scripture declares that by the hands of the Prophets were many signs and wonders wrought among the people. The sick were healed in great numbers, some being brought in their beds to be

SELF-HELP STUDY NOTES

**SELF-HELP
STUDY NOTES**

placed where Peter's shadow would fall upon them (Acts 5:15). Remarkable healings and miracles were taking place *by* the Power of the Holy Spirit, *through* the lives of the Spirit-filled Apostles.

The Early Church experienced resistance to this move of God and, as still happens today, it was the religious leaders who led the opposition to the Holy Spirit movement. It was the Sanhedrin, the local *"Church Council,"* which seized Peter and the Apostles and had them placed in prison (Acts 5:17-21). But here again the Power of God was demonstrated.

An Angel of the Lord came by night, opened the prison doors, and instructed them to go to the Temple and speak the Word of Life to the people (Acts 5:19-20). They did return to the Temple and resumed their preaching. Of course, the religious leaders again demanded that they cease preaching as they had been ordered previously (Acts 5:27-28).

Peter and the other Apostles told the Council that when there was a conflict between the orders of God and man that they would prefer to obey God. And then Peter went on to preach about Jesus. The Disciples defended themselves by declaring that they were obeying God. And this was the point where Gamaliel — the learned man of the Laws — tried to persuade the Council not to fight against God but rather to wait and see what the final outcome would be.

The Apostles were beaten and released, but they rejoiced that they had been found worthy to suffer for the Name of Jesus Christ. And they went daily to the Temple and to every house teaching and preaching about Jesus (Acts 5:40-42). The Holy Spirit Power demonstrated in the Early Church is not apparent in many churches today.

A SPIRIT-FILLED DEACON — STEPHEN

In the Early Church the number of Believers multiplied, and practical needs arose (Acts 6:1). It was decided that the Spiritual Leaders of the Church were to give themselves entirely to the study of the Word of God and to Spiritual Ministry. So they selected out certain deacons who were to concentrate on more practical matters — procurement and preparation of food, accommodations, and so forth. *"Seven men of honest report"* were selected; men who were *full of the Holy Spirit and Wisdom"* (Acts 6:3).

One of the first of the deacons chosen was Stephen, a man *"full of Faith and power"* who *"did great wonders and miracles among the people"* (Acts 6:8). The ministry of this Spirit-filled deacon reached far beyond the basic duties of his deacon's role. In addition to his concentration on fulfilling his practical functions, he ministered, preached, and performed miracles as he went about his normal duties.

Of course, the Devil doesn't appreciate having the Gospel brought forth with power, people being delivered from demons, and the sick being healed in the Name of Jesus Christ. So resistance soon developed as Stephen went about preaching under the Power and Anointing of the Holy Spirit. Members of the synagogues plotted against Stephen and brought him to trial for heresy because he preached Jesus Christ. They were cut to the heart by his words (no doubt having been put under conviction), but their reaction was to *gnash on him with their teeth* (Acts 6:9-15 and 7:54).

Scripture goes on to say in the next Verse, *"But he, being full of the Holy Spirit, looked up steadfastly into Heaven, and saw the Glory of God, and Jesus standing on the Right Hand of God, And said, Behold, I see the Heavens opened, and the Son of man standing on the Right Hand of God. Then they cried out with a loud voice, and stopped their ears, and ran upon him with one accord, And cast him out of the city, and stoned him: and the witnesses laid down their clothes at a young man's feet, whose name was Saul. And they stoned Stephen, calling upon God, and saying, Lord Jesus, receive my spirit"* (Acts 7:55-59).

This man of God was so hated of the Devil for the works he had done that the Jewish religious leaders gnashed their teeth, rushed him out of the gates, and stoned him to death.

To declare the unsearchable riches of God and the Gospel of the Lord Jesus Christ in the Power of the Holy Spirit will certainly evoke a response. Many accept, believe, receive — and are gloriously changed. But tragically, others harden their hearts, growing indignant and antagonistic. They become violent in their reaction to individuals who pray for the sick, believe God for answers to prayer, and believe in the Power of Almighty God. Even physical violence is not unknown because the spirit causing these reactions comes from the Devil.

Satan despises the Work of the Holy Spirit because it wreaks havoc on *his* kingdom. Satan's kingdom is *not* hurt by churches that operate as social clubs. Neither is his kingdom hindered by preachers who find *"religion"* an ego trip and who are only *intellectually* involved in the *technicalities* of Scripture. Such know nothing about the Power of the Holy Spirit.

Satan's kingdom is not bothered by the size of a church's membership roll. It's a question of whether *lives* are changed and transformed by the Spirit of God. The *"proper"* churches don't pose a threat to Satan, for they concentrate on the same old *safe* places and involve themselves only in matters that are *"socially acceptable"* to the broadest possible cross-section of the population. It is only when Spirit-filled Christians move in unity of fellowship and in the Power of God that there's a threat to the kingdom of Satan. *Then* he fights against it with all the powers of Hell.

Being Spirit-filled does not render immunity to difficulties created by Satan. As in the case of Stephen, a strong stand for Christ has resulted in

SELF-HELP STUDY NOTES

SELF-HELP STUDY NOTES

martyrdom for many. It is evident from Scripture that Stephen was not only Spirit-filled but that he was *working* at his relationship with the Lord. He proclaimed the Gospel every chance he could. The sick were healed and the lives were transformed.

It was the same religious leaders who had crucified Christ who engineered Stephen's death (Acts 6:11-12). The same is true today. It is the community leaders of the *"establishment"* churches who stand up and denounce the mighty moving of God's Spirit. And all too often, it is the influence of the organized religions that discourages the impressionable and prevents them from moving forward to the true power and might of God as demonstrated through the Holy Spirit.

ANOTHER DEACON — PHILIP

Philip was another Spirit-filled deacon of the Early Church. Philip preached Christ to the city of Samaria (Acts 8:5). Scripture says that with one accord the people gave heed unto the things which Philip spake. They had seen the miracles he had performed under the Anointing of the Holy Spirit (Acts 8:7-8).

The people gladly received the Word of God, and many believed and were baptized when Peter and John arrived to continue Philip's ministry (Acts 8:14).

Besides preaching, Peter and John prayed for the people to receive the Holy Spirit (Acts 8:15). Scripture describes their relationship with the Holy Spirit in this way: *"(For as yet he was fallen upon none of them: only they were baptized in the Name of the Lord Jesus.) Then laid they their hands on them, and they received the Holy Spirit"* (Acts 8:16-17). The people believed and had been baptized, so when hands were laid on them and prayers made, they were baptized with the Holy Spirit.

Some churches teach that when you become saved, there is nothing else to receive. They claim that there is no more, that you *have* received the Holy Spirit. But in Acts 2, 8, 9, 10, and 19, we read of Christians being filled with the Holy Spirit some time *after* they have been saved. Of course, the Holy Spirit plays an essential role in a person's salvation, but this is *not* what is referred to in Acts 1:8. This says, *"But you shall receive **power**, after that the Holy Spirit is come upon you."*

This is not the relationship in the Holy Spirit which *brought* you to Salvation. This is not the *drawing* spoken of by Jesus in John 6:44. This is an *immersion* in His Being and Power — which is generally referred to as *"the baptism with the Holy Spirit."*

The baptism with the Holy Spirit must *follow* Salvation. While it can occur just minutes or seconds later, it must come *after* Salvation and is not an *"automatic"* part of Salvation.

The sinner comes forth to receive Salvation. It is the *saved* person who comes forth to receive the Gift of the Holy Spirit. Every single account in Acts demonstrates this. Acts 8 *clearly* states that the people believed and were baptized. But it wasn't until after Peter and John came — and prayed for them to be baptized with the Holy Spirit — that this actually took place.

They had been baptized in water, and they had experienced the joy of Salvation. Great things had been happening through the Holy Spirit Power residing in Philip. Demons had been cast out, sick bodies had been healed, and the signs of a great revival were present. But the Holy Spirit had not yet fallen on these people prior to the visit of Peter and John. All this occurred, of course, *after* the Day of Pentecost and the initial outpouring of the Spirit. So when Peter and John prayed for the people, they were baptized with the Holy Spirit.

SIMON'S REQUEST

Among the Believers in Samaria (and also baptized in water) was a man named Simon, a sorcerer who had amassed great wealth by bewitching people with his sorcery. When he saw hands laid on the Believers and their receiving the Holy Spirit, Simon offered money to the Apostles if they would teach him to deliver the baptism of the Holy Spirit by the laying on of hands (Acts 8:17-18).

Obviously something unusual had to have happened to these people or Simon would not have been willing to pay hard cash for a *"franchise"* offering it. There had to be *evidence* that something tangible had occurred. Simon the sorcerer was not, of course, properly motivated, nor did he understand what was involved. Peter rebuked him severely and advised Repentance (Acts 8:20-23). It is apparent from this account that they were praying for people to receive the Holy Spirit *after* conversion — and that something *unique* (which a man like Simon could misunderstand and desire for selfish purposes) had occurred.

Simon did have powers, and as a sorcerer he had seen unusual things done. He was not particularly impressed with healings and some of the other phenomena, but this experience impressed him.

In Acts, Chapters 2, 10, and 19, the people spoke with other tongues as they were baptized with the Holy Spirit. There are other evidences characterizing Spirit-filled Believers, but this was the basic, *common* evidence which was initially demonstrated by those baptized with the Holy Spirit. It was immediately recognizable by all observers as an evidence of the baptism. Quite obviously what impressed Simon was this same evidence that had occurred on the Day of Pentecost.

SELF-HELP STUDY NOTES

SELF-HELP STUDY NOTES

THE APOSTLE PAUL

Saul (later to go by the name Paul) was severely persecuting the Believers in Christ when he met the risen Lord on the road to Damascus. As Jesus spoke to him, Saul was blinded by a light from Heaven, and his vision was lost for three days. During this period he fasted. Then the Lord spoke to Ananias (not the husband of Sapphira mentioned earlier), a devout Disciple who was directed to the place where Saul was abiding.

Ananias went to Saul and prayed for him to receive his sight again, and also to be baptized with the Holy Spirit. His sight was restored, and he was also filled with the Holy Spirit. As in Acts 8, it can be *concluded* that the initial evidence was speaking in tongues, because he is later recorded (in I Corinthians 14:18) as saying, *"I thank my God, I speak with tongues."*

Transformed by Christ, and empowered by the Holy Spirit, Paul went on to become what is generally conceded to be the greatest missionary statesmen of all time. He was led by God to bring *many* to Christ, to establish churches on his missionary journey, and to write many of the books of the New Testament under the Anointing of the Holy Spirit.

A MAN NAMED CORNELIUS

In the Tenth Chapter of Acts, we find a discussion of the Work of the Holy Spirit in the Early Church. Much of this chapter deals with a man by the name of Cornelius. A centurion (the captain over a troop of Roman soldiers) and a devout man who feared God *"with all his house,"* Cornelius was a man who gave much alms to the poor. He also spent much time in prayer.

Cornelius received a vision. An Angel spoke to him and told him about Peter (Acts 10:1-7). Simon Peter had a vision at the same time, and this concerned Cornelius who was at that moment dispatching messengers to bring Peter to him. As Peter pondered the meaning of his vision, the Spirit of God informed him that three men were seeking him (Acts 10:19) and that he was to go with them. When Cornelius met Peter, he fell down at his feet and worshiped him (Acts 10:25-26). Peter was embarrassed and told him to stand up since he too was just a man.

Cornelius described to Peter how for four days he had fasted and prayed, and how God had sent him a vision (Acts 10:30-33). A number of people had gathered at the house of Cornelius, and as Peter spoke the Holy Spirit fell on them. The Bible records that those who experienced the baptism at this time *spoke with other tongues, and magnified God* (Acts 10:44-46).

Though the Hebrews were surprised that the Holy Spirit had thus fallen upon the Gentiles, they now realized that Jesus came not only for the Jews but for all mankind. Gradually, this point was becoming evident to the Hebrew Believers, but it proved a difficult lesson for some of them to absorb.

Many of those who walked with Jesus would remember His words, as well as those of John the Baptist. John had declared that he would baptize with water, but that the Messiah (whom he was proclaiming) would baptize with the Holy Spirit (Mk. 1:8).

The realization of this promise was delivered not only on the Day of Pentecost, but also subsequent to it, right up to this day. And it should be obvious from reading the Word of God that *associated* with this baptism is the fact of speaking in tongues.

ANOTHER GROUP SPEAKS IN TONGUES

Another account of great significance is found in Acts 19. While Apollos was at Corinth, Paul — having passed through the upper coasts — came to Ephesus and found a group of Disciples. Paul asked these Believers, *"Have you received the Holy Spirit since you believed?"*

They told Paul that they had *"not so much as **heard** whether there would be any Holy Spirit."* They further informed him that they had received John's baptism, the water baptism of Repentance. As Believers in the Lord Jesus Christ, they were saved and baptized. But suddenly, *"When Paul had laid his hands upon them, the Holy Spirit came on them; and they spoke with tongues, and prophesied"* (Acts 19:6). Once again, it is absolutely evident that the experience of baptism with the Holy Spirit was *accompanied by speaking in other tongues!* This is the initial evidence!

It is also obvious that these Believers were asked if they had received the Holy Spirit. The question takes into consideration that they *were* Believers (saved and baptized). So by asking the question, Paul documents that Salvation and the baptism with the Holy Spirit are *not* simultaneous experiences. You can be saved and *not* filled with the Holy Spirit!

As we have discussed previously, there are those who insist that a person *does not need this experience*, claiming it is automatically received at the time of Salvation. But obviously, based on the question asked by Paul, the baptism with the Holy Spirit is a separate and unique experience for Believers. And Paul is, I believe, a Christian authority second only to Jesus Christ Himself.

Others claim that the only time the Holy Spirit came upon individuals in a dramatic fashion (as they were filled with the Holy Spirit) was on the Day of Pentecost. But some of these experiences we have been relating happening long after the Day of Pentecost. And these were not isolated

SELF-HELP STUDY NOTES

SELF-HELP STUDY NOTES

occurrences; they happened all through the Book of Acts which describes the history of the Early Church over an *extended* period. This, plus the fact that the same phenomena are happening today, would seem to satisfy all but the most obstinate that the baptism with the Holy Spirit is not an *unusual* occurrence; that it was not for a short or isolated period in history; that it is indeed associated with speaking in tongues unknown to the speaker; and that it *is* happening today!

A SPIRIT-EMPOWERED CHURCH

The Early Church experienced *mighty* moves of the Holy Spirit as people were baptized with the Spirit. It happened to individuals and entire groups, and it would appear that all spoke with other tongues and prophesied.

These manifestations continued to be observed throughout First-century Christianity, and they are happening today.

The Believer, in the time of the New Testament, came to understand what the baptism with the Holy Spirit involved. It is sometimes overlooked that the Epistles (which constitute a major part of the New Testament) were written *to* Spirit-filled Believers *by* Spirit-filled Believers.

Sometimes correction and instruction are necessary to correct abuses, as in the Epistles to the Corinthians. But the early Believers understood the Spirit-inspired Scriptures for they were Spirit-filled themselves.

The Early Church was indeed Spirit-led, Spirit-filled, and composed of Believers baptized with the Holy Spirit. The great advances they accomplished were indeed the acts of the Holy Spirit working *through* Spirit-filled Believers.

Chapter 6

The Holy Spirit In The Believer

SUBJECT	PAGE
DOES ONE RECEIVE THE HOLY SPIRIT AT CONVERSION?	99
AN EXPERIENCE FOR OUR DAY	101
THE NEED TO BE FILLED WITH THE SPIRIT	102
CONDITIONS FOR RECEIVING	103
BAPTISM OF POWER	104
INITIAL EVIDENCE	105
THE BAPTISM WITH THE HOLY SPIRIT AS A DEFINITE AND DISTINCT WORK OF GRACE	106
INDIVIDUALS ARE BAPTIZED WITH THE HOLY SPIRIT *AFTER* CONVERSION	108
EVIDENCE THAT ONE HAS RECEIVED THE BAPTISM WITH THE HOLY SPIRIT	111
WHY TONGUES?	112
WHAT GOOD DOES IT DO?	114
DO ALL SPEAK WITH TONGUES?	116
TO SUMMARIZE	118
IS THERE A NEED TO TARRY IF ONE IS TO RECEIVE?	119
THE PRECIOUS PRESENCE OF THE HEAVENLY GUEST	119

CHAPTER SIX

THE HOLY SPIRIT IN THE BELIEVER

"He said unto them, Have you received the Holy Spirit since you believed?" (Acts 19:2).

"That the blessing of Abraham might come on the Gentiles through Jesus Christ; that we might receive the Promise of the Spirit through Faith" (Gal. 3:14).

DOES ONE RECEIVE THE HOLY SPIRIT AT CONVERSION?

When the Apostle Paul came to Ephesus he asked some new Disciples a significant question: *"Have you received the Holy Spirit since you believed?"* (Acts 19:2).

These were Believers who had been baptized by John the Baptist (the baptism of Repentance) but who were completely unaware of the Holy Spirit. Paul told them fully of the Redemptive Work of Christ, and they were then baptized in water unto Repentance. Following this, Paul laid his hands on them and they were then instantly baptized with the Holy Spirit, speaking in tongues and prophesying.

As in the other recorded cases in Acts, the baptism with the Holy Spirit was experienced *subsequent* to their accepting Jesus Christ as Saviour.

There is a great deal of controversy today as to whether one receives the Holy Spirit at the moment of conversion. Actually, the only proper answer to this question is, *"Yes and no!"*

The responsibilities of the Holy Spirit are many and varied, and one of the most important is that of Regeneration. Our Lord said, in John 6:44, *"No man can come to Me, except the Father . . . draw him."* And who acts as the Father's *instrument* in drawing him? Paul states in I Corinthians 12:3 that *"no man can say that Jesus is the Lord, **but by the Holy Spirit.**"* This demonstrates without question that the Holy Spirit is definitely involved in bringing the sinner to conviction, Repentance, and Salvation. So, does a person *"receive"* the Holy Spirit at Salvation, as many preachers insist? Certainly. But the question remains, what does *"receive"* mean? Is it the same as being *baptized* with the Holy Spirit?

In order to clarify the difference between the relationship of the Holy Spirit in the baptism with the Holy Spirit and in Salvation, let's draw an analogy.

A person is walking in the wilderness on a warm day. Off in the distance this person hears the bubbling of a brook. The sound *draws* this

SELF-HELP STUDY NOTES

SELF-HELP STUDY NOTES

person approaching the stream. At this point he has been *influenced* by that *"living water,"* and spiritually affected by it, but that person and the stream remain two separate entities.

But now if that person decides to *enter* that stream, immerses himself in it, and swims along *with* the stream, (becoming in effect, part of the stream), the relationship of the stream and the man is a totally different one. And so it is in the difference between the Holy Spirit's role in Salvation and baptism.

The Holy Spirit *is* a factor in Salvation and *must* be present in order for a person to become convicted and to *accept* Salvation. The Scriptures quoted earlier (Jn. 6:44 and I Cor. 12:3) demonstrate this according to the Word of God.

But in the *baptism* with the Holy Spirit, the Spirit and the individual become, in a sense, one. The person is immersed (baptized) with the Spirit, and the Holy Spirit actually takes up residence *in* the person.

So the question raised a moment ago *must* be answered *"yes and no."* Yes, at Salvation the individual *does "receive"* the Holy Spirit, because it is the Holy Spirit who convicts and draws that person to Salvation. But, *no*, the person does *not* receive the Gift of the baptism with the Holy Spirit at Salvation because the deeper, more permanent relationship of the baptism can only come *after* Salvation.

The activities of the Holy Spirit are many and varied. He is a Comforter, Leader, Teacher, Communicator, and Guide. He is the director of all God's activities on Earth today.

When the sinner comes to the moment of Salvation, he *"receives"* the Holy Spirit — within the context of being *"Born-Again"* under the *influence* of the Spirit. However, assuming that being born of the Spirit is the same as the baptism in power can lead to erroneous doctrine. Unfortunately, untold numbers of Christians fail to receive this deeper relationship with the Holy Spirit because of this teaching.

This widespread but erroneous doctrine can handicap a Christian in his efforts to walk fully in harmony with the wishes of God. Unfortunately, not every Believer has received the baptism of the Holy Spirit — even though all Believers *can* have it if they wish. There is a definite difference between being *born of* the Spirit and being *baptized with* the Spirit.

At Salvation, life is imparted to someone who was formally dead in sin. The baptism with the Holy Spirit *empowers* someone who was formerly a weak, ineffectual Christian. The Believer is then fitted for God's service. It is clearly the mandate of God that every Christian *should* receive the baptism with the Holy Spirit. Jesus *commanded* the Disciples to *wait until they received the baptism* before starting out in their ministries.

Salvation and the baptism with the Holy Spirit are two separate and distinct experiences. They are different as to source, time, and nature. A person may experience Salvation without experiencing the baptism with the Holy Spirit. They can *not*, however, experience the baptism without first experiencing Salvation. The baptism with the Holy Spirit must, therefore, be *preceded* by Regeneration (Salvation). Only *then* can the Holy Spirit actually take up residence within us. It is the indwelling of the Holy Spirit that endows us with power and enables us to be of greater service to God.

AN EXPERIENCE FOR OUR DAY

Great numbers of people are currently experiencing the baptism with the Holy Spirit. All over the United States, Canada, and around the world, Christians of many denominations are coming to know the thrill of a personal experience with God. The Holy Spirit is being revealed as a vibrant, dynamic force within the lives of individuals. This is precisely what God intended from the beginning. God and man were never intended to lead separate existences. God created man for *His* companionship.

Many, many people have become dissatisfied with cold, formal religion and have hungered for a greater Spiritual Reality. They long to experience a *dynamic* Christian life. I have found over the years that many people attending our crusades around the world are there because they are tired of dead preaching, dead sermons, and congregations which are not quickened by the Power of the Holy Spirit. Their prayers are now being answered. Their desires are being fulfilled. The Holy Spirit is moving dynamically in lives, just as He did in the lives of the early Christians of the New Testament.

And an interesting point is the fact that I have never met a Spirit-filled Christian who has been *disappointed* in the experience of the baptism. There are very few times in life that the actual realization of something lives up to our *anticipation* of it. The baptism does!

It is a tragedy that legions of pastors warn their flocks *against* the baptism without ever discussing the experience with an actual Spirit-baptized person. Of course, it's difficult to discuss something with someone after you've *banished* them from your fellowship. And all too often that's what happens to those who dare venture forth into a deeper relationship with God. This is, however, a *sure* way to ensure stunted Christian Growth and a bored and passive congregation willing to accept milksop services.

Sometime ago, I spoke with a professional man, a member of an honorable profession and very comfortable financially. God had just filled him with the Holy Spirit, and he told me that *before* he was filled with the Spirit he had suffered a nervous breakdown. This forced him to take a leave of absence from his work.

He had reached the end of his rope physically and mentally. He knew

SELF-HELP STUDY NOTES

SELF-HELP STUDY NOTES

nothing about God the Father, the Lord Jesus Christ, or the Holy Spirit. He had come to the point where his life had no meaning. It was nothing more than going through the motions in a shattered travesty of what he had once *hoped* his life might be. But now he was rejoicing in the Lord, and life had taken on a completely new perspective and meaning.

He, like so many, was bubbling with excitement, and the joy of the Lord glowed forth from him. I have never beheld a happier man in all my life. He had committed his life to the Lord Jesus Christ and experienced the baptism with the Holy Spirit.

Just a few hours after God had filled him with the Spirit of God, his physical problems vanished, his mental problems disappeared, and his Spiritual problems evaporated. The Lord Jesus Christ became a glorious reality to him — more than just some historic figure who had hung on a Cross. Suddenly He had become the living, dynamic, *risen* Christ.

The Holy Spirit is also more than a religious concept, a vague symbol. He is a vibrant force within one's life, as any who have stepped forward to invite Him into their lives will so testify. The Spirit of God is being poured out on *"all flesh."* Believers from all denominations are experiencing the baptism in the mighty Holy Spirit, and I have never met *one* who has regretted moving forward to accept this blessed new relationship.

The baptism with the Holy Spirit is valid for today. Peter, speaking in Acts 2:38-39, said *"the Promise* (stated first in Joel 2:28-32 and repeatedly by Peter in Acts 2:16-18) *is unto you, and to your children, and to all who are afar off."* This Promise is being beautifully and abundantly fulfilled in our day.

THE NEED TO BE FILLED WITH THE SPIRIT

Numerous times in the Book of Acts we read of people being *"filled with the Holy Spirit"* (Acts 2:4; 4:8; 4:31; 9:17, and 13:9). *We* are told to be *"filled with the Spirit"* (Eph. 5:18). Now let's think about this: In order to be *filled*, there must be first a space or void. You can't *fill* a bottle that is already *full*.

Believers aren't *automatically* filled with the Spirit. Believers are commanded, in the New Testament, to be filled with the Spirit. The Holy Spirit moves on individuals, drawing them to Christ and strengthening them many ways. But there is something infinitely unique and complete when one experiences the baptism with the Holy Spirit — the *Immersion* in Him — which finally *removes* the void that previously existed. The *command* (because that's what it is) to be filled is still valid for today. God does not meet the needs of man differently at different times. Man is always man, and God is always God. God's response to man's needs in New Testament times is *precisely* His response to *our* needs in *this* day.

CONDITIONS FOR RECEIVING

There are *conditions* for receiving the baptism with the Holy Spirit. The *first* condition is Salvation. A person *must* be saved (Born-Again) before he can aspire to receiving the baptism with the Holy Spirit. Of course, the person who has committed his life to Christ has experienced the *convicting* power of the Holy Spirit. He is already a son of God and adopted into the Family of God.

In that sense, the Holy Spirit has indeed been present in his life. But one still needs God's Spirit to *energize* his Christian walk with *power*. Without question, the singular most important step any soul can take in life is Salvation. Without this there *is* no more. But *having* been saved, what then? A drab, spiritless, ineffectual *plod* through life? Years of being a go-nowhere, do-nothing Christian? What about feeding the carburetor some *High-Test*? Just as filling up with *premium* can rejuvenate a hic-coughing, balky car, — accepting the baptism with the Holy Spirit can put new life into your *Christian* travels.

Of course, a person never *merits* the Gift of the Holy Spirit — just as no person merits Salvation. Jesus paid the price for our Redemption on Calvary, and He promised the Holy Spirit to activate our Christian lives. The baptism with the Holy Spirit is *not* available to sinners, and only *after* sinners are saved can they move forward into the Holy Spirit baptism. Jesus made it abundantly clear that the sinner, the unbeliever — in fact, the *world* — cannot receive Spiritual things. A person must be saved as the first condition for the baptism with the Holy Spirit.

The *second* condition is Faith. Once a person has Faith, he can receive anything else he needs from God. In Galatians 3:2 Paul confronts that church with a question as to the *source* of the Spirit. Did they receive it by *"works of the Law, or by the hearing of Faith?"* The answer, obviously, is *by Faith*. And we are told, in Galatians 3:14, *"That the blessing of Abraham might* (will) *come on the Gentiles through Jesus Christ; that we might receive the Promise of the Spirit through Faith."*

Several years ago, the Lord directed me to conduct a Holy Spirit service in one of our crusades. This is a service set aside to bring the infilling, or baptism, of the Holy Spirit to anyone who is seeking it. We have subsequently seen multiplied thousands baptized with the Holy Spirit in these services.

There is no specific pattern or ritual for receiving the Holy Spirit. On the Day of Pentecost the Disciples were sitting down, while in other cases they received while standing. Obviously the posture or position of an

SELF-HELP STUDY NOTES

SELF-HELP STUDY NOTES

individual is of no importance. People have received the baptism with the Holy Spirit under all imaginable conditions and circumstances.

But while there are no *set* procedures, there is a general pattern of factors which can be winnowed from the Word of God. One of the most effective is *"the laying on of hands."* Many times, in services, the one leading the service will call people forward and lay hands upon them, bringing about the baptism with the Holy Spirit. Sometimes, however, there is a mass of people pressing forward, making this an impossibility.

Years ago, when our crowds were small, we laid hands on individuals. But God showed me that I did not have to personally lay hands on those coming forward for the baptism. Any person who is Spirit-filled can perform this service and individuals will receive the Gift of the Holy Spirit. There are people who have been used in a special way — praying for those seeking the baptism and bringing it on by the laying on of their hands.

Of course, anyone can pray for the person who is hungering for the Holy Spirit, and there are times when individuals are filled with the Spirit without the laying on of hands. However, in Acts 8, after Peter and John came to Samaria, the people were filled with the Holy Spirit when Peter and John laid hands on them. Again, in Acts 9:17, the Bible tells us that Ananias prayed for Saul *and laid hands on him* to receive the Gift of the Holy Spirit.

In the Nineteenth Chapter of Acts we see Paul laying hands on the Disciples at Ephesus — and they immediately received the Gift of the Holy Spirit. But then again, in the Second and Tenth Chapters, there were no hands laid on the Believers. The Holy Spirit fell on those present with no special physical contact on the part of any other person.

There is no concrete rule. You can receive the Holy Spirit *without* the laying on of hands, but it is often expedient and desirable.

BAPTISM OF POWER

Jesus gave the promise to the Disciples, *"But you shall receive power, after that the Holy Spirit is come upon you."* This promise was realized by the early Disciples, and examples of that power were soon evident. The Disciples had fled when Jesus was being tried and in some cases (like that of Peter) denied even *association* with Him. But suddenly, the Disciples who had been fearful and timid became dynamic, courageous messengers of the Good News of Jesus Christ. What brought about this dramatic change? The infilling with Holy Spirit Power as promised by the Lord. This was obviously a result of their receiving the Holy Spirit baptism.

Naturally, there is a *reason* for granting power to the Believer. It is for service — to make us effective witnesses. The blessings of the baptism with the Holy Spirit are not meant as an ego trip or for a personal Spiritual *"high."* Neither are the *Gifts* of the Spirit toys intended for our amusement.

The dynamic power realized in the baptism with the Holy Spirit is clearly intended for witnessing and service — and *not* just to make us *"feel good."* The baptism provides us with power to dominate circumstances, to be victorious, and to spread the light of the Gospel to a sin-darkened world.

INITIAL EVIDENCE

Prior to the demonstration of Holy Spirit Power in healings and miracles, the Disciples exhibited the *primary* evidence of the baptism which was speaking in tongues. Most Christian churches and denominations believe (to one degree or another) in the Holy Spirit. This doesn't create any major problem. But when it comes to receiving the baptism with the Holy Spirit, *with the evidence of speaking in tongues*, great controversy erupts.

The question is often asked, *"Is speaking in tongues scriptural and relevant for this day?"* The matter of speaking in tongues is probably the most controversial subject within the Body of Christ today. *"The Body of Christ"* is, of course, the overall, worldwide mass of those who believe in the fundamentals of Faith.

This matter of glossolalia — or speaking in other tongues — has caused a divisive line to be drawn right down the center of most Bible-believing bodies. When the term *"filled with the Spirit"* is used, little or no controversy ensues. Altering this however, to be *"baptized with the Holy Spirit"* causes a much more pronounced reaction. And using the phrase *"baptized with the Holy Spirit with the evidence of speaking in other tongues"* causes tremendous turmoil and controversy. Obviously the problem doesn't arise over the question of the *infilling* of the Holy Spirit; the conflict stems rather from the issue of speaking in tongues.

Many say tongues *never* existed — or that it passed away with the Early Church. Some insist that it is not relevant to today's world — while others go so far as to attribute tongues to the Devil.

Still others (and we are speaking of literal multitudes) proclaim it as a valid Scriptural Manifestation of Holy Spirit Power as evidence on the Day of Pentecost — when God's Holy Spirit overflowed the 120 Disciples gathered in Jerusalem. Modern proponents insist that, as an example of both Holy Spirit and Godly Power, it has been a *proper* manifestation from that day to this.

Many opinions could be quoted from teachers of the Bible. Different schools of thought could be cited. We are on safe ground, however, if we turn to *Scripture* and form our opinions so they are in agreement with those

SELF-HELP STUDY NOTES

SELF-HELP STUDY NOTES

of our Heavenly Father.

Before we launch into a Biblical, Scriptural discussion of this subject, we would like to give a few relevant thoughts which will do much to clarify our position.

WE BELIEVE THIS:

- We teach and believe, *from the Word of God*, that speaking in tongues is a valid, Scriptural expression as given by the Holy Spirit. As such, it is relevant to the day and age in which we live.
- We do not believe and teach that speaking in other tongues will automatically produce a better Christian.
- We do not believe or teach that anyone *has* to speak in tongues to be saved.
- We do not believe or teach that speaking in other tongues has anything to do with a person making Heaven his eternal home.
- We do not believe or teach that anyone becomes *"more saved"* as a result of speaking in tongues. When a person accepts Jesus as his Lord and Saviour, he is *saved*. Prayerfully, he will *grow* in his walk with the Lord, but at the moment of Salvation he is as *saved* as he will ever be.

WE FURTHER BELIEVE:

- That speaking in other tongues is ordained by God.
- That it was a *common* manifestation in the Early Church, and it is just as widespread (and proper) today. (Actually, it never ceased from that day to this.)
- That it is a valid manifestation and demonstration of the *initial* infilling with the Holy Spirit.
- That it is a great *help* to the believer, a giver of strength, and a builder of Faith.

THE BAPTISM WITH THE HOLY SPIRIT AS A DEFINITE AND DISTINCT WORK OF GRACE

Many churches teach that the infilling of the Holy Spirit *automatically* accompanies the fact of Salvation at the *moment* a person is Born-Again. In essence, that is correct. A person does *receive* the Holy Spirit when he is saved, but there is a vast difference between being *born of* the Spirit and being *baptized into* the Spirit.

We believe there is a definite and separate experience *subsequent* to

Salvation. We believe this experience is not comparable to, nor simultaneous with, Salvation. It does not make a person *"more saved;"* it does not better prepare one for Heaven. But we do believe it gives one *power for service*. And this *"subsequent experience"* that we are discussing is, of course, the mighty baptism with the Holy Spirit.

In Acts 1:4, when Jesus assembled together with those who were to observe His departure from Earth, the Bible says He *commanded* that they should not depart from Jerusalem but should wait for the promise of the Father.

Some have fastened on this reference to Jerusalem and have (no doubt humorously) suggested that everyone perhaps should go to Jerusalem if they wish to be filled with the Holy Spirit — in the manner of the Early Church. Of course, anyone who would make such a statement is really revealing the *shallowness* of his or her knowledge of the Bible.

There was a reason why Jesus told His Disciples to await the Comforter in the city of Jerusalem. Jerusalem was literally *the city of the King*. This was the proper place for the *initial* outpouring of the Holy Spirit to take place. After this original incident, however, the Holy Spirit fell *wherever* hungry hearts reached out to God.

Acts (Chapter Ten and Verse Twenty-four) speaks of Cornelius and his household calling unto God in the city of *Caesarea*. Of course, to those familiar with the Word of God, it is recognized that the Holy Spirit fell upon the Gentiles then and there in the city of Caesarea, and that none of them had to go to Jerusalem.

In the Ninth Chapter of Acts, the Apostle Paul was outside the city of *Damascus* when the Holy Spirit came upon him. In *Samaria* the Spirit of God was poured out on those upon whom Peter and John laid hands. The Eighteenth Chapter of Acts also mentions the district of *Phrygia* and *Galatia*, where Paul spoke to the Disciples of John who were later (Chapter 19) filled with the Holy Spirit. Chapter Eighteen also speaks of the church at Corinth (and in fact, of *all* the churches pertaining to the early move of God on this Earth).

So anyone who would attempt to isolate a single Passage of Scripture (Acts 1:4) and try to use this as proof that individuals must go to Jerusalem to receive the Holy Spirit is ignoring the far greater mass of contrary evidence elsewhere in Scripture.

But let's turn back to our original thesis — that the Holy Spirit baptism is a separate Work of Grace. We find that the individuals referred to in Acts 1:4 were already saved. There's no doubt about this, yet they were specifically told to *wait for the Promise of the Father*. In Luke 11:13, Jesus spoke of the Holy Spirit being given by the Heavenly Father *to those who ask it of Him*.

SELF-HELP STUDY NOTES

SELF-HELP STUDY NOTES

So from these Passages (and from many other Passages that might be cited), we maintain that the reception of the baptism with the Holy Spirit is a separate and distinct Work of Grace and not an element in the Salvation process. By the term *"work of grace"* we mean, of course, something that is freely given by God — something that is actually a gift (Acts 2:38). Just as Salvation is an unmerited Work of Grace, the baptism with the Holy Spirit is *also* a Work of Grace.

INDIVIDUALS ARE BAPTIZED WITH THE HOLY SPIRIT *AFTER* CONVERSION

This is, of course, another area of tremendous controversy. As mentioned above, many teach that the Holy Spirit comes *automatically* at conversion, and there is nothing else to be sought, or asked for, after this. They say, in effect, that our relationship with God is then complete. There is much disagreement, even among non-pentecostals, regarding this Doctrine. Many non-pentecostals state that there *is* a filling with the Holy Spirit, *after* conversion, and that one must seek the Lord for this and overtly *ask* for it. At the same time, however, they deny that it is accompanied by speaking in tongues.

In order to avoid wandering too far afield, let's confine our discussion to the *Scriptural* basis for the appraisal of the question of receiving the Holy Spirit *after* conversion. And we believe that it is theologically and Scripturally correct to state (as was discussed earlier) that a person *receives* the Holy Spirit after conversion — but the action of the Holy Spirit in regenerating the heart and the life of the unsaved is far different from the *baptism* with the Holy Spirit. This is a completely different action and is manifested by a baptism of *power*. We emphasize again — there is a definite difference between being born *of* the Spirit and being baptized *with* the Spirit.

Acts 2:4 describes the filling of the 120 with the Holy Spirit. I think it would be completely unrealistic to say that these people were not already saved. They obviously were. The 120 included eleven of the Apostles (and actually the *twelfth*, who had just been chosen), and it also included Mary, the mother of Jesus. The Master had also told His Disciples (in Luke 10:20), when they were rejoicing over the fact of devils being subject to them (within the authority of Jesus), that they should rather *rejoice because their names were written in Heaven*. This, of course, confirms that they were *already saved*, with their names written in the Lamb's Book of Life.

So these were all previously saved people. They were receiving this *additional* gift in compliance with the commandment of the Lord

(Acts 1:4). It was not to *become* saved — nor to become *"more saved"* — but as a *baptism of power!* It was definitely subsequent to Salvation.

We read in the Eighth Chapter of Acts of Philip going to the city of Samaria and preaching Christ unto the people there. It says, in the Sixth Verse, that they *"gave heed unto those things which Philip spoke."* It tells of unclean spirits coming out and of many being healed. There was great joy in the city. Then in Verse Twelve it tells of the Samaritans believing what Philip was preaching — concerning the Kingdom of God and the Name of the Lord Jesus Christ — and how they were being baptized, both men and women. This is exactly what the Word *tells* us to do in John 3:16, Acts 10:42-43, and in other Scriptures. When anyone does this, *that person is saved!*

So these individuals were saved. They were washed in the Blood, their names written in the Lamb's Book of Life. Then the Fourteenth Verse talks about the Apostles (who were in Jerusalem) hearing about the Samaritans receiving the Word of God. They then sent unto them Peter and John. In the Fifteenth Verse, we are told that Peter and John *prayed that they might receive the Holy Spirit.*

Now if an individual receives *everything* at conversion, *what was happening here?* Why were Peter and John there? What was the point of going down and preaching the Holy Spirit and praying for them if they had *automatically* received it at conversion — as it is commonly taught today? The *Bible* says (in Vs. 16) that *none of them* had been filled with the Holy Spirit. They had been saved, they had been baptized in water, but in the Seventeenth Verse it says that hands were laid on them and only *then* did they receive the Holy Spirit!

The Ninth Chapter of Acts describes the conversion of Saul of Tarsus (Paul), and the Twelfth Verse recounts God's command to Ananias to go and pray for Paul and put his hands on him that Paul might receive his sight. Ananias was not directed to lay hands on him that he might be saved — because Paul had *already* accepted the Lord Jesus as his Saviour, as a result of the great vision recorded in the Third through Seventh Verses of the Ninth Chapter of Acts.

The Seventeenth Verse states that when Ananias met Saul, he called him *"Brother Saul."* He would *not* have done so if Paul had not accepted Jesus. But Paul *had* already accepted Jesus; he *was* saved; his name *was* written in the Lamb's Book of Life; he was *already* washed in the Blood of the Lamb. Ananias was sent to pray for him that he might receive his sight again (since Paul's blindness was caused by the great light coincident with the vision on the road) *and* that he might be filled with the Holy Spirit. If one is baptized with the Holy Spirit at conversion, *what* was Ananias doing, and *why* was he praying for Paul? I believe that without question the

SELF-HELP STUDY NOTES

SELF-HELP STUDY NOTES

baptism with the Holy Spirit does not take place *at* conversion but is an act *subsequent* to Salvation.

In the Tenth Chapter of Acts, it would seem that the outpouring of the Holy Spirit took place almost immediately after conversion — which is also a common occurrence today.

The Nineteenth Chapter of Acts describes the Apostle Paul as speaking to the Disciples of John at Ephesus. He asked them (as recorded in Vs. 2) *"Have you received the Holy Spirit since you believed?"* And they replied that they didn't even know what Paul was talking about. He then explained to them, and in the Sixth Verse it says he laid hands on them, and *"the Holy Spirit came on them."*

Let's make this point very clear. Every Christian receives the *Holy Spirit of adoption into sonship with God* at the time of Salvation (Rom. 8:9, 14-16). This was not, however, what Paul was referring to when he addressed John's Disciples at Ephesus. He was asking about the Spirit baptism that John had preached — describing how Jesus would baptize them with the Holy Spirit and fire (Jn. 1:31-34 and Acts 1:4-5). This had nothing to do with *new birth* by the Spirit — it is the endowment of power for service.

When one reads this, one must see that a person can be saved by the Blood of Jesus and believe for Salvation, yet be in ignorance of the baptism with the Holy Spirit. It is clearly stated that such was the case here, and millions are in the same condition today. They have been saved by the Blood of Jesus, yet know little or nothing about the baptism with the Holy Spirit.

Read St. John 14:17. Here Jesus stated plainly that a *sinner* could not receive the baptism with the Holy Spirit — it is simply impossible. The vessel must be first *cleansed* (through the Born-Again experience) and only *then* will the Spirit of Truth (whom the world cannot receive) enter in.

Consequently, individuals who insist that a person *automatically* receives everything at Salvation (and does not have to seek anything further from the Lord) are not correctly interpreting the Word of God. There *is* an experience after Salvation — it is the baptism with the Holy Spirit. And the point I want to stress is that this must occur *subsequent* to Salvation. It is not simultaneous; it must *follow* Salvation (although it can occur almost *immediately after* being Born-Again).

Further, one must *ask* to receive this second grace experience. It is not an automatic gift from our Heavenly Father (Lk. 11:13). It is something *every* Christian should seek after he is Born-Again — although he cannot receive it *until* he is reborn.

Neither the church that teaches, nor the pastor who preaches, that an individual receives *everything* at conversion, is conforming to the Word of God. The sad fact is, however, that the majority of churches in this country (and in most countries for that matter) lead their people down a primrose path by telling them that once they are saved they have everything God has to offer. In reality, no one *ever* has it all. One must *continue* to grow in grace and in the knowledge of the Lord. And then, of course, there is the great experience we've been discussing — the mighty baptism with the Holy Spirit which Jesus, in Acts 1:4, *commanded* all to receive. And again, let's emphasize this: the Holy Spirit baptism is an experience that *follows* Salvation, and it must be sought. It does *not* come to the Believer automatically.

EVIDENCE THAT ONE HAS RECEIVED THE BAPTISM WITH THE HOLY SPIRIT

We teach, according to the Word of God, that the only way one can be assured that one *has* been baptized with the Holy Spirit is by the act of speaking with other tongues as the Spirit of God gives the utterance (Acts 2:4). This, to be sure, is not the *only* sign. There are any number of additional signs, but we do believe that tongues are the *initial* sign and evidence that will take place in the Believer's life when he is baptized with the Holy Spirit. And let's look at the Word of God to confirm this.

There are five separate incidents in the Book of Acts which describe individuals being baptized with the Holy Spirit. These incidents cover a time period of over twenty years. Then, there is also a lengthy dissertation in the Fourteenth Chapter of I Corinthians covering the use of tongues.

ACTS 2:4

This particular Verse states, *"And they were all filled with the Holy Spirit, and began to speak with other tongues, as the Spirit gave them utterance."* This needs no further explanation. It is clear, concise, and to the point.

ACTS 8:16-23

In the Eighth Chapter of Acts, Peter and John came from Jerusalem and prayed for the Samaritans to receive the Holy Spirit. It doesn't say anything about them speaking with tongues, but it *does* state (in Verses 18-19) that Simon the sorcerer *saw* that through the laying on of the Apostles' hands, the Holy Spirit was given. He then offered the Apostles money that he might also have this power — that *he* might lay hands on people so that they would receive the Holy Spirit.

It seems obvious that this greedy individual would not offer money if there weren't some tangible manifestation of results. If the laying on of hands had no visible evidence following it, why would he offer to pay the Apostles for their *"secret?"* The only logical conclusion is that the recipients *"spoke with other tongues as the Spirit of God gave them utterance."*

SELF-HELP STUDY NOTES

SELF-HELP STUDY NOTES

ACTS 9:17

When Ananias laid hands on Paul (who was later to become one of the greatest Apostles who ever lived), he was filled with the Holy Spirit. And, to be sure, it doesn't say anything about speaking in tongues! But — over in I Corinthians 14:18 — Paul says, *"I thank my God, I speak with tongues more than you all."*

So, the evidence is there that the Apostle Paul *did* speak with other tongues as he was baptized with the Holy Spirit.

ACTS 10:44

The Bible describes, in the Tenth Chapter of Acts, the circumstances as the Holy Spirit fell upon the household of Cornelius. The Bible says that the Jewish brethren were astonished because *"on the Gentiles also was poured out the Gift of the Holy Spirit."* It then says in the Forty-sixth Verse, *"For they heard them speak with tongues and magnify God."*

ACTS 19:6

This Passage states, *"They spoke with tongues, and prophesied."*

Now, in three of five Passages given — where experiences are related concerning the infilling of the Holy Spirit — it says that they spoke with other tongues. And the Word tells us that *"at the mouth of two witnesses, or at the mouth of three witnesses, shall the matter be established"* (Deut. 19:15). Joining this with the implied evidence discussed above, in relation to the other two incidents (Acts 8 and Acts 9), we can properly conclude that *they* spoke with other tongues also.

Any honest seeker after Truth, upon studying the Word of God in this regard, must come to the conclusion that *something* happened when these individuals were filled with the Holy Spirit. That *"something"* obviously had to be speaking in other tongues as the Spirit of God gave them utterance. Acts 2:4 says *"They . . . began to speak."* Acts 10:46 says *"They heard them speak."* Acts 19:6 says *"They spoke."* And Ephesians 5:18-19 says, *"Speaking to yourselves."*

WHY TONGUES?

First, let's address the question of what's *behind* speaking in tongues. Some have spoken disparagingly of this great gift by saying it is nothing more than babble, chatter, or incoherent jabbering. However, one should be very careful in saying anything about the Holy Spirit — or anything connected with the Holy Spirit — because speaking in other tongues is not jabber or babble or incoherent prattle.

It is generally a language spoken *somewhere* in the world and known by some people in the world or Heaven. We are given insight in the Second Chapter of Acts that there were devout men *from every nation under Heaven* (and, of course, this referred to the world known in those days). It says they had come together and were confounded because *"How hear we every man in our own tongue, wherein we were born?"*

It then goes on to list the people who were there. This included Parthians, Medes, Elamites, and at least thirteen additional nationalities. Yet all these disparate people said, *"We do hear them speak in our* (own) *tongues the wonderful Works of God"* (Vs. 11).

Now these individuals were not preaching to these people to become saved. They were merely praising the Lord in other tongues. They were speaking a language they had not learned. Some skeptics have tried to explain this away as some language the 120 had just learned. In other words, they had suddenly become linguists and were praising God in languages other than Aramaic, Hebrew, or Greek — the common local tongues. This is not true, however. These were uneducated Galileans who were *not* students of languages.

Of course, this is the way it *always* is when individuals speak in tongues. There are hundreds and perhaps *thousands* of languages and dialects in this world, and many of them sound very strange to our ears. They are not strange, of course, to the people who routinely converse in them. So it is not just jabber, or chatter, or babble — it is always a language that is spoken and understood *somewhere* in the world, but *not* spoken and understood by the individual who has been filled with the Holy Spirit.

If you will notice, whenever it was time to preach to these people about the Lord Jesus Christ and give an invitation to be saved, Simon Peter (as is recorded in Acts 2:14) did not continue speaking in tongues. He then preached in the common language of the day, which was either Aramaic or Hebrew. Of course, all those present understood.

It is easy to see how so many people could know the Hebrew language (being Jews themselves) and *also* the language of the country in which they resided. This is common among many people today. And it is also possible that *some* of the 120 had learned more than one language — but the language spoken as they were baptized with the Holy Spirit was *not* a language that was known to them. It was a supernatural utterance, given by the Holy Spirit, which always accompanies this baptism. So tongues refers to languages known either on this Earth or in Heaven.

In I Corinthians 13:1 the Apostle Paul said, *"Though I speak with the tongues of men and of Angels, and have not charity."*

Paul is talking here about speaking in *other* tongues — on which he is to give an extensive dissertation later in the Fourteenth Chapter. And he uses the term *"of Angels,"* implying the possibility that sometimes a language that is spoken could be an angelic language. We do not want to be continuous on this point; we cannot be entirely *positive*, but this might well

SELF-HELP STUDY NOTES

SELF-HELP STUDY NOTES

be what Paul meant.

Let's look further at why God chose tongues. He certainly has had good reasons for doing *all* the things He's done over the millennia, and the same would be true in this matter. It was prophesied by Isaiah (and quoted in I Corinthians 14:21) that men *would* speak with other tongues. Isaiah then went on to add that even though the Lord would arrange this mighty sign, men would not listen to Him. As you will note, this is a terrible indictment — but it's exactly what's happening today. Following are some of the reasons why we believe God chose speaking in tongues as the initial sign pointing to one who has been baptized with the Holy Spirit.

SUPERNATURAL — First of all, it is always a *supernatural* utterance that takes place when a person is baptized with the Holy Spirit. It must be exercised by *Faith*, but it is not of the individual's doing. It comes from the Lord Jesus Christ and was promised as long ago as Isaiah — which documents its tremendous importance.

GIVEN BY GOD — Careful reading of I Corinthians 14:21 and Isaiah 28:11 would infer that when men speak with other tongues, it is actually God speaking *through* them to the people. Obviously, anything becomes of tremendous importance when we realize it is given by God.

UNIVERSAL — This is a single evidence the world over. It is not one evidence for one country and something else for another (as some foolishly insist). It is the same evidence everywhere. It was the same evidence in the New Testament days as it is today. It is the same across the world and across the years — which makes *excellent* evidence — if one is willing to view it without prejudice.

INSTANTANEOUS — The *moment* the baptism with the Holy Spirit comes to the individual, he starts to speak with other tongues. It happens that same way with everyone. It's not something that involves an interaction with other individuals. It is strictly a *personal* experience between the individual and God. It always happens instantaneously, the *moment* the baptism with the Holy Spirit occurs.

There are many other reasons why I am certain that God chose tongues, but really it is not our position to *question* why He chose tongues. Rather, it is our responsibility to *accept* what God has decreed and then to be thrilled and delighted with it.

WHAT GOOD DOES IT DO?

Many have asked this question. *"How can it be of any help or service to anyone?"* Some preachers say this and *laugh*. Of course, those who could ask such a question are really revealing their lack of knowledge on the subject. There is *much* good accomplished when one speaks in tongues, and we will endeavor to enumerate specific benefits.

USHERS IN THE HOLY SPIRIT — I think it is apparent (Acts 2:4) that God is telling us that the moment individuals are filled with the Holy Spirit, they will begin to speak with other tongues as the Spirit gives them utterance. And if tongues does serve to usher in the Holy Spirit (as we believe it does), it becomes of extreme importance in this great Work of Grace in the hearts and lives of Believers.

IS A REFRESHING — In Isaiah 28, as he gave Prophecy concerning the Holy Spirit (in Vss. 11-12 — as quoted by Paul in I Corinthians, Chapter 14), Isaiah mentions something of extreme importance. He said, *"This is the rest wherewith you may cause the weary to rest; and this is the refreshing."*

Only those having experienced the Holy Spirit baptism and who speak devotionally in other tongues regularly, understand what this means. It is like the Spiritual recharging of one's batteries. Jude spoke of this in the Twentieth Verse of his short Epistle when he used the phrase *"building up yourselves on your most Holy Faith, praying in the Holy Spirit."* This is what he was talking about. It *is "the refreshing."* It lifts one up Spiritually.

HELPS ONE TO PRAY — Romans 8:26 tells us that *"we know not what we should pray for as we ought: but the Spirit itself makes intercession for us with groanings which cannot be uttered."* The Greek says *"which cannot be articulated in a normal or natural voice."* Naturally, this refers to speaking with other tongues. It helps us to pray. When we don't know how to pray in reference to some problem, it is often because we don't understand or recognize the *complexities* of the problem.

Thus, when we go before God in the natural, we can ask for what *we* see as solutions — but which, in fact, aren't. But as we pray in the Spirit (in other tongues), it is not only a great refreshing, but God is actually enunciating our prayers in a form that will lead to a complete solution. The Holy Spirit moves upon our hearts and says things to the Heavenly Father where we would not know what to say or how to say it. Therefore, God's Holy Spirit truly makes intercession for the Saints — according to the Will of God.

A SIGN TO THE UNBELIEVER — This term *"a sign to the unbeliever,"* has a number of meanings. One of them is that it is a sign to the unbeliever (or to those who do not know or understand) that the individual *has* been baptized with the Holy Spirit. In other words, speaking in other tongues is just the sign we've been discussing throughout this Chapter. It is also a manifestation of the Power and Presence of God; a sign that God is working mightily and that the unbeliever should get right with God.

EDIFIES THE BELIEVER — I Corinthians 14:4 speaks of a person speaking in tongues as edifying himself. This is sorely needed, as we

SELF-HELP STUDY NOTES

SELF-HELP STUDY NOTES

mentioned. It strengthens the Believer, builds his Faith, and lifts him up — not in selfishness (the Holy Spirit never does that) but in just the way the Believer *should* be lifted. The Holy Spirit always does this perfectly — in a *healthy* manner — and never makes a mistake by edifying the Believer in a way that could corrupt the carnal ego. This is *perfect* edification — and this is why it is so desperately needed.

A DIVINE MEANS OF COMMUNICATION — In I Corinthians 14:4, the Apostle Paul said that when he prayed in an unknown tongue his spirit prayed, even though his understanding was unfruitful. His spirit thus united with the Holy Spirit and sought the Face of God in exactly the right manner. Consequently, this is a divine means of communication. It makes one's prayer life much more effective and infinitely more powerful.

ELIMINATES SELFISHNESS IN OUR PRAYING — As we have discussed (as seen in Rom. 8:26), there are many times we do not know how to pray about something. And I'm persuaded that oftentimes a Christian will pray things into existence that ought not to be asked for. When we pray in the Spirit, however, we automatically eliminate selfishness from prayer. In other words, when we pray in the Spirit, we pray according to the precise Will of God and never according to our own.

Of course, there are many *other* reasons we could give for speaking in tongues and much we could discuss on the benefits derived. The above should serve as sufficient examples, however.

DO ALL SPEAK WITH TONGUES?

A man once asked me, *"Do I have to speak in tongues to be baptized with the Holy Spirit?"* My answer to him was this: *"No sir, you do not* have *to speak in tongues to be baptized with the Holy Spirit, but when you* are *baptized with the Holy Spirit, you will speak in tongues."*

That answer may surprise some, but, you see, this individual was concentrating on tongues instead of the Holy Spirit. We should avoid this. While tongues are important, one never asks for *tongues*. One asks for the Holy Spirit, and tongues will automatically follow.

Yes, we do teach and preach that every recipient of the Holy Spirit, without exception, speaks with other tongues as he is baptized with the Holy Spirit. I think Acts 2:4 pretty well confirms this.

However, many people are confused in respect to the initial evidence of having received the Holy Spirit (which we believe to be speaking in other tongues) and the *Gift* of Tongues (which is one of the nine Gifts of the Spirit). These are two different entities. Admittedly, everything received from God is a gift. But there is a difference between *speaking* in other tongues (in our own devotional praise to the Lord — which might even include praying in the Spirit) and the *Gift* of Tongues — as outlined in I Corinthians 12:10. This confuses many, so I will attempt to clarify the difference.

It may well sound confusing at first, but I believe you will understand as you mull over it a bit. One could *speak* in tongues every day of his life and still not have the *Gift* of Tongues. Admittedly, what he has *is* a gift — but I'm discussing an individual *praying* in tongues. Now, he might pray every day (or every hour, for that matter, just as he prefers) in his daily devotions to the Lord. The *Gift* of Tongues, on the other hand, as discussed in I Corinthians 12, is one of the *nine Gifts of the Spirit*. Its usage is totally different from that of individual praying in tongues. This is another matter entirely, and the two should not be confused.

Some ask why the Word of God tells us that *not all* speak in tongues. And this *is* precisely what it says — but it is not referring to *praying* in tongues; it is referring to the Gift of Tongues. This is one of the nine Gifts of the Spirit.

In I Corinthians 12, starting with Verse 28, the Apostle Paul describes how God has set these gifts in the church. Then he asks the following questions: *"Are all Apostles? Are all Prophets? Are all Teachers? Are all workers of Miracles? Have all the Gifts of Healing?"*

Now, the answer to *all* these questions is obviously *"No!"* All are *not* Apostles, all are *not* Prophets, all are *not* Teachers, and all are *not* workers of Miracles.

And *next* Paul asks the questions, *"Do all speak with tongues? Do all interpret?"* Taking a cue from the preceding examples, the answer is again *"No, all do not speak in tongues, and all do not interpret."*

So what's going on? Well, obviously, the *Gift* of Tongues — one of the nine Gifts listed (a Word of Wisdom, the Word of Knowledge, the Discerning of the spirits, the Gifts of Faith, the Gifts of Healings, the Working of Miracles, the Gift of Prophecy, the Gift of Tongues, and the Gift of Interpretation) — is not a *universal* gift any more than the other nine Gifts listed.

Some speak of tongues ceasing (as recorded in I Cor. 13:8) and try to use this Passage to imply that *"when the Word of God becomes effective"* — that is, when the Bible is compiled — there will no longer be a *need* to speak in tongues. They contend that the Early Church had many immature and undeveloped Christians and that tongues were necessary then. Now, however (according to their view), Christians — being *mature* in the Lord — do not need to speak in tongues. This is not the case.

The Apostle Paul, in the Thirteenth Chapter of I Corinthians, is talking about love. He says in the Tenth Verse *"But when that which is perfect is come, then that which is in part shall be done away."* Some contend that he is talking here (*"when that which is perfect is come"*) about the

SELF-HELP STUDY NOTES

SELF-HELP STUDY NOTES

Bible! Quite obviously, Paul was *not* referring to the Bible; he was referring to the Return of our Lord Jesus Christ to begin His Millennial Reign.

Paul goes on, in the Twelfth Verse, to talk about how we see through a glass darkly now but will see then face to face. Obviously, this refers to the time when our Lord returns and there will no longer be a need for Tongues, Interpretation of Tongues, Prophecies, or *anything* of this nature — because the Prince of Peace will be here personally. He is *"that perfect"* — the very personification of all good things.

Paul also mentions in this Verse that knowledge will cease. Some individuals who use this Verse as *"proof"* that *tongues* will cease when the Bible is compiled, refuse to address the question of whether knowledge *also* ceased at the same time. Of course, we *need* knowledge. It has *not* ceased today, and Paul is merely stating that when Jesus Christ comes — and we as the Saints of God put on our Glorified Bodies — we will have *perfect* knowledge and will not have to continue to *learn* as we do today.

At that time, there won't be a need to speak in tongues either. More of today's necessities will no longer be required. For instance, there have been many times that I have cried before the Lord to ask forgiveness for something I've said or done in error. When the Lord returns, we won't have to do this.

Paul is saying here that love will never fail. It will always abide. We need love now; we needed it yesterday; we will need it tomorrow. Even when Jesus comes, love will still be the foundation, the bedrock, the basis for all that is good — because God is love!

TO SUMMARIZE

We believe:
1. The baptism with the Holy Spirit is valid today;
2. It is a definite Work of Grace;
3. It is an experience that is received *after* Salvation;
4. *Every* recipient of the Holy Spirit will speak in other tongues as the Spirit of God gives them utterance;
5. Tongues are not just babble or chatter, but are actual languages spoken in the world, but not understood by the speaker (unless God gives the interpretation); and,
6. That speaking in tongues is very valuable to the Believer — that *anything* given of God is of great consequence. We further believe it to be a tremendous importance in one's personal walk with the Lord Jesus Christ.

As one wise man said, *"Those who are opposed to the baptism with the Holy Spirit (with the evidence of speaking in tongues) have an argument. Those who have received it have an experience."*

IS THERE A NEED TO TARRY IF ONE IS TO RECEIVE?

Over the years, many have struggled, pleaded, labored, and agonized, waiting to receive the baptism with the Holy Spirit. But all you *need* to do is be saved, and you can then be baptized with the Holy Spirit. It is not necessary to wait and tarry to speak in tongues. The early Disciples were told to wait, or tarry, for the coming of the Holy Spirit. But the moment He came, they were *filled*. The Holy Spirit is here and available today, so a person need no longer *wait* to be baptized with the Holy Spirit.

There was a very fine, earnest man who waited for ten years to be baptized with the Holy Spirit. He tried again and again, going to countless altars as invitations were given. He finally reached the point where he decided that he would either be baptized in that very service or he would give up.

He went to the altar, knelt for prayer . . . and felt *nothing!* He thought it wouldn't hurt to try to make some sounds or give some form of audible expression, so he went ahead and did just that. The people around him began rejoicing because they thought he had *finally "broken through"* and received the baptism. As they crowded around him rejoicing, the man stopped them and said, *"Nothing has happened. I haven't felt anything. I just went ahead and did this speaking."*

A large group had gathered around him, and among these were two fine ladies he knew well. They had been missionaries in China. They pointed out to him that he had known them for some time, and had known of their missionary work in China, and that he could therefore trust what they were about to tell him. Then they told him that he had just been praising God, in Chinese!

All *he* had done was to *"blurt it out!"* And while he had not experienced a great emotional sensation, he *was* speaking in the Spirit! When this was revealed, he and the group about him became excited. It was so simple. All that had to be done was to *give expression* to what the Spirit had done within. The Spirit gives the utterance, but the individual *must do the speaking.* This is plainly stated in Acts 2:4. *"And they were all filled with the Holy Spirit, and began to speak with other tongues, as the Spirit gave them utterance."*

THE PRECIOUS PRESENCE OF THE HEAVENLY GUEST

Man was made for fellowship with God. Due to man's fall in the Garden, fellowship with God was severed. The Presence of God is of extreme importance to His People. When the people of Israel were led out of

SELF-HELP STUDY NOTES

SELF-HELP STUDY NOTES

Egypt and toward the Promise Land, they were instructed to build the Tabernacle. It was a movable place of worship, and within it (in the Holy of Holies) the Shekinah (or Glorious Presence of God) dwelt.

In the Gospel of John, we are told that Jesus (the Word) became flesh and dwelt (literally *"tabernacled"*) among us (Jn. 1:14). God *will* communicate with us. Jesus promised that the Holy Spirit would come after He returned to the Father. And He did come — on the Day of Pentecost.

The Promise of the Spirit had previously been given by the Old Testament Prophets. Ezekiel said, *"And I will put My Spirit within you, and cause you to walk in My statutes, and you shall keep My judgments, and do them"* (Ezek. 36:27).

When His Spirit indwells us, He will show us the way to walk. It is also stated in John 14:17 that the Spirit of Truth will be *in us*. *"Even the Spirit of Truth; Whom the world cannot receive, because it sees Him not, neither knows Him: but you know Him; for he dwells with you, and shall be **in you**."* We are to be His Dwelling Place, His Temple: *"Know you not that you are the Temple of God, and that the Spirit of God dwells in you?"* (I Cor. 3:16).

The Body of Believers is to be a holy habitation of the Spirit. Not only are we *collectively* the Temple of the Holy Spirit, but we can be a Temple of the Holy Spirit individually too! *"What? Know you not that your body is the Temple of the Holy Spirit which is in you, which you have of God, and you are not your own?"* (I Cor. 6:19).

The abiding presence of the Holy Spirit within one is wonderful and precious. But the Holy Spirit comes only when He is welcome, and Scripture warns us not to grieve the Holy Spirit. The Spirit never uses force or coercion, but is always meek and gentle. You can be *"renewed in the spirit of your mind"* by Him (Eph. 4:23).

This is, in fact, a *command*; and many other requirements are also listed, by way of exhortation, to Spirit-filled Believers. It is His Presence that makes the difference if one's life is to develop in purity, holiness, and in the Fruits of the Spirit: Love, Joy, Peace, Longsuffering, Gentleness, Goodness, Faith, Meekness, and Temperance (Gal. 5:22-23 and Eph. 4:23-32).

The Holy Spirit in the Believer gives not only power for service and witnessing, but Victory in one's life. The Holy Spirit's Presence in a person's life is transforming. Spirit-filled Believers experience a greater love for God's Word than ever before. New insights and applications replace the former blindness. The reality of Christ Jesus is much greater as He is revealed by the Holy Spirit. There is a new joy, peace, liberty, and happiness — plus an enhanced response in praise — once one is baptized with the Holy Spirit.

Chapter 7

The Gifts Of The Spirit

SUBJECT	PAGE
INTRODUCTION	123
FOR THE BODY	124
ALL THE GIFTS ARE IMPORTANT	125
FOR THE CHURCH TODAY?	125
THE GIFTS OF THE SPIRIT AND THE GREAT COMMISSION	128
A SPIRIT-FILLED CHURCH	130
THREE CLASSIFICATIONS OF GIFTS	131
REVELATION GIFTS	131
POWER GIFTS	142
THE VOCAL GIFTS	150
DEVOTIONAL TONGUES AND THE GIFT OF TONGUES	156
SIX TIMES IT IS NOT PROPER TO SPEAK IN OTHER TONGUES	160
GIFTS WITHOUT THE BAPTISM	164
OTHER GIFTS AND MANIFESTATIONS	165
PURPOSE OF THE GIFTS	166
ANTICIPATIONS	170

CHAPTER SEVEN

THE GIFTS OF THE SPIRIT

"Now concerning Spiritual Gifts, Brethren, I would not have you ignorant. You know that you were Gentiles, carried away unto these dumb idols, even as you were led. Wherefore I give you to understand, that no man speaking by the Spirit of God calls Jesus accursed: and that no man can say that Jesus is the Lord, but by the Holy Spirit.

"Now there are diversities of gifts, but the same Spirit. And there are differences of Administrations, but the same Lord. And there are diversities of Operations, but it is the same God which works all in all. But the manifestation of the Spirit is given to every man to profit withal.

"For to one is given by the Spirit the Word of Wisdom; to another the Word of Knowledge by the same Spirit; To another Faith by the same Spirit; to another the Gifts of Healing by the same Spirit; To another the working of Miracles; to another Prophecy; to another Discerning of spirits; to another Divers Kinds of Tongues; to another the Interpretation of Tongues:

"But all these work that one and the selfsame Spirit, dividing to every man severally as He will. For as the Body is one, and has many members, and all the members of that one Body, being many, are one Body: so also is Christ" (I Cor. 12:1-12).

SELF-HELP STUDY NOTES

INTRODUCTION

This subject of *"The Gifts of the Spirit"* is a matter of great importance and relevance. Of course, the Work of the Holy Spirit is wonderfully important in *every* facet of Christ's ministry. But when we come to the Gifts of the Spirit, we find a particularly exciting area of examination.

The Gifts of the Spirit, to Spirit-filled Believers, are scarcely of less importance than the primary reason for the baptism — the endowment of the Believer with *power*. This is because the Spiritual Gifts are, in effect, the *tools* of power. Tragically, prejudice and opinionated thinking have caused many to forfeit these Blessings of God, as they fail to pursue (and thus to receive) all that God has for them. The baptism with the Holy Spirit (and its ensuing Gifts of the Spirit) is without question life's greatest experience — after Salvation. The Gifts of the Spirit are a source of tremendous enrichment to all Spirit-baptized Christians.

As we begin to examine this subject, we might logically see what the Word of God has to say about it. For those who are hungry for God and

SELF-HELP STUDY NOTES

desire everything that God has for them, there should be a continuing desire to search the Scriptures to find what God has to say on *every* subject. Whatever might be taught by anyone, it should always be checked out against the Word of God.

The Gifts of the Spirit are discussed in I Corinthians, Chapter 12. This is the great *"Spiritual Gifts Chapter,"* in which the nine Gifts of the Holy Spirit are presented. There are other gifts and other ways in which individuals are used (as empowered and inspired by the Holy Spirit), but these nine gifts receive primary attention.

In the First Verse of this Chapter, Paul states: *"Now concerning Spiritual Gifts, Brethren, I would not have you ignorant."* The Greek word translated here as *"Spiritual Gifts"* is *pneumatikton* and literally means *"Spiritual Matters"* or spiritualities. This Chapter does, however, refer to Spiritual *Gifts*, because the Greek word for gifts (charismata) is used specifically in verses 4, 9, 28, 30, and 31.

Two words are used Scripturally to refer to the Gifts of the Spirit. One is *charisma* (plural — charismata), which is the Greek word from which we get the word *"charismatic,"* and refers to a gift we receive from God because of His Love and Grace. The other word is *phanerosis*, which means *"a manifestation."*

The word charisma refers to the Gift of Grace, a *favor* which one receives with no merit of his own. It is a Gift of Divine Grace and reminds us that these blessings are not necessarily a reward for good behavior but are a sign of a relationship (e.g., that of a parent giving a child a gift on a special occasion). The word for *"Manifestation"* (*phaneros*) simply refers to something that is open to view, visible, or made known.

The Gifts and Manifestations of the Holy Spirit are meant to help Christians meet needs. A Christian, walking in the Spirit, ministers to another individual by utilizing specific gifts. For example, a person suffering from a physical ailment is ministered to by means of the *"Gifts of Healings."*

FOR THE BODY

We are to be informed on all Scriptural subjects, and we should fully understand what is revealed in this particular portion of God's Word. The Gifts and Manifestations of the Spirit are given that *"every man may profit."* The various gifts are listed, and it is declared, divided *"to every man severally as He will"* (I Cor. 12:11).

It is then added (in I Cor. 12:27) that *"Now you are the Body of Christ, and members in particular."* Paul repeated this in his letter to the Church at Ephesus, that we are the Body of Christ. It appears in Ephesians 1:19-23.

*"And what is the exceeding greatness of His power to us-ward who believe, according to the working of His mighty power, Which He wrought in Christ, when He raised him from the dead, and set him at His Own Right Hand in the Heavenly places, Far above all principality, and power, and might, and dominion, and every name that is named, not only in this world, but also in that which is to come: And has put all things under His Feet, and gave Him to be the Head over all things to the **Church, Which is His Body,** the fullness of Him that fills all in all."*

Jesus Christ is the *Head* of the Church, and we, as His Children, are the *Body*. And this does not refer to any special denominational group. It refers instead to everyone who is Born-Again and washed in the Blood of the Lamb — regardless of which church they may belong. Everyone who is in Christ is a member of the Body of Christ.

Being *parts* of the Body of Christ, we are members in particular. And into that Body have been ordained and established various ministries and gifts: *"And God has set some in the Church, first Apostles, secondarily Prophets, thirdly Teachers, after that Miracles, then Gifts of Healings, Helps, Governments, Diversities of Tongues"* (I Cor. 12:28).

ALL THE GIFTS ARE IMPORTANT

In dealing with the Gifts of the Spirit, it is well to remember that all are important. Some have stated that the Gift of Tongues is the least important of the gifts. But looking at it from a slightly different view, the most important gift is always the one that is needed at any particular moment.

If you are praying for someone to be healed, the Gifts of Healings would be of utmost importance at that moment. And if God wanted to give an utterance in an unknown tongue to a congregation or a Christian gathering, *that* would be the utmost important gift at *that* moment. If an occasion demanded a word of wisdom, the Gift of Wisdom would be of premier importance at that instance. So we should never assume that *any* gift is insignificant, because everything that God gives is vital, significant, and important.

Of course, some of the gifts are more controversial than others — particularly the Gift of Tongues. This has caused many people to stumble and have difficulty in accepting the Gifts of the Holy Spirit in general.

FOR THE CHURCH TODAY?

One of the problems that people encounter in regard to the Gift of Tongues — as well as with the other Gifts of the Spirit — springs from this

SELF-HELP STUDY NOTES

SELF-HELP STUDY NOTES

very question. Many think that the Gifts of the Spirit — miracles and other divine manifestations — were only for the First-century Church. They feel these gifts have *"passed away"* and are not for the Church today. So this is a crucial question. In fact, few subjects involving the New Testament are as important as that of the latter-day legitimacy of the Gifts of the Spirit.

As we said, Paul tells us (in Chapter 12 of I Corinthians) that the Church is the Body of Christ. He then goes on to point out that the *parts* of the Body are Believers exercising their various gifts — even as members of the human body have different functions and purposes. Paul says this is important because *all* members must work in concert if the mystical Body of Christ on Earth is to function as a whole.

Without the Gifts of the Spirit in today's Church, the Body of Christ becomes something quite different from what God intended. Instead of being the supernatural organization God designed (functioning *with* the Gifts of the Spirit), it becomes a merely *human* organization with all the problems and inadequacies inevitably displayed by *all* human organizations.

Churches that don't *practice* the Gifts of the Spirit, that indeed do not *have* the Gifts of the Spirit and don't even *want* the Gifts of the Spirit, are doomed to become *"just another human organization."* This has happened to the vast majority of churches today. A church may consist of a beautiful building, an ambitious program, and a paper organization that makes it appear to be perfection itself, but without the Power of the Holy Spirit, it will have little impact on the lives of the individuals with which it comes in contact.

I know a young man who was in torment from drug dependency who attended a number of churches. They delighted in marching him down the aisle as they tried to persuade him to join their church — and all the time he was crying out in anguish for *help*. What he was seeking was deliverance from his addiction, but they didn't know *how* to deliver him. Each made him a member of their fellowship, but he was still bound by his problem. All he wanted was to be set free. He was actually at the stage of contemplating suicide when he saw a sign in front of a church that said, *"Jesus Saves."*

He went in and the preacher of the Gospel — who knew the Power of the Spirit in his life — laid hands on him and rebuked the demon powers of Hell that bound this man. He was instantly delivered. Today he is a preacher of the Gospel. He had been to many churches, and his name had been entered on various church rolls. They had involved him in church activities, youth groups, and any number of additional activities, but his problem persisted. It wasn't until he found a Body of Believers who knew the Power of the Spirit — with the Gifts of the Spirit in operation — that he was delivered and set free.

Joyfully, there are more and more people realizing this in all denominations. The Spirit of God is being poured out on all flesh, and the Holy Spirit is demonstrating that this was *not* for some limited time during the First Century.

The Word of God tells us that the Lord *"gave some, Apostles; and some, Prophets; and some, Evangelists; and some, Pastors and Teachers"* (Eph. 4:11). This was for the building up and edifying of the Saints, for the work of the ministry. The Gifts of the Spirit were also given for the strengthening of the Body of Christ (I Cor. 12). Now Pastors, Teachers, Evangelists, and Prophets were *not* done away with after the First Century. They are still vitally needed and glaringly apparent in this day and age — *and so are the Gifts of the Spirit!*

These positions and responsibilities within the Church, *together* with the Gifts of the Spirit, are for the perfecting of the Saints for the work of the ministry — and for edifying the Body of Christ. As such, they are needed as much today as they ever were. The Body of Christ needs edifying today, and without question the Saints need perfecting.

The Gifts of the Spirit are sorely needed to deliver people from the bondage of sin. It would be absurd to say that these Early Church manifestations are no longer necessary.

There are many preachers and churches that no longer preach or teach the Born-Again experience, conversion, and the new birth. Of course, the Devil doesn't want people to know that they need to be Born-Again — and that they can be saved through the Blood of Christ — so he has promoted this view. And he would also like to see the modern Church working blindly and ineffectually without the baptism with the Holy Spirit or the Gifts of the Spirit. Naturally he doesn't want the precious Truths of God's Word declared to the people.

There is a drought of God's Word in all too many churches today, but there are still many who do experience new life in Christ, the mighty baptism with the Holy Spirit, and the great blessings of the Gifts of the Spirit. People from all denominations are experiencing new dimensions of Divine Glory as they experience the move of the Spirit in the mighty baptism with the Holy Spirit.

Just one example is a Baptist minister who spoke to me sometime ago. His face was aglow, his whole being illuminated. He said, *"I just received the mighty baptism with the Holy Spirit. My church is coming alive. I am praying for the sick now, and for the first time in my ministry they are being healed!"*

He went on to say that he was praying for those bound by demon spirits and they were being set free. He was rejoicing in having had such a

SELF-HELP STUDY NOTES

SELF-HELP STUDY NOTES

wonderful and beautiful experience with his entire ministry magnified. He felt that he was finally doing what God wanted him to do, according to the New Testament patterns.

As Children of God, it is our responsibility to preach the Gospel to sinners, pray for the sick, cast out devils, and fulfill the Great Commission. As previously stated, the Gifts of the Spirit are not only *needed* today, they are indeed *for* today. They have, thank God, been much in evidence among many groups in recent years.

THE GIFTS OF THE SPIRIT AND THE GREAT COMMISSION

The Lord, in His Great Commission (Mat. 28:18-20 and Mk. 16:15-18), gave the promise of miraculous signs following and confirming the preaching of the Word. No one denies that this Commission is to the Church, and to the Church *as it exists today*. All who profess to believe the Word of God refer to this Great Commission. In it Believers are commanded to *"teach all nations, baptizing them in the Name of the Father, and of the Son, and of the Holy Spirit"* (Mat. 28:19). And Jesus then added, *"Teaching them to observe **all** things whatsoever I have commanded you"* (Mat. 28:20).

All of Jesus' commands, and all that He taught, were meant to be preserved and taught to Believers over the centuries. In the account given to Mark (16:15-18), Jesus said that Believers are to go into all the world and preach the Gospel to every creature. And *then* He said, *"And these signs shall follow them who believe; In my Name shall they cast out devils; they shall speak with new tongues"* (Mk. 16:17).

Now the reason these signs are *not* following the majority of church ministries today is that they do not *believe* in divine healing, miracles, and deliverance!

One of the signs that should follow Believers is: *"In My Name shall they cast out devils"* (Mk. 16:17). The powers of Satan and demonic activity are absolutely *inundating* the world today. Not only do we need to *preach* on the terrible destructive forces surrounding us, but we should also have the power within our Christian hearts and lives to *cast out* these demonic powers! And this applies to both ministers *and* Spirit-filled Believers. We are truly involved in a Spiritual Warfare (Eph. 6:12). The hold that demonic forces have on individuals is awesome. Multitudes need deliverance from demonic influence, and there is only one way to accomplish this. That is in the *Authority* of Jesus Christ, through the *Power* of the Holy Spirit.

Also, in this same reference in Mark 16:17, it is written, *"They shall speak with new tongues."* Many wish that this particular Scripture was not there. Admittedly, there *is* some dispute among scholars as to the ending of the text of Mark. Some textual critics believe that Mark 16 ended with Verse 8. However, there are excellent early manuscripts which do contain the entire Twenty Verses that we have in our Bibles. It is completely consistent with the rest of the Scripture, and this is perhaps the single best method for determining the validity of anything Spiritual. Speaking in tongues is emphasized in a number of additional Passages as we have noted previously.

Another part of the Great Commission of the Sixteenth Chapter of Mark states that Believers *"shall take up serpents; and if they drink any deadly thing, it shall not hurt them; they shall lay hands on the sick, and they shall recover"* (Vs. 18).

This matter of taking up serpents has been misunderstood and has resulted at times in unbelievably foolish activities among certain groups. The serpent is primarily presented in Scripture as a type of the Devil, so the basic application of this deals with people being delivered from satanic forces. It in *no* way encourages taking up poisonous snakes in an attempt to demonstrate Faith. Our Lord said, in Matthew 4:7, *"You shall not tempt the Lord your God."* He was quoting Deuteronomy 6:16 and other earlier Scriptures here. We, as Christians, have the power and authority (in Jesus Christ) over satanic forces, and *this* is the primary import of this Passage.

Neither should a person swallow poison as a demonstration of Faith, just because this Verse says, *"if they drink any deadly thing, it shall not hurt them."* There have been times, however, when hostile forces have tried to physically harm Christians by poisoning them, and there are miraculous accounts of deadly poisons having no harmful effects on these Believers. And, of course, we are all familiar with the incident of the serpent striking Paul in Acts 28:1-6. But these were all situations *imposed* on the Believers, in such cases God protected the victims.

The Scripture continues on to say that Believers shall *"lay hands on the sick, and they shall recover."* This is consistent with other Scriptures, such as James 5:14: *"Is any sick among you? Let him call for the Elders of the Church; and let them pray over him, anointing him with oil in the Name of the Lord."*

This is for the Church today. Some would erroneously conclude (and declare) that the world has already been evangelized and there is no further need for these demonstrations of God's Power. Now this assumption, on the grounds that the Gifts of the Spirit are no longer needed because the world is evangelized, is far removed from the truth. The world is *not* evangelized as yet and *desperately* needs the Message of Saving Grace, with the Power of God demonstrated in every way possible.

SELF-HELP STUDY NOTES

SELF-HELP STUDY NOTES

One of the most successful means of mass evangelism is through the ministry of Healing and Miracles. It is good to send medical missionaries to build hospitals and schools, but the Gifts of the Spirit go far beyond this in their demonstration and proclamation of the Gospel Message. Today's Church desperately needs the Gifts of the Spirit.

The Gifts of the Spirit are absent from the Church today because the Church has largely been satisfied to stumble along without them. The Church has become comfortable, reclining in their big buildings, schools, money, power, fame, and popularity. It is absolutely essential that the Church realize her position as the Body of Christ. The Church, trying to operate without the Gifts of the Spirit, can never fulfill the destiny for which she was intended by Jesus Christ. We, as Children of the Most High God, *must* have the Gifts of the Spirit.

A SPIRIT-FILLED CHURCH

Sometime ago, I was talking to a missionary who helped establish a *huge* church in Korea whose numbers run into the tens of thousands in every Sunday morning's services. And there's a reason for this phenomenal growth.

This missionary told me that some Presbyterian people were helping him. These were people who had been saved by the Blood of Christ and who had experienced the baptism with the Holy Spirit. The Gifts of the Spirit were in operation within this church, for they had eagerly accepted the baptism with the Holy Spirit.

They were seeing the sick healed, people set free from the bondage of Satan, from drug addiction, from prostitution, from thievery, and from every vile, vulgar sin imaginable. This is what the Church is all about and what every church should be doing.

Churches and Christians filled with the power are found throughout the world and in all denominations. The Church is *meant* to be a repository of power. The New Testament and the entire Word of God is *filled* with power. *We* can have this power — this Anointing of the Holy Spirit.

There are some who object, however, because they have witnessed fanaticism and excess on the part of certain Christians who have misused the things of God. Unfortunately, there *are* those who have gone off into various deviations, bringing reproach upon the cause of Christ. But just because you once received a counterfeit twenty-dollar bill doesn't give grounds to demand that banks throw away *all* twenty-dollar bills.

Wherever there is a counterfeit, there has to be a corresponding *genuine* article. Certainly Satan enjoys seeing counterfeits functioning within the Church to discredit the genuine. It is the legitimate that threatens Satan, so naturally he tries to hinder the True Move of God by encouraging excess, fanaticism, and counterfeit.

Gifts of the Spirit operating within the Church have been a tremendous aid to evangelism and in distributing the Gospel to the ends of the Earth. Some of the greatest evangelical efforts have been accomplished by those baptized with the Holy Spirit. They have prayed for the sick and cast out demons as they proclaimed the Gospel Message. And *wherever* this has been done, people have responded in great numbers.

In the great Spiritual battle in which we are engaged, we need the *"whole armor of God"* as described in Ephesians 6. And this indicates, as of primary importance, the basics of the Gospel and the power of the Gifts of the Holy Spirit. Where these essential gifts are operational, we hear impressive reports of real progress in putting forth the Gospel in fulfillment of the Great Commission.

THREE CLASSIFICATIONS OF GIFTS

Theologians have separated the nine Gifts of the Spirit into three classifications. *First*, there are the *"Revelation"* Gifts. These are the Word of Wisdom, the Word of Knowledge, and the Discerning of spirits. These all fall into a similar category, and, in fact, tend to work together more often than not. In many situations, they tend to interrelate and overlap to the point where it can be difficult to separate them. Sometimes two of these gifts will operate simultaneously in a certain situation, but frequently all three will come into play. All three of these gifts operate in the area of revelation; which is to say, they expand our ability to *know*.

Secondly, we have the *"Power"* Gifts. These are the Gift of Faith, the Gifts of Healings, and the Gift of the working of Miracles. These all involve the power to perform — to *do*.

And, *finally,* in addition to the Power Gifts, there are the *"Inspiration"* Gifts — which come vocally. There are the Gifts of Prophecy, Divers Kinds of Tongues, and the Interpretation of Tongues. The Inspirational or Vocal Gifts have to do with the power to *communicate*.

REVELATION GIFTS

WORD OF WISDOM — The first Gift of the Spirit which we will discuss is the Word of Wisdom. This is different from the wisdom James discussed in James 1:5 where he said, *If any of you lack wisdom, let him ask of God, that gives to all men liberally, and upbraideth not; and it shall be given him."* Here James was talking about *"normal"* wisdom — the type we need for the day-to-day operation of our lives. This is not

SELF-HELP STUDY NOTES

SELF-HELP STUDY NOTES

the Gift of *the Word* of Wisdom.

The reason we do not use the term *"gift of wisdom"* is because this would give credence to the erroneous theory that this gift refers simply to being wise, clever, or quick-witted. As stated in the Bible, it is *"the Word of Wisdom."* This can be seen in operation when a particular word of revelation or fact is given to an individual. It is simply a matter of day-to-day wisdom, for the Word of Wisdom concerns a supernatural revelation regarding the Plan and Purpose of God.

The Gift of the Word of Wisdom is the Mind of God pertaining to *futuristic* events. It has been called the greatest of the gifts. And why not? Anyone that can have prior knowledge to events that are going to transpire in the future, has the knowledge that is beyond human ability to ascertain. Only God can give that kind of knowledge, because only God knows the future.

Many of the Prophecies in the Old Testament actually were Words of Wisdom. They were given by the Prophet, but they pertained to futuristic events. And please notice, the term is *"Word of Wisdom."* God only gives a small part of His Knowledge to us concerning these futuristic events. He doesn't tell us all that He knows — only a part of it. Hence, the term *"Word of Wisdom."*

In the Seventh Chapter of Isaiah, the Bible tells us of Ahaz, the king of Judah that was fearing an attack by Syria and Israel. Isaiah went out to meet Ahaz and told him certain particular things. He then told him to ask for a sign from the Lord that this thing would be done. Ahaz was so corrupt and wicked in his heart that he was not really interested in asking God anything. And then Isaiah gave the great Prophecy, beginning with the Fourteenth Verse where he said, *"Therefore the Lord Himself shall give you a sign; Behold, a virgin shall conceive, and bear a son, and shall call His Name Immanuel."* This was actually a Word of Wisdom concerning the birth of the Lord Jesus Christ by the virgin Mary. It was something that would happen hundreds of years in the future.

So God gave to Isaiah a futuristic Word of Wisdom concerning something that would happen in coming years.

The Old Testament is full of incidents of this nature; actually, there are many in the New Testament as well.

For instance, in the Twenty-first Chapter of Acts, we are told of the Apostle Paul who, on his way to Jerusalem, stopped at Caesarea and entered into the house of Philip the Evangelist. And the Bible tells us that Agabus, a certain Prophet, took Paul's girdle and bound his own hands and feet and said, *"Thus saith the Holy Spirit, So shall the Jews at Jerusalem bind the man that owns this girdle, and shall deliver him into the hands of the Gentiles."* Actually, this was a Word of Wisdom. It concerned futuristic events that would transpire.

I realize that some may think, "Well this is Prophecy and not a Word of Wisdom. However, New Testament Prophecy is different from Old Testament Prophecy, and we will explain this when we discuss the Gift of Prophecy.

When I was nine years old (1944), the Lord spoke through my lips of the inventions of the atomic and hydrogen bombs. Of course, the general public knew absolutely nothing about these monster weapons in 1944. The Manhattan Project was then being worked on, but the general public knew nothing of it. Scientists had not yet invented this lethal weapon that would change the direction and course of history, but God spoke through my heart of one weapon that would completely destroy an entire city. I remember as it was given out to the people, telling in exact detail how the fire would burn from this one bomb and destroy tens, even hundreds, of thousands of human beings in one detonating blast. No one then understood, but it was announced to the world that the United States had dropped its first atomic bomb on Nagasaki and Hiroshima, and people were killed by this one bomb, then we knew this was the fulfillment of that particular revelation from God. It was actually a Word of Wisdom.

THE WORD OF KNOWLEDGE — There are many opinions as to just what the Word of Knowledge is. Let's begin by stating what the Word of Knowledge *isn't*. It is not the things you know, but pertains rather to the things you *don't* know. This particular gift can be of real support and assistance to every Christian. This is not to minimize the other gifts (such as the Gifts of Healings) — for *all* are important. The different gifts are to meet different needs, but there is an undeniable and common need for the Gift of the Word of Knowledge.

It should be noted that this Gift is not *"the gift of knowledge"* but rather *"the Gift of the Word of Knowledge."* It doesn't relate to one's education or things learned by study or experience. Both the Word of Knowledge and the Word of Wisdom are supernatural revelations from God. The Word of Knowledge is the Mind of God concerning people, places, things, or events pertaining to the past or the present. Whereas the Word of Wisdom deals with futuristic events, the Word of Knowledge deals with present or past events.

I recall, some years ago, when we were constructing some of the original buildings for our Baton Rouge offices. Huge trucks arrived one morning loaded with massive concrete beams intended to top the buildings to serve as the roof. The engineer in charge examined their proposed location and called me over.

He explained that the beams wouldn't work because of some error in the supporting structure. The huge crane was prepared to set them up on the walls, and the workmen were all standing around ready to work. But because something had been done wrongly, a real problem existed.

SELF-HELP STUDY NOTES

SELF-HELP STUDY NOTES

There were thousands of dollars worth of beams sitting on the truck, and I asked if they couldn't just be set on the ground until the situation could be remedied. He said they couldn't be stored on the ground as they would become damp and the uneven contour of the land might cause them to break. The engineer, one of the best in the city, continued to think about the situation. Finally, he said they couldn't be installed because they just wouldn't work. Everyone standing there was in a quandary, and of all present I was probably the *least* capable of proposing a solution.

For a long time, I had studied God's word concerning this matter of the Word of Knowledge. In our revival meetings, radio ministry, and numerous other activities, God had often given direction. This was going through my mind as I walked toward the back of the building, away from the men discussing how the situation might be handled. As I walked along I said, *"Lord, thousands of dollars are being wasted, money I don't have."* As I talked to God, I said, *"There must be a way to use that material."* I asked the Lord for a Word of Knowledge — direction from the Lord in our dilemma.

I have no knowledge whatever concerning building construction. The engineer had rattled off figures he had carefully worked out on a piece of paper, and told me that the displacement weight and other problems would place unacceptable loads on the walls. The building codes wouldn't accept the situation, and if they were put up, the building would no doubt collapse.

As I was seeking the Lord, He told me to suggest to the engineer that he lay plates on the walls where the beams would rest. This would distribute the load over a much larger area. I suggested this to him and he thought a few seconds. *"No,"* he finally said, *"that won't work. We just can't do it."*

I continued to pray under my breath and walked over to the side of the building with bowed head. *"Lord,"* I said, *"I told him what to do and he said it won't work."* And at that moment, the Lord revealed to me that the Devil was blinding his thoughts and clouding his mind. Satan is the god of this world and the prince of the powers of the Earth. God instructed me to rebuke the foul spirit blocking his mind and causing him confusion.

So I took authority over the demon powers of Hell, and, standing right there in the middle of that building, commanded that all spirits of darkness depart. It was like a light shining all about me and warm oil flowing over me. I had no control over the engineer, but in the Power of Jesus Christ I had taken authority over the spirits of darkness.

In Matthew 18:18 our Lord said, *"Verily I say unto you, Whatsoever you shall bind on Earth shall be bound in Heaven: and whatsoever you shall loose on Earth shall be loosed in Heaven."* This refers to the binding of spirits of darkness. I felt good in my heart, went back, and made the suggestion again. And suddenly his whole countenance changed. He took off his hat, scratched his head, and stared off into the distance. After a moment he said, *"You know? I forgot something. I believe it will work."*

The plates were put on, and he gave the signal to the crane operator. The huge engine roared into action, picking up the first of the beams and swinging it into place. As it settled into place, nothing gave way. The beam was sturdy and strong. I rejoiced in my heart and tears rolled down my cheeks. The engineer walked over and laid his hand on my shoulder, saying, *"Preacher, don't worry about anything. I don't know why, but I know the thing will work."* He shook his head. *"I just don't know why I didn't think of this sooner."* Then he gave me some figures concerning displacement as he said, *"Don't worry about it, it will pass every code."*

God had given the Word of Knowledge in instructions in this situation which had nothing to do with *Spiritual* Matters but was completely in the practical realm. Often the Gift of the Word of Knowledge will come to solve just such problems. I've seen this happen many times. We have often asked for words of knowledge and have thus been able, on any number of occasions, to solve problems in all areas of life. How thrilling and exciting it is to receive these insights and revelations when, in the natural, you know nothing about the project at hand.

This Gift of the Word of Knowledge has been used to help protect Christians in a variety of ways. It shows us how to pray more effectively, how to help others, and is in general a tremendous comfort in all kinds of problems.

There are various kinds of knowledge. *First,* there is the natural human knowledge which is being increased at a tremendous rate. In this area, there are computers that store unbelievable stockpiles of facts that go beyond the capability of the human mind to absorb or utilize. While natural worldly knowledge is essential for survival in our present situation, it unfortunately can become a source of pride in a man.

Then there is a *second* kind of knowledge. This is the fallen world's supernatural knowledge. There are many things known by the occult, psychics, and metaphysical investigators which brings one into close contact with Satan. There are religious experiences through drugs, cults, psychics, and other occult sources which are expanding dramatically in this day and age. This fallen knowledge from the spirit world is outside the limits of God's permission, and Christians are *not* to become involved in this area. (This is the type of knowledge that Jeanne Dixon and others like her possess.)

In the *third* place, there is true intellectual knowledge. This comes by knowing God personally through Jesus Christ (Jn. 17:3, Phil. 3:10). As a person is filled with the Holy Spirit and comes to know God's Word

SELF-HELP STUDY NOTES

135

SELF-HELP STUDY NOTES

thoroughly, there is a knowledge of Gods' Will and Ways for which there is no earthly substitute. Christians will grow in this knowledge only as they study God's Word, pray, and live totally for Him.

Then there is a *fourth* type of knowledge referred to as *"the Gift of a Word of Knowledge."* Here are examples in Scripture which give insight into this gift. A supernatural revelation, a Word of Knowledge, was given to Nathan regarding the affair between David and Bathsheba. Nathan was also given the wisdom to deal with the king in this matter (II Sam. 12:7-13). Elisha, by special revelation, was shown the location of the Syrian army and was thus able to save Israel from almost certain defeat (II Ki. 6:8-23).

Jesus knew the hearts of individuals and declared such when He spoke to them. This was by the Word of Knowledge, not by mind-reading. Jesus knew a great deal about Nathanael before He ever met him (Jn. 1:47-50). The Gift of the Word of Knowledge may thus reveal hidden facts about an individual. When Ananias and Sapphira endeavored to deceive the Early Church, the Holy Spirit revealed to Peter (by the Word of Knowledge) the true nature of their actions.

There are many present-day situations where this Gift of the Holy Spirit has been in operation and has been of great value in helping Believers. Through the Gift of the Word of Knowledge, much has been revealed which has proved both necessary, and of assistance, in resolving difficult situations.

THE DISCERNING OF SPIRITS — The Discerning of spirits is a spectacular gift which few people really understand. The Gift of the Word of Knowledge and the Gift of the Discerning of spirits often work hand-in-hand. They are closely related, and thus often work in conjunction. Of course, there are also times when they are not both needed, and then they work independently.

The Gift of the Discerning of spirits is more than just heightened discernment. And there are, of course, different levels of discernment. There is, first of all, what we might call *"natural discernment."* Believers and non-believers alike possess this. It is a matter of using ingrained judgment and common sense to evaluate certain circumstances, people, activities, and situations.

Then there is a deeper intellectual discernment, which is evidenced as deeper perceptions of those who have the Mind of Christ by being renewed in Him. This discernment develops as a person receives Christ, grows in Him, and increases in the knowledge of His Word. The Book of Hebrews states in 5:13-14, *"For every one that uses milk is unskilful in the Word of Righteousness: for he is a babe. But strong meat belongs to them who are of full age, even those who by reason of use have their senses exercised to discern both good and evil."*

As one grows and matures in the Christian life, the Holy Spirit enables him to sift matters and project their logical conclusions on the basis of their foundations — either in good or evil. The Gift of Discerning of spirits naturally pertains to the spirit world. It deals in the area of evil spirits — which would include demons, fallen angels, and Satan himself.

It would also include angelic spirits and the Hosts of Heaven — which would include Angels, Cherubims, Seraphims, or even the Lord Himself. It would also include the discerning of human spirits, because mankind is a tripartite being — spirit, soul, and body — so it is dealing on a threefold level concerning the spirit world — and it is always in the spirit world.

The *Gift* of the Discerning of spirits does not come, however, simply through training and development. It is a specific gift, given at the moment it is needed. Through this gift, a Believer is enabled to immediately sense the motivating force behind an individual or beneath the surface of a particular situation. There is an unnatural recognition of the Spiritual forces at work, to the point where individuals have even *seen* demonic spirits at work.

Sometimes this comes as a keen sense of awareness of a particular type of spirit, and the accompanying ability to recognize that spirit's influence over certain situations. Sometimes as the Holy Spirit reveals the background in certain cases, there is such interplay of all three Revelation Gifts that it is difficult to sort them out specifically. But the point is, this is a Gift of the Spirit and the insight given is supernatural in nature.

The Gift of the Discerning of spirits is extremely necessary in this day and age. It can function as a form of protection from the influence of the enemy and from problems within the fellowship. Sometimes individuals are included within local fellowships who have the wrong kind of spirit. The Gift of Discerning of spirits is also useful when other gifts are being exercised in a meeting. When a Prophet speaks, his prophecies are to be judged on the basis of their source (I Cor. 14:29 and I Jn. 4:1-3).

One of the greatest problems in today's world involves evil spirits at work. We are involved in serious Spiritual Warfare, and there is a great need for the Discernment of spirits as a result. It is something that is being used, or *should* be used, regularly.

People bound by demonic forces need desperately to be freed. Those with the Gift of Discerning of spirits are often powerfully used in liberating individuals from this bondage. Sometimes this is the *only* means of setting the captive free.

In this world, with so many Spiritual needs and with such intensified Spiritual activity, the Gift of the Discerning of spirits is crucial. It is being used and experienced more now than at perhaps any time in history.

Encounters within the Spiritual realm certainly demand the Discerning of spirits because Satan can appear as an angel of light. The majority of cases involving this gift do pertain to evil spirits. In this matter of the Devil

SELF-HELP STUDY NOTES

SELF-HELP STUDY NOTES

appearing as an angel of light, it must be noted that many people are deceived. They are deluded into believing many things are of God, when in truth they are of the Devil.

The Gift of the Discerning of spirits does indeed involve discerning of *evil* spirits, but that isn't the whole story. There are occasions when good spirits are discerned as well. When the Lord is endeavoring to help an individual, guiding him in certain areas of life and providing strength, there have been occasions when Angels have appeared unto God's people.

There are many close to God who may have operated with the Gift of the Discerning of spirits, without ever realizing that this was the actual gift at work. They have used this gift, and seen the results, but without realizing just what it was that brought about their sudden, supernatural perceptions.

An interesting illustration of the use of this gift relates to a great man of God whom I have known for many years. He was preaching a revival in Texas, and praying for the sick on certain specified nights of his crusade. Of course, he prayed for the sick *every* night, but certain services were specifically devoted to healing. People were especially urged to bring their sick to these meetings.

This preacher said that there was one woman in particular who was related to the pastor. She was brought in on a stretcher as her doctors had sent her home to die of cancer. She was in the final stages, and it was a matter of only having a short time remaining. The preacher prayed for her during this special healing service, but there was no outward indication of healing. She was terribly emaciated and actually gave off the smell of death.

The second week of the revival she was brought back again in great pain. Once again she was prayed for, with no apparent results. And this is an area where we can go awry. People often think if someone is prayed for once without receiving an answer, that prayer will no longer avail. They feel they shouldn't continue to *beg* God over and over again. But there *are* times when we must seek God's face again and again. And while I don't know precisely why this is, the account of the importuning widow in Luke 18:1-8 demonstrates this principle. It's not that God is deaf or because we have a *"bad connection,"* but simply because Satan will do everything he can to hinder us. Thus, as Children of God, we must *persevere*.

This woman was prayed for more than once. The evangelist was closing the meeting that week, but the pastor asked him to extend the revival for another week. It created some difficulty for the evangelist, but he felt God's leading so agreed to remain for another week. He scheduled one or two more healing services, and this same woman was brought for healing for the third time. Again, after preaching the message, he prayed for her; but again there was no sign of healing. Then, as he began to move on from her to another waiting person, the Holy Spirit suddenly revealed the spirit realm to him.

The Gift of Discerning of spirits came into operation, and he suddenly saw a demon spirit sitting on this woman's shoulder. This loathsome spirit was responsible for the physical problems she was suffering. He was trying to kill her and, in fact, had just about succeeded.

Once the evangelist recognized this spirit, he immediately commanded it to depart in the Power and Authority of Jesus Christ. This demonic presence had laid siege to her body and was determined to kill her. But as soon as the evangelist took authority over it in Jesus' Name, it departed and she was healed.

This doesn't mean that every physical disability is the direct result of demonic activity that must be discerned and dealt with. But this undoubtedly is true in many cases. Jesus commanded many spirits of infirmities to leave the individuals who were having physical problems when He ministered here on Earth. And, of course, the Devil *is* the author of all sickness. Demon powers — the powers of darkness — always afflict people whenever they can, and in whatever *way* they can.

At first the evangelist *prayed* for healing and the woman was not healed. He had seen many others healed through prayer, but prayer was having no effect in her case. But then, when the Discerning of spirits came into play and he recognized the *cause* of her problem, he was able to deal with this cause and she was instantly healed. This woman needed *deliverance*. She had breast cancer which had spread to the lymph glands under her arm. It was in this (shoulder) area that the evangelist saw the demon clutching her body. When he commanded it to leave, he saw that its claws were fastened to her body right at the spot of the cancer.

The demon whined and protested for a moment and refused to leave. Please realize, the crowd present couldn't see this, only the evangelist could. He was directly addressing the demon and those present were aware of this.

Jesus said that, *"In My Name they will cast out devils."* This demon was commanded to leave the woman's body. The evangelist, through the Discerning of spirits, saw the demon walking out the door after he released himself from her body. The woman began shouting praises to God.

When the demon left, the disease also left. She immediately sprang out of her bed, and the glory of God flowed all over her as strength began to return to her body. She went to her doctors the next day and was thoroughly x-rayed and tested with no trace of cancer present. This woman was alive and well — and all as a result of the Discerning of spirits coming into play. It was a life-giving force for this woman and has been for countless others.

SELF-HELP STUDY NOTES

SELF-HELP STUDY NOTES

If the Gift of Discerning of spirits had not begun operating here, this woman would have died in a matter of days. To be sure, her soul and spirit would have been in Heaven, but she would have died and would not have been able to remain with her loving family.

It is revealed at times, to those who have ministered, that on occasion there is a need for divine healing and, on other occasions, a need for deliverance from the powers and forces of Hell. In each of these cases the problem is manifested physically, but the source lies in the Spiritual Realm. Demon powers can cause migraine headaches, ulcers, and many other illnesses, although these illnesses are not *necessarily* caused by demonic activity.

The Gift of Discerning of spirits is not necessarily something for the newer Christian to seek. Sometimes people feel *led* to ask the Lord for some specific gift when it is not the leading of the *Spirit*. We can also be influenced by human, *worldly* leadings. There can be an ego element in sitting in a service and seeing a member of the congregation singled out for prominence in the proceedings. And when we see more experienced Christians utilizing certain gifts, we can't help but note the *attention* focused on them. This is when our natural, human desires can enter in.

"How wonderful it would be," we might say to ourselves, *"if God would use me as He uses Brother Smith."* But is it a question of envying Brother Smith the *attention* he receives? The powers of darkness will use any weakness as a wedge to break down our spirituality. And it is *most* important that we sort out *all* of our motives to make sure that we keep pace with God's timetable for our development. When the Holy Spirit is ready to use us for His Purpose, He will make it obvious to us that it *is* time for whatever gift is then required. We should be patient and concentrate on exercising the Gifts the Holy Spirit has entrusted to us for any given time and for any given stage in our Christian development. When great needs present themselves, however, it is certainly proper and logical to seek the Gifts of the Spirit which will meet those needs. The Gifts are entrusted to us as they become necessary.

I recall something that happened several years ago. It may seem odd, but the Gift of the Discerning of spirits was involved in recognizing demonic influence in a matter completely removed from the Spiritual Realm. Demonic forces can affect not only people, but physical objects as well.

This incident involved a piece of machinery in our office that had been plagued with mechanical problems. It just wouldn't work. We called in professional repairmen and engineers to go over it and one finally said, *"I just don't know what it is."* He actually did more harm than good, although he had a reputation as being an expert in this particular field.

Next they flew in a man from a distant city who was supposedly the top man in this field. He had no sooner left town again when the machine returned to its former, paralyzed state. Needless to say, I was completely discouraged. Then one night after work, when everyone had gone home and the office was closed, I remained behind. I was troubled in my spirit as I walked into the room containing this large piece of equipment.

At the time we needed it desperately in our work, and I was praying as I walked up and down beside it. I had reminded the Lord that we had done everything we knew to get it operating properly, but something just wasn't right. Then the Spirit of God began to move and the Gift of the Discerning of spirits began to manifest itself. The Lord spoke to my heart and said, *"It is a demon spirit causing this equipment to fail. Rebuke it and cast it out. Once you command it to leave, the machine will work."*

I stood there, and as the Presence of the Lord began to overshadow me, I took authority. I said, *"In the Name of Jesus Christ, I rebuke this foul spirit that is causing this equipment to malfunction, and I command it to leave these premises, immediately and forever."* The next morning when the operator started it up, it worked beautifully, and it has *continued* to function properly ever since.

You see, demon powers — the forces of darkness — can get in and effect things, but by Discerning these spirits, we can take authority over them. It is both simple and beautiful. Of course, there are things that wear out and break down, and that's an entirely different matter. Everything that happens is not the result of demonic activity. There can be a tendency to *"go overboard"* on these matters — either ignoring demon spirits completely — or seeing them as the controlling force of just about *everything*. We should always strive for balance, but there *are* times when demon forces can affect objects, people, or situations.

The Gift of the Discerning of spirits and insight into the demonic influences behind certain situations can solve these problems in a moment. When the Spirit of God gave discernment in the situation of our equipment, there was an immediate and total victory. We are in a state of constant Spiritual Warfare, and we must be ever aware of demonic activity as a possible factor.

I remember once when trying to cut an album with RCA Victor that the master kept coming up completely unusable. I finally reached the point of complete despair. I just didn't know what to do. Finally I turned to prayer. *"Lord,"* I said, *"it's costing thousands of dollars, and we have done everything within our power."* Then, one afternoon, as I stepped into my car to go to church to pray, the Lord spoke to my heart.

He said, *"Son, it is the spirit of the Devil that's causing the problems with your album. Take authority over it right now!"*

You see, it was the Gift of the Discerning of spirits that had suddenly come into operation, and only *then* was the problem brought into focus. It

SELF-HELP STUDY NOTES

SELF-HELP STUDY NOTES

wasn't the machinery down at RCA, or the engineers, or the technicians. They were all capable men doing their best to deliver a good final product. But they just couldn't get the job done because the Devil was throwing the proverbial monkey wrench into the situation. The spirit of darkness was there to hinder everything we did.

But then the Lord opened my heart and mind to see what was going on, through the Gift of the Discerning of spirits. And although I was several hundred miles away from Nashville at the moment, I took authority over the situation and rebuked the demonic forces in Jesus' Name. At that moment I *knew* it was solved, so I immediately began rejoicing. When we received the next master, it was perfect. Thank God for the Gift of the Discerning of spirits.

This Gift of spirit Discernment was present in the Life of Jesus. On one occasion, as recorded in Mark 5, Jesus came into the country of the Gadarenes and was met immediately by a man from the tombs who had an unclean spirit. He had been dwelling among the burial places and no man could bind him with chains or fetters. He used his supernatural strength to break any chains placed upon him and went out about the area crying and cutting himself with stones.

Jesus was immediately aware of the principal demon spirit involved and actually talked to him. This man's problem was not psychological but Spiritual. Jesus took authority over these demonic forces and the man was instantly delivered, set free, transformed.

Similar occurrences are happening today. The Spirit of God still works, and the Gifts of the Spirit are in operation. Demonic forces are also at work and need to be dealt with. The Gift of the Discerning of spirits is not only *needed* today, it is present and available for our use.

POWER GIFTS

There are three Gifts of the Spirit commonly referred to as *"the Power Gifts."* These are the Gift of Faith, the Gifts of Healings, and the Working of Miracles.

We have mentioned that the Gifts of the Spirit sometimes work in conjunction with each other. When it appears that *one* is in operation it may be that two or three are actually involved, while we are only conscious of the one predominant at the moment. This is often true of these three gifts, perhaps more so than with any of the other gifts. There can be an unusually close relationship here, and the possibility of more than one of these gifts working together to meet a special need.

THE GIFT OF FAITH — Many people talk about Faith, and it is probably the most sought-after of all the gifts. Yet few people really understand what Faith is. The Word of God places such great emphasis on Faith that an entire Chapter (Chapter 11 of the Book of Hebrews) lists those of special Faith of the Old Testament.

Faith is emphasized over and over again in Scripture and by everyday Christians in everyday conversation. In the Book of Hebrews we read, *"Now Faith is the substance of things hoped for, the evidence of things not seen"* (11:1). That would be a pretty good definition of Faith if we didn't say another word about it.

Many things can be said about Faith. Faith is a present-tense matter because it is a present-tense activity — while Hope is future tense. Faith is believing *before* seeing the accomplishment of a situation. Faith eventually brings into reality what a person starts out by believing. Faith is not passive, it is active.

The *Gift* of Faith is different from ordinary faith. There are many kinds of faith. Natural *human* faith is exercised everyday of our lives, by both Believers and unbelievers. Faith is exercised by an individual every time he drives through a green light, believing that the cross-traffic will stop on their red. Faith is exercised every time we sit down in a chair, trusting that it will hold us. Natural human faith and trust are demonstrated every day by every one of us.

Then there are other kinds of Faith, which are from God and are supernatural. Salvation does not come from our good deeds, but comes through *Faith* in Jesus Christ. Scripture says, *"Believe* (have faith) *on the Lord Jesus Christ, and you shall be saved"* (Acts 16:31). This is *"saving Faith."* *"For by Grace are you saved through Faith"* (Eph. 2:8).

The Bible tells us that without Faith it is impossible to please God (Heb. 11:6). The Faith that saves is itself a gift from God and not something we generate within ourselves (Eph. 2:8-9).

But God's Word also says that *"Faith comes by hearing, and hearing by the Word of God"* (Rom. 10:17). For those who have received Jesus and have become Christians, it is said that there is given to everyone a *"measure of faith"* (Rom. 12:3). In the Christian life, everyone has a measure of Faith. God has an unlimited store and will supply as we continue to trust in Him.

But there is a second kind of Faith. And this is the Faith that comes as a *"fruit of the Spirit"* (Gal. 5:22 — faithfulness). As we abide in Christ and grow in Him, we can bring forth much fruit (Jn. 15:5). Thus, as the Spirit of God works in an individual's life, there is the growth of various fruits, and among these is Faith.

But there is still *another* kind of Faith, and this is the Faith that concerns us within this study of the Gifts of the Spirit. This is the *Gift* of Faith. There is a potential here for every person who is in Christ, but it

SELF-HELP STUDY NOTES

SELF-HELP STUDY NOTES

becomes much more active following a person's receiving the baptism with the Holy Spirit. This is not like the Faith that we receive as a *Fruit* of the Spirit, which takes time to grow and develop: the Gift of Faith is given instantaneously.

With the Gift of Faith, there is a sudden *surge* of Faith (special Faith). It generally occurs in a crisis situation and within the pressure of a great need. Suddenly there is a great confidence and belief — usually coupled with the irresistible urge to *declare* something in Jesus' Name — with the absolute *certainty* that it will come to pass.

Jesus told the Believers to *"have Faith in God."* Actually in the original Greek this reads, *"have the Faith of God."* And then He went on to say: *"For verily I say unto you, If you have Faith as a grain of mustard seed, you shall say unto this mountain, Remove hence to yonder place; and it shall remove; and nothing shall be impossible unto you"* (Mat. 17:20).

There are countless examples of Faith in the Old Testament, such as that of Elijah who appeared on the scene in I Kings 17:1 to announce to Ahab that it would not rain for three years. And what happened? It *didn't* rain for three years!

Everyone who names the Name of Jesus and is truly Born-Again has Faith. But this is not the *Gift* of Faith. The Gift of Faith — one of the nine Gifts of the Holy Spirit — is Faith above and beyond the normal measure of Faith given to every Believer.

You can encourage and nourish your Faith by *acting* upon it. But this is still not the Gift of Faith. The Gift of Faith is not necessarily something ladled out to the individual on request. There must be a specific need in order to activate this gift. You will not receive the Gift of Faith, precious as it is, simply by desiring or requesting it.

Just because a person might plan to be an evangelist or missionary, he won't automatically receive the Gift of Faith to help him in his work. An individual must first *step out* on the Faith God has already given him. Then, *after* he has believed God for great things, this Gift of Faith will come into operation — but only in answer to a momentary need.

I remember years ago preaching a great revival meeting at a wonderful church in Illinois. There were marvelous people there and we acquired many lifelong friends. The meeting went on for six weeks with a large number of people saved. Scores were filled wonderfully and gloriously with the Holy Spirit.

Since that time, I run into people all over the country who tell me that they came to the Lord Jesus Christ during that meeting — or who were affected by God moving in their hearts and lives at that time. God poured out Faith in my heart during that meeting, and I can say without exaggeration that the Gift of Faith for revival went into operation in my life at that meeting. Prior to that, I had constantly prayed, sought God, wept, pleaded, and believed God for a great outpouring of the Holy Spirit. I wanted so *badly* to see people saved, lives changed, sick bodies healed, and a great move for the Kingdom.

The results, however, up until then, were very limited. We had labored and worked and wept for God. But at this meeting, something special occurred in my life. God gave me the Gift of Faith to *believe* for great results in a revival crusade. I didn't plead for this gift or harangue God importunely for it. It just suddenly fell into my life; and that, more often than not, is the true sign that this particular Gift of the Spirit is working.

From that moment on, I never again worried about *"drawing a crowd."* Suddenly it became necessary to find ever bigger buildings to seat the people. Most of the time, the churches offered weren't large enough. God gave me Faith for revival, and I believe with all my heart that it was the Gift of Faith that came into my life at this time. It is still there, and God is continuing to bless. How precious and wonderful are His Gifts, and how glorious it is to see people responding to the miraculous power that has changed and transformed their lives.

In this ministry, we have moved on to greater and greater outreach. The only way I can explain it is that through the operation of the Gift of Faith, God has moved in this ministry touching hearts and lives. The Lord has led and provided; He has spoken and directed. He told me that the impact of the Holy Spirit upon our rallies would be ever greater and that thousands of Baptists, Methodists, Catholics, Presbyterians, and other faiths would hunger for the Holy Spirit in our meetings.

Just as the Bible promised, God was pouring out His Spirit in the latter days. Multitudes would be saved. Literally hundreds of thousands would be baptized with the Holy Spirit. The Spirit of God was gloriously at work in an outreach that was to expand beyond my wildest imagination. And all, I believe, due to the operation of the Gift of Faith.

One of the most precious things happening is that thousands are receiving the baptism with the Holy Spirit. This has been going on the past several years in a mighty way. I remember quite some time ago meeting in a large city in Texas where several hundred received the Gift of the Holy Spirit. There wasn't any special tarrying. There were no loud noises or running up and down the aisles. There was no one beating on another's back or screaming in their ears trying to elicit a response. Instead, it was just a beautiful time. People just stood quietly, waiting and listening for instructions. And when I prayed for them, scores were instantly baptized with the Holy Spirit — speaking in other tongues as the Spirit gave the utterance.

SELF-HELP STUDY NOTES

SELF-HELP STUDY NOTES

It was not a wild, boisterous display of unbridled emotion. After they were filled with the Spirit, many did exhibit joy and happiness. But they were, in general, just raising their hands, praising the Lord, or weeping quietly for joy. This is one of the beautiful results of the Gift of Faith in operation. It functions in *many* areas and situations, and great things are accomplished for God's Glory.

THE GIFTS OF HEALINGS — There are a multitude of questions concerning the matter of divine healing. Why does God heal some while others fail to be healed? Why is it good that Christians sometimes fail to receive their healings, while those who may not even *profess* to be Christians are healed? It seems on the surface to be totally illogical and even unfair.

The word for *"healing"* in some of our texts is singular, but in the original Greek it reads *"Gifts of Healings."* There are certainly great needs in the area of healing. When the Gifts of Healings are operating, many wonderful miracles take place.

There are individuals who have had ministries where *many* healings have been experienced. While physical healing is not as important as Salvation or the healing of a person's *spirit*, there is still a great need for the healing of physical infirmities. And where there have been many physical healings, great numbers have had their Faith increased. Because they were exposed to the miracles of healing, many have reacted by accepting Jesus Christ into their hearts and lives.

Healing comes by Faith. We can't merit or buy healing. We can, of course, lay hands on the sick and pray for them to recover. Reference is made to anointing for healing in James 5:14.

Where the specific Gifts of Healings are in operation, great and dramatic healings do take place. There are, however, cases of individuals needing healing and failing to receive it. I know a very fine man of God who died of cancer at the age of forty, leaving behind five children. As far as I know, he did everything he could, asking the Lord a number of times for healing.

This was a tremendous preacher of the Gospel, and I have no idea *why* he didn't receive his healing. It certainly wasn't because of sin in his life, because he was clean and pure and sought God earnestly. There are no simple answers to these cases where healing is withheld.

There are any number of cases where healing comes instantly, dramatically, and miraculously. I thank God for the people healed in our meetings, but not all are healed. I wish they would be. I continue praying to God to use me more in this area, and I thank God there are people alive today who wouldn't be if we hadn't prayed for them with resultant healing. They are now serving God and giving a beautiful testimony.

Any time anyone receives healing in his body, that healing comes about through Faith in God's Word. John 15:7 says, *"If you abide in Me, and*

My Words abide in you, you shall ask what you will, and it shall be done unto you."

In James 5:14-15 we read, *"Is any sick among you? Let him call for the Elders of the Church; and let them pray over him, anointing him with oil in the Name of the Lord: And the prayer of Faith shall save the sick, and the Lord shall raise him up."*

A lady came forward in one of our crusades whose complexion was strikingly pale. Her body was emaciated, and it was obvious that she was a very sick woman. Her husband told me, *"My wife has leukemia."* I prayed for her — and for others, actually for scores of people that night. This woman instantly received her healing.

I received a letter from her husband following this incident. He was overjoyed as he wrote, *"Her doctors have taken all kinds of tests and they're just shaking their heads in amazement. They said they can't find any trace of leukemia."* He said they were thanking God for this miracle.

Obviously, at the moment she was healed, the Gift of Healing was in operation. Usually when the Gifts of Healings operate through a preacher (or anyone), that individual may not *will* it to operate, it just happens. God has been dealing with me concerning this matter. This gift has operated though me at times, but at other times those present and in need of healing have not been healed.

I have discussed this with others God has used a great deal in this area, and it does not work automatically for them either. Obviously, it is as the Spirit wills. It is not a gift that any man or woman of God — regardless of how close they may be to God or how much the Lord has used them in the past — can turn on or off at will. When the Spirit chooses to deliver the Gift of Healing, people are healed. Saint or sinner — it doesn't seem to matter.

Many unsaved people are healed, while often times believing people are not. Some love God and serve Him with all their hearts but fail to receive healing. Why does it operate in this way? I don't know. But when the Gift of Healing is in operation, people are instantly healed.

The gifts within the area of demonstration of God's *Power* are Healings, Miracles, and Faith. Jesus performed many miracles during His earthly Ministry, and there is a continuation of this compassionate ministry to those in need today. Multitudes are interested in the Gifts of Healings — just because there is such great need for healing today. It is a gift of great benefit to man, and is greatly sought by those who are ill.

A great part of Jesus' Ministry dealt with healing the sick. When Jesus instructed His Disciples, one of His first commands was to *"heal the sick"* (Mat. 10:8). Later He told His Disciples, *"He that believes on Me, the Works that I do shall he do also; and greater Works than these shall he do; because I go unto My Father"* (Jn.14:12).

SELF-HELP STUDY NOTES

SELF-HELP STUDY NOTES

The Gifts of Healings are for *supernatural cures*. Untold numbers have been healed of injuries and cured of diseases in supernatural ways. The Holy Spirit works through compassionate human channels to minister to those in need.

There are numerous accounts of healings performed by Jesus in the Gospels, and by the Early Church in the Book of Acts. There are unusual cases of healings where the ailing simply had the shadow of a Spirit-filled person (like Peter) pass over them (Acts 5:15). In other cases, items of clothing (or cloths) from anointed individuals were brought to the sick for healing (Acts 19:11-12). Needless to say, some of these situations have been misused and even abused, but real and valid healings have taken place upon such unusual demonstrations of Faith.

God moves marvelously in meeting man's needs today, just as He did in the First Century. Great numbers of people have been healed in recent decades as the Gifts of Healings have been demonstrated in the lives of individuals. Not everyone who is prayed for is healed, however. There are many unanswered questions; but, nonetheless, all kinds of disease and conditions have been healed supernaturally by the Power of God through the Gifts of the Holy Spirit in this day and age.

THE WORKING OF MIRACLES — This is the third and the last of the Gifts of the Spirit which are termed the *"Power Gifts."* The word *"miracles"* should be understood by almost everyone, but there are times when incidents are described as miracles when they actually aren't. The miracle of conversion is perhaps the greatest miracle in the world today, but when the Gift of the Working of Miracles is discussed, this is *not* the type of *"miracle"* that is meant.

Properly, miracles are incidents or events that seem to defy what we generally refer to as *"the natural laws."* In nature, events generally operate in a predictable pattern. Unique events and miraculous happenings have taken place, however, in both the Old and New Testaments. They are happening in our present-day society as well.

There are many miracles in the Old Testament including the following:
- The dividing of the Red Sea for the Children of Israel to pass through (Ex. 14:21-31).
- The sun standing still for Joshua (Josh. 10:12-14).
- The widow's barrel of meal and cruse of oil that did not diminish during the famine (I Ki. 17:8-16).
- The sun going backward ten degrees on Hezekiah's sundial (II Ki. 20:8-11).
- The great number of miracles recorded in the Old Testament in the lives of Moses, Elijah, and Elisha.

Jesus performed many miracles in the New Testament. These include:

- Turning the water into wine (Jn. 2:1-11).
- Walking on water (Mat. 14:25-33).
- Miraculous feeding of the multitudes (Mk. 6:38-44).
- Causing the storm to cease (Mk. 4:39-40.
- Such other incidents as miraculous catches of fish and finding money in the mouth of the fish (Jn. 21:5-12 and Mat. 17:27).

Jesus performed more miracles than anyone else in the Bible. But then He said, *"Greater Works than these shall he do; because I go unto My Father"* (Jn. 14:12).

The Gift of Miracles is a gift which brings much glory to God. God delights in performing miracles and using His Children to deliver this gift. When Jesus told His Followers they would do greater works than these, this was made possible by His Ascension into Heaven. He subsequently provided the full Power of the Holy Spirit at Pentecost for all Christians.

Jesus further declared that signs would follow the Believers (Mk. 16:17), and many miracles occurred in the Early Church following His Ascension. Philip, the Evangelist, was transported bodily from Gaza to Azotus by the Power of the Holy Spirit (Acts 8:39-40). Elymas, the sorcerer, was miraculously struck blind to prevent his opposing Paul's ministry (Acts 13:8-12). Paul was bitten by a deadly snake but was unharmed (Acts 28:3-11). Many miracles took place in the lives and actions of Peter and Paul and the other Apostles. Deacons also, like Stephen and Philip, performed a number of miracles.

In I Corinthians 12, the Gift of Miracles is spoken as one of the nine gifts — and is to be regularly manifested by Believers. When Jesus said that those who believed would do *greater* things, He indicated that wondrous events were forthcoming. Some prefer to believe this to mean greater *numbers* of things would be done because of the greater numbers of people, while others feel it means unique and unusual things.

There is a definite need for caution in this area of miracles as more and more people experiment with occult and psychic powers. These are, of course, from Satan. Christians are not to be involved or deceived by these. One is always to follow the Scriptural Patterns and do only what Jesus did. Miracles *are* occurring today according to Scriptural Patterns. With so many more Believers becoming Spirit-filled every day, even more can be accomplished as time goes by, just as Jesus promised.

Believers have reported seeing weather altered and other supernatural events taking pace — all due to the Gift of Miracles. Sometimes miraculous events are *"supernaturally natural"* and a person must be alert with anticipation, allowing God to manifest His Power.

Miracles are interesting, exciting, and are a Gift of the Holy Spirit — but they are never to be the main focus of attention. A person must always

SELF-HELP STUDY NOTES

SELF-HELP STUDY NOTES

keep their eyes on Jesus. There is always a subtle temptation for people to flock to supernatural events and to follow miracles rather than following Jesus. Those who follow Jesus *first* find miracles following *them*.

THE VOCAL GIFTS

There are three Gifts of the Spirit which are called the *"Inspiration"* Gifts or the *"Vocal"* Gifts. These are Prophecy, Divers Kinds of Tongues, and Interpretation of Tongues.

THE GIFT OF PROPHECY — Prophecy is supernatural speech in a known language. It is not basically a *"private"* gift but is generally brought to a group of Believers — although it may be for one or more of the individuals present.

Significant emphasis is given to Prophecy. Paul said, *"Follow after charity, and desire Spiritual Gifts, but rather that you may prophesy . . . he who prophesies edifies the Church"* (I Cor. 14:1-4). Later in this Chapter he says, *"Covet to prophesy"* (I Cor. 14:39).

Prophecy is primarily for Believers but is also, to a lesser degree, for unbelievers (I Cor. 14:22). It can be of considerable significance for unbelievers in certain cases. We are told in I Corinthians 14:3 that Prophecy ministers to Believers in edification (building up), exhortation (urging on), and comfort (consolation).

Prophecy has by no means passed away, and it may be demonstrated under various circumstances. Fairly often, when men of God are preaching, the Gift of Prophecy will be interjected suddenly and unexpectedly into the middle of a sermon. Thus the preacher suddenly finds himself delivering a prophetic message from God. This is not at all uncommon for Spirit-filled preachers.

A prophetic utterance may last for ten or twenty seconds or for a minute or more. There is no *"standard"* time limit, and the minister of the Gospel is actually the vessel through which God's Message flows as the Gift of Prophecy appears. The preacher himself has no idea of the length of the utterance until he actually delivers it.

Many times while preaching, I have felt a special anointing as a message *"comes through"* from the Lord. I recall one time in particular as I was ministering, when in the middle of the message the Spirit of God fell on the congregation. I realized that what I was saying was heavily inspired, and the congregation sensed it too. I made the statement at the time that the Spirit of God would be poured out on the world in a measure never experienced before.

This, of course, pertained to the outpouring of God's Holy Spirit which we have since experienced. The Gift of Prophecy operated here for several minutes in the middle of my planned message. This happens time and time again when some special word from the Lord arrives suddenly in the midst of our more usual service. It is a *special* word, and the Gift of Prophecy is definitely in operation.

Don't misunderstand, however. All preaching is by no means prophecy. In truth, very little preaching is prophecy. Some speak of ministers as having a prophetic message when they mean they are delivering the Word of God in a dynamic fashion. This is not what we are discussing. Prophecy is not just inspired preaching. The Gift of Prophecy operates only when there is a special *unction* placed upon an individual by the Holy Spirit to deliver a specific message of divine inspiration.

Prophecy isn't just a matter of foretelling the future, nor is it a matter of routine preaching. The operation of the Gift of Prophecy is the bringing forth of a specific message from God.

We should devote special attention to certain aspects of this matter of prophecy. It is not primarily for giving predictions. As stated in I Corinthians 14:3, it is for edification, exhortation, and comfort. Some people have mistakenly assumed that their gift can be *"used"* as a personal bludgeon. They feel they can stand and prophesy doom, damnation, and judgment on individuals and groups. This is not what Scripture says.

Much of the personal emphasis and misuse of this gift is either of Satan or a reflection of the speaker's opinions or desires in the flesh. Scripture plainly declares that Prophecy is for *edification*. It is rarely harsh denunciation. Some individuals seem to enjoy delivering *"doom and gloom,"* warning *"unfortunates"* that they are about to suffer personal disasters. Just such an incident involved my sister. It was *"prophesied"* that she and her entire family would experience a calamity that (naturally) never happened.

God speaks to individuals to prepare them for good fortune or to inform them of how they will be used. Paul wrote in his first letter to the Thessalonians *"Despise not prophesyings. Prove all things; hold fast that which is good"* (I Thess. 5:20-21).

Sometimes the Gifts of God are misused. Without question the enemy has counterfeits, but misuse or counterfeit should not deter our Faith in the *True* Manifestations of God. There *has* been misuse of the Gift of Prophecy. Individuals have been directed to sell their homes and businesses and move to foreign lands. More often than not, this has not been of God, and it has been devastating to the individuals involved. Great tragedies can result from such situations.

A number of people have gone about prophesying to others, telling them that God has called them to preach, to be missionaries, or to do any number of things. Of course, God *does* use individuals to lay hands on and prophesy over other persons. But Prophecy should be judged. Directive

SELF-HELP STUDY NOTES

SELF-HELP STUDY NOTES

Prophecy should *always* be confirmation of what the person has already felt in his heart — or else confirmed in at least one other clear and definite way. Scripture states in Deuteronomy 19:15, *"At the mouth of two witnesses, or at the mouth of three witnesses, shall the matter be established."* We are therefore always within the Will of God and in conformance to His Word when we remain patient until anything of importance is established by at *least* two, and preferably *three*, witnesses. One of these may, of course, be our own spirit witnessing to the legitimacy of the other two. A person should *never* alter the course of his life based on the word of one individual professing to prophesy.

Prophecy is to be judged by the Church, as it is given within the Body. This doesn't mean that a person is necessarily being judgmental of the prophecy or of the one giving it, but the prophecy itself *is* to be *"judged."* This ensures that it is in accord with the Word of God and the moving of God's Spirit. We are told in I Corinthians 14 that we are to judge prophecy because some prophecies are not of God.

You may personally believe that the prophet is a fine person and a good Christian who loves the Lord with all his heart. And he may well be. By extension, you might, therefore, assume that what he is saying is of God. But a person can easily wander off on a side road in the flesh. Prophecy therefore must be judged. Tongues and interpretations are also to be judged when they intrude into this area, because tongues and interpretations are equal to prophecy.

The question should be raised as to when the Gift of Prophecy may be used. And, yes, it *can* be used in one's personal devotion, during one's daily prayer time. This doesn't mean, however, that every time you pray you ought to prophesy. In fact, there is no *infallible* way to say just how or when you should prophesy.

There are Christians of many years standing who have only uttered one or two brief words of prophecy in their whole lives. On the other hand, there are those who are frequently used of the Holy Spirit to deliver prophetic words to the faithful. What it all amounts to is this: If you feel a strong compulsion to deliver a word you feel is true — deliver it. It may well be that the Lord has chosen you, in this case, to serve as His instrument in the operation of the Gift of Prophecy.

The second use of prophecy is in the public assembly; that is, when people gather for worship. Many times the Spirit of God will fall, and it will be an appropriate time for a message to come forth in the form of prophecy. This might be given by an individual directly, or it may come as tongues and an interpretation, either by one or two persons. Many times during the song service or in the worship segment before the sermon, the Spirit of God falls. Then while the people are worshipping the Lord, there might be an utterance and a prophecy.

Sometimes this occurs when people are praying before an altar at the conclusion of the service, or in a prayer meeting. At times this will be during a special type of service and there will be a *direct* prophecy, or by means of an utterance in tongues with interpretation. Remember, though, all things are to be done in an orderly manner. We must be led by the Spirit in this matter, and one must take particular care not to wander off into the world and do something that might hinder others present. Above all, we should be ever conscious of our guiding principles: the Word of God and the *Work* of God.

The Gifts of the Spirit are only manifest through God's desires and motives — and never through our own. We are exhorted to desire prophecy, not despise it. We should nurture and promote it. We should encourage the manifestation of this Gift of the Spirit, and while misuse of the Vocal Gifts is not unknown, they are of great importance and can provide a special blessing for the listeners.

TONGUES AND INTERPRETATION — The Vocal Gifts, or Gifts of Utterance, include, *"Divers Kinds of Tongues," "Interpretation of Tongues,"* and *"Prophecy."* These help to turn us Godward and create a greater reverence for the Lord and the things of the Lord. They are primarily designed to guide and direct our lives, but they do help to reveal God to us and enhance our responses to Him.

The Gifts of Tongues and Interpretation are presented together and are referred to in I Corinthians 12:7-11. When the Gift of the Spirit operates and a message is delivered in an unknown tongue, the utterance *is* to be interpreted.

Speaking in tongues is basically manifested in one of two ways. The most common is the *devotional* language an individual is given, in which he speaks in tongues for private edification. This does *not* require an interpretation (I Cor. 14:2). This *"devotional tongue"* is referred to as the initial *evidence* of the baptism with the Holy Spirit.

This is completely different from speaking in tongues within the context of delivering a *public* utterance in an unknown tongue. To be sure, we may properly use our devotional tongue publicly in a worship service, aloud, but it would still be within the *"private"* context — that of direct communication with God.

On the other hand, a public utterance *"in tongues"* is completely different. Here, when the Spirit leads, the subject speaks out boldly, and the gathering almost always falls immediately silent as an air of expectancy comes over the service.

What we here are referring to is the Gift of Tongues as demonstrated by a Spirit-filled Christian who feels inspired to speak in tongues in the

SELF-HELP STUDY NOTES

SELF-HELP STUDY NOTES

presence of others — with the Interpretation of that utterance following it (I Cor. 14:27-28 and 12:10).

As this Gift of Tongues is received by the listeners, they are edified both by the initial message *and* by the interpretation which follows. There are also times, however, when this tongue is a sign to an unbeliever — spoken in a language understood by that unbeliever — with God speaking directly to him in this language.

In one memorable case of this type, a young oriental lady married an American serviceman and, living in this country, went to the altar to pray. She was not, however, praying to Jesus; she was praying to her oriental God. Near her a woman was speaking in tongues whom God used to address the young oriental woman in her own language. The young lady's specific religious temple name was used, and she was encouraged to accept Jesus. Needless to say, she responded immediately and accepted Jesus as her Saviour.

There are other cases where the message is not understood in the natural, but where an interpretation is given. These tongues are a message from God as well as a sign to the unbeliever that God is real and concerned about the individual. Most often the Gift of Tongues and Interpretations is a message from God to bless and exhort Christians.

Sometime ago, I was talking to a preacher I consider to be a great man of God. I asked him what he thought about Full-Gospel people and speaking in tongues. He started out by saying that since he had been baptized with the Holy Spirit he had learned many things. At the time we spoke, he had built a tremendous church where hundreds had been saved and filled with the Spirit. But we were discussing the period *before* he had become Spirit-filled.

"Before God baptized me with the Holy Spirit," he said, *"I didn't think Spirit-filled people believed in getting saved—or even believed in the Blood of Jesus. I thought that all you lived and breathed and talked about was speaking in tongues. Of course, I found out later that you concentrate on Salvation and only then on being filled with the Holy Spirit."*

People who are not of the Pentecostal, Full-Gospel, or Charismatic faith spend so much time discussing tongues that they become convinced that it is our primary emphasis. Of course, winning souls to Christ and being saved is first and foremost. We can certainly agree with those who emphasize being saved, accepting Jesus as Lord and Saviour, and being cleansed by the Blood of Christ. But we do consider the baptism with the Holy Spirit of vital importance, and we are convinced that speaking in tongues is a *part* of that experience.

There are many who ask the question: what is meant by the term *"unknown"* tongues? The word *unknown* was not in the original Greek text. It was later added by the King James translators for a specific reason. It is to help explain and clarify the text and meaning. This is done any number of times in the Bible translations we use.

The reason for using the term *"unknown"* is because the individual speaking in another tongue does not know or understand the language in which he is speaking. Most of the time, it is unknown to the listeners too, but it is a definite language. The majority of the time, when an individual is speaking in tongues, he is speaking in a language that is understood in some part of the world.

A close friend, who is a tremendous minister of the Gospel, was in Texas preaching a meeting. He holds great revivals all over the country. At this particular service the Lord gave him a message in tongues. It came at the latter part of the service after the preaching was over and the people were worshipping around the altar.

He gave the message, and the interpretation afterward. After the service a Jew came forward and told him he had spoken in a perfect Hebrew dialect. This preacher had no knowledge of Hebrew. *"Do you mean I spoke in Hebrew?"* he asked.

The Jew nodded. *"Yes, you spoke in perfect Hebrew."*

The pastor then asked, *"And what about the interpretation? Was it as it should be?"*

Again the Jewish gentlemen nodded. *"Yes,"* he said, *"the interpretation was exactly as it should have been."*

At another time this same man was praying, with several other ministers of the Gospel present. He spoke in tongues during the devotional and worship segment of the meeting. He spoke softly, more or less to himself, and did not give an interpretation since this was his own private devotion.

There was a missionary there who had spent many years in China and after it was over he said to the preacher, *"Do you know what language you used when you were speaking in other tongues?"* The preacher said he had no idea.

"Well," the missionary said, *"You spoke in Chinese. I am very familiar with the Chinese language, especially one dialect in which I have preached many times. And that was the dialect you just prayed in."*

There are many such cases. People pray and worship God in the Spirit and speak in tongues, and someone happens to be present who understands the language they are using. Many times there are unusual languages or rare dialects. By and large, though, the tongue is unfamiliar to the speakers as well as the listeners. It is, however, a language that is known somewhere in the world, in *most* cases.

There may also be another kind of language. Paul suggests this in I Corinthians 13:1. Here he says that an individual may speak in *"a Heavenly*

SELF-HELP STUDY NOTES

SELF-HELP STUDY NOTES

language." He states, *"Though I speak with the tongues of men and of Angels"* (I Cor. 13:1).

Notice that he uses the plural for tongues of men and of angels. While we prefer not to make a major issue of this, it does appear that there are times when an individual may speak in *angelic* tongues if this is what the Holy Spirit chooses to give as the utterance. Whatever the Holy Spirit may do in this regard — whether it be the tongues of men or Angels — it is a miracle, and we thank God for it.

Sometimes tongues have been employed in public gatherings involving praise and prayer directed toward God. There are also times when Spirit-filled Believers *"sing in the Spirit."* This is also a form of speaking in tongues. Sometimes an entire group may blend together as the Holy Spirit moves through the assembly, and there are occasions where it sounds like an angelic choir. Many unbelievers have been touched by God at such moments.

All Gifts of the Spirit are precious, and this is no less true of the Vocal Gifts. Due to the problems and difficulties regarding *"tongues,"* we will add some additional thoughts.

DEVOTIONAL TONGUES AND THE GIFT OF TONGUES

It needs to be clearly understood that there is a difference between private *devotional* tongues and the *"Gift of Tongues."* We have been dealing primarily with the Gift of Tongues as mentioned in the Twelfth Chapter of I Corinthians. This says, *"To another the working of Miracles: to another Prophecy: to another Discerning of spirits: to another Divers Kinds of Tongues: to another the Interpretation of Tongues."*

Obviously, this has to do with *different languages.* But this does not refer to something like preaching to a heathen people in their own language; nor should it suggest that one can suddenly receive a special gift without language study. It would be so much simpler if we could prepare ourselves to minister in heathen countries in this fashion, but unfortunately it just isn't so. These are gifts, given by Almighty God — the Gift of Tongues and the Gift of Interpretation. Private devotional tongues, however, are for prayer and worship and communication with God. These do not require interpretation.

Paul exhorted the Corinthians concerning the usage of tongues and interpretation in I Corinthians 14:13. *"Wherefore let him who speaks in an unknown tongue pray that he may interpret."*

This refers to the *Gift* of Tongues, or speaking in unknown tongues in situations where interpretation is called for. There are a number of conditions where this is applicable. By and large, Tongues and Interpretation are used in almost the same circumstances as the Gift of Prophecy.

There are times in my own private devotional life when I worship in tongues — praying in the Spirit. This is *not* the Gift of Tongues. At other times, however, in my private devotions, I will speak in tongues and then the *Gift* of Tongues comes into operation. In these cases, the Lord always gives the interpretation of the utterance. These are, more often than not, situations of some importance. Certainly, these incidents cannot be described as insignificant or unimportant.

Some people like to stress the thought that the Gift of Tongues or the Gift of Interpretation are the lesser gifts. This isn't really true. *Any* gift that is needed at a particular time is the most *important* gift at that moment. I've seen many situations where an utterance in tongues, either public or private, would edify and encourage in a marvelous way. These are like the Breath of God moving upon an individual or congregation as a special blessing.

If a person is just speaking in his own devotional language, worshipping the Lord, there is seldom an interpretation. The *Gift* of Tongues is not present here. Sometimes in worship situations people hear an individual near them praying in tongues and wonder what is called for. This is simply use of the devotional tongue in a public situation, however, and is not an expression which demands an interpretation.

Many times as I preach, the Spirit of God flows over the congregation in the midst of the message, and for a moment or two the people begin to worship the Lord. This will not prove loud or boisterous, but hands will be raised in praise. During such worship incidents lives are touched.

I, like many others, have spoken in tongues during such times of worship. Some have become critical because there is no interpretation in these situations. But this is not what Paul referred to in regard to the Gift of Interpretation. This is not an utterance in tongues with the Gift of the Spirit in operation, so an interpretation is not called for. It is simply a matter of *worship* in tongues which happened to be public rather than private. This was what Paul was referring to when he said, *"I thank my God, I speak with tongues more than you all"* (I Cor. 14:18). He obviously prayed and worshiped a great deal, privately, in tongues.

There is one Scripture that has caused considerable confusion. This is, *"Have all the Gifts of Healing? Do all speak with Tongues? Do all Interpret?"* (I Cor. 12:30). This question, *"Do all speak with tongues?"* is often referred to by critics of speaking in tongues. The context of the question suggests that Paul's answer to it is *"No!"* This does not refer, however, to speaking in tongues as *evidence of the baptism with the Holy Spirit. All* who are baptized in the Holy Spirit demonstrate this type of utterance. It comes from within and is an expression in other tongues in the *devotional* language or praise and worship. It is not the *Gift* of Tongues, which is for public (or even personal) use, and

SELF-HELP STUDY NOTES

SELF-HELP STUDY NOTES

requires the Gift of Interpretation. Of course, as noted, those speaking devotionally in tongues *can* suddenly find the Gift of Tongues in operation, and an interpretation will then follow.

This question, concerning *all* having the Gifts of Healings, Interpretation, or speaking in Tongues, has to do with the *Gifts* of the Spirit where individuals are chosen to demonstrate specific gifts. Again, is must be noted that this is different from *the initial expression of the baptism with the Holy Spirit*. Here speaking in tongues is the initial evidence, as indicated in Acts 2, 8, 9, 19, and 20. (This was also discussed more fully in the previous section.)

In each of these references, individuals baptized with the Holy Spirit spoke in tongues. In two of the references this is implied rather than explicitly stated. But in the other cases, tongues are specifically mentioned. This is, therefore, the *evidence* of their baptism with the Holy Spirit. It must be strongly emphasized that there is a difference between a *devotional* expression in tongues and the *Gift* of Tongues — which should always be accompanied by the Gift of Interpretation.

Many who argue against speaking in tongues use this Scripture (I Corinthians 12:30) as a proof text for contending that speaking in tongues is not for all. The people who introduce this question, saying that not *all* speak in tongues, tend to bitterly oppose *all* speaking in tongues, therefore destroying their own argument against *all* tongues — because Paul's statement definitely states that *some* speak in tongues. Unfortunately, there is much misunderstanding in regard to tongues, and with misunderstanding often comes outright rejection of the whole concept. This results in forfeiting one of the most precious gifts that God has for us.

It is a serious matter to deny anything Scriptural, or to try to explain it away. And for some it doesn't stop with just explaining away related phenomenon. They go to the point of rejecting the very fundamentals of God's Word. Not only do they deny tongues and the baptism with the Holy Spirit, but many deny even the basic fundamentals of the Faith — the inspired Word of God, Salvation through the Redemptive Work of Jesus, and forgiveness of sin through His shed Blood.

We do sometimes see gifts improperly used, and this can cause some to reject the total picture. Doctrines must be based on the Word of God, and one should not allow his view of God to be distorted by individuals. For example, someone rises and blurts out something in tongues, interrupting the service and disturbing everyone present. This person is in the flesh and certainly out of order. Such action discredits one of God's great Gifts.

We should not, however, allow one misguided soul to intrude into our relationship with God. As we have established, the Gifts of the Spirit can be misused and even counterfeited. Such incidents in no way negate the legitimacy of the authentic and true. But occasional misuse of the gifts can cause great problems and disturb the weak in faith. Those who are seeking and searching, however, will see and appreciate the value of the gifts when they are used in a proper manner.

Because so many problems have centered around tongues — and because such great misunderstanding exists — we have repeated certain points for example.

As has been explained, speaking in tongues is the initial evidence of the baptism with the Holy Spirit. As an individual prays in tongues, this is devotional tongues as used for private prayer and communication with God. It is *not* the Gift of Tongues and does not require interpretation.

- A Spirit-filled person should speak in tongues every day of his life, and he may well do so and still not have the *Gift* of Tongues. The *Gift* of Tongues comes into evidence when the Holy Spirit delivers a message to an individual group. Here, interpretation *is* required.
- Personal worship of the Lord in tongues is *generally* done in private. Sometimes, however, devotional tongues *will* be used in a *public* environment, such as a prayer meeting or worship service, and here no interpretation is necessary.
- It should be understood that these are the two *basic types* of tongues. Not everyone has the *Gift* of Tongues any more than everyone has the Gift of Prophecy, the Gift of Miracles, or any of the other gifts. One should, however, desire these gifts.
- It might also be noted that, just because the person does not possess the Gift of Tongues (or *any* of the nine gifts), this *doesn't* mean this person isn't Spirit-filled or close to God.
- All Spirit-filled Believers should use tongues daily in their prayer life, but not all will minister to the Brethren through the Gift of Tongues (I Cor. 12:30). In the public situation, there are those quickened by the Spirit and operating within the Gift of Tongues to deliver a message to the gathering. Here the Interpretation of Tongues must follow to explain the content of the message.
- God moves in marvelous ways through the Gifts of the Spirit operating in public meetings. Of course, this must be done decently and in order — as Paul exhorted the Corinthians. Just because Paul gave correction to the Corinthians in the *employment* of their gifts, some have concluded that it was the gifts themselves that were out of order. This isn't so. It was, rather, the Corinthian practice of allowing confusion to intrude. There is never to be confusion. Things are always to be done decently and in order. Paul never suggested that the gifts themselves were to be suppressed, but rather that improper practices be corrected.

SELF-HELP STUDY NOTES

SELF-HELP STUDY NOTES

All the Gifts of the Spirit are precious, including the Vocal or Inspirational Gifts: Prophecy, Divers Kinds of Tongues, and the Interpretation of Tongues.

SIX TIMES IT IS NOT PROPER TO SPEAK IN OTHER TONGUES

It is never proper to speak in tongues without being motivated by love, according to Paul in I Corinthians 13:1 *"Though I speak with the tongues of men and of Angels, and have not charity, I am become as sounding brass, or a tinkling cymbal."* Paul declares that, even when speaking in other tongues, if we aren't motivated by love (or extended in a spirit of love) we are like a sounding brass or tinkling cymbal. Anything done without love is unprofitable, sometimes even harmful. There are individuals who have received the Holy Spirit baptism and have spoken in tongues, but have allowed bitterness or even hatred to creep into their lives. This is a tremendous hindrance to their Christian walk.

God is love, and walking in Him means that a Christian must walk in love. A saved person is the Temple of the Holy Spirit. Love is to motivate the Gifts of the Spirit. Unless a person is motivated and immersed in love, he should not seek to exercise the Gifts of the Spirit. If he does, it will be as a sounding brass or a tinkling cymbal — in other words, empty noise.

Sometimes a person starts off on the wrong track and becomes motivated by *self-interest*. It is possible for the Christian walk to become an ego trip — a compulsion to be *heard and seen* when functioning in the Gifts of the Spirit. In this case, love is not present as it should be, and these people can sometimes even speak harshly of others. When such a situation exists, the person should cease speaking in tongues, go to the altar, get down before God, and pray the problem through. A Child of God should never speak in tongues when he is not motivated by love with a heart filled with love for *everyone*.

The *second* situation where it is not proper to speak in tongues is in a regular church service when no interpreter is present. If an utterance in tongues is given before those assembled in a service, and interpretation must be given. In I Corinthians 14, Paul made it clear that individuals *could* speak in an unknown tongue, but it must be done in order and there should be an interpretation. And if there is no interpreter present? *"Let him keep silence"* (I Cor. 14:28).

This does not mean, however, that the young Christian who has just received the baptism with the Holy Spirit is obliged to wander up and down church aisles asking whether an interpreter is present. Scripture makes it clear that the *Elders* in the Church should set the example. Once the newer Christian has participated in few services, it will become apparent just which members possess the Gift of Interpretation of Tongues. When these are present, the new member may deliver the utterance with confidence that it will be interpreted.

It is important that everything be done in order. Confusion is of the Devil, and basically he is the author of all confusion. But if a message is delivered in tongues with no ensuing interpretation, there is no need for embarrassment. Sometimes when no interpretation is given, the person delivering the message may feel he has been out of order despite a strong leading to deliver the message. This doesn't mean, however, that it was not of God. It may have been perfectly proper and in order, with the interpreter resisting God's call to deliver the interpretation. This does happen on occasion. But as a general rule, Scripture does call for an interpretation of messages given to the Body.

The *third* case where tongues should not be used is when Truth is to be delivered. There are occasions when plain expressions of Truth and instruction are to be shared with the congregation. In I Corinthians 14, Paul speaks of coming to them to deliver Truth and to teach. He wanted to speak *directly* to them, so this had nothing to do with speaking in foreign languages or praying in tongues. He said that if he *had* come speaking in tongues, it would have been of no profit to them without some special revelation or understanding.

If he had just spoken in tongues, with no understanding or interpretation, they would have gained nothing. He further said he would rather speak five words with his understanding than ten *thousand* words in an unknown tongue. Now, he wasn't telling them *not* to speak in tongues, but was referring them instead to the proper method for giving truth in a public assembly.

Some of these expressions and teachings by Paul have been twisted to suggest that tongues are of no value or nothing more than gibberish. But this isn't what Paul said. Everyone at the church in Corinth spoke in tongues — but not at the proper times! So Paul was giving explicit instructions for correction. He clearly stated that they were not to *forbid* speaking in tongues. He was not criticizing them *for* speaking in tongues, but rather was exhorting them to do so in the right manner, place, and time.

He said next that if the whole Church came together in one place speaking in tongues and there were unbelievers present, they would consider the Church *mad* (I Cor. 14:23-25).

The Gifts of the Spirit do not follow the same pattern as speaking in the personal, private devotional situation. Here a person can (and should) speak in tongues at any time. We can even carry on prayer time in tongues in the presence of others by doing it silently.

There are times when the Spirit of God is moving in a service and someone interjects something that completely interrupts the preacher and

SELF-HELP STUDY NOTES

SELF-HELP STUDY NOTES

the flow of the service. This has happened to me. It can be necessary in such cases to admonish the party causing the interruption. Much as we might dislike doing this, it can be necessary because such actions interrupt the service and hinder the Work of God.

There are times, during teaching or preaching, when the message and the interpretation come at exactly the right moment and place in the service. This is done by the Holy Spirit, and it is always proper. This generally occurs in smaller gatherings where the number of people is limited and where there is a less formal atmosphere.

Unfortunately, when services are disrupted, people sometimes say they just couldn't restrain themselves. They state that they didn't want to *"quench the Spirit."* Generally, however, this is not a matter of *"quenching the Spirit,"* it is a matter of controlling the flesh. The Holy Spirit is *never* the author of confusion.

The phrase *"I couldn't help myself"* is self-deception. God doesn't compel anyone into bringing forth an utterance. There may be a strong anointing; there may be a feeling of definite *direction*; but there is never coercion.

The Spirit of God moves gently. The Lord will impress something on our hearts. He will move upon us and speak quietly to our spirits. He will touch and urge — but He will never drive or force us. So when a person claims that they can't help themselves, they are obviously in error somewhere.

Moving to the converse, Satan *does* coerce and compel. While the Word of God states that the spirit of the prophet is subject *to* the prophet, Satan does not abide by this restraint. He places irresistible desires in people who can overcome them only with great willpower. And please note that the *"spirit"* mentioned here is with a small "s." This refers to the prophet's own spirit, not the Holy Spirit (with a capital S).

If the Holy Spirit moves upon you, and the preacher is delivering a sermon, don't worry about *"quenching the Spirit"* — wait for the *suitable* moment. Once the sermon is finished, God will arrange the proper moment. He is never pressed for time. Just be patient and be prepared to share at the *appropriate* time, perhaps during prayer. If such a moment *doesn't* present itself, you can be assured that you weren't *meant* to participate in that particular service.

Also when delivering an utterance, there is no need to shout or to deliver the message in a special tone of voice to make it sound *"spiritual."* Many of these things are self-induced — of the flesh — and instead of helping the Holy Spirit may actually be a hindrance.

People instantly sense when something is not of God. When God is moving through the Gifts of the Spirit and speaking through an individual, it touches hearts. People instantly perceive that all is in the Spirit and is a wonderful blessing to those present. It is never necessary to scream, shout, or wave your arms. It is surprising, but no matter how softly and sweetly we might speak, God's Message always comes through.

The *fourth* time one should not speak in tongues is when he is invited to say grace at the table. Paul said, *"Else when thou shalt bless with the spirit, how shall he that occupies the room of the unlearned say Amen at the giving of thanks, seeing he understands not what you say? For thou verily give thanks well, but the other is not edified"* (I Cor. 14:16-17).

Following this, Paul says that he thanks God that he speaks in tongues *"more than you all."* Paul is pointing out here that there *are* occasions where we should *not* speak in tongues, and table grace is this type of occasion. Giving thanks is something that should be edifying to all present, and is *not* edifying to those who don't understand what is being said. One should simply give thanks clearly and directly so it will be understood by all present.

The *fifth* situation where it is not proper to speak in tongues is when the whole Church is present, and all (or most) would like to speak in tongues, but there are individuals present who might stumble over such actions. Paul states (I Cor. 14:23-24): *"If therefore the whole Church be come together into one place, and all speak with Tongues, and there come in those that are unlearned, or unbelievers, will they not say that you are mad? But if all prophesy, and there come in one who believes not, or one unlearned, he is convinced of all, he is judged of all."*

There are those who say they are going to do what the Lord directs no matter what *anyone* thinks. But we must remember, the Spirit of God does not cast His pearls before swine. He will not promote a situation that will lead to rejection or confusion. There may be incidents in a service involving Spirit-filled people, which the public would misunderstand. But this isn't what we're discussing here. We're talking about those matters that should be controlled by the Spirit of God, and not by individuals who brazenly insist on their way, thus placing themselves in the limelight.

As an example, I would not appear on the radio speaking in tongues. In this case, as in many others, some might misunderstand and might well conclude that I was trying to impress others with my spirituality or holiness. Rather than *impressing* some, it might rather *harm* many.

Speaking in tongues is wonderful and precious — but it should be done in the right place at the right time. Paul was reproving the Corinthian church because a number of them were speaking in tongues simultaneously. It is never correct for one to say, *"I am going to speak in tongues, and I don't care who likes it or who doesn't like it."* This lacks concern for the sensitivity of others and can cause a brother to stumble. It should never be done.

But this doesn't mean we are *never* to speak in tongues in public assembly, just because there *are* services where we *shouldn't* speak. As an

SELF-HELP STUDY NOTES

SELF-HELP STUDY NOTES

example, if I were invited to speak at a church that did not believe in speaking in tongues, it would be a gross discourtesy to force my actions and beliefs upon them.

Pentecostals should try the spirits, and always walk *in* the Spirit. Satan operates in the spirit realm and well-meaning Pentecostals have done things that result in Satan stealing the glory that belongs to God. This happens whenever things are done that hurt the Kingdom. There are any number of actions that can hinder the Work of God, so we should be vigilant, discern the spirits, and determine whether they are of the Lord.

In talking about the public assembly where a worship service is being held, Paul gave these instructions: *"If any man speak in an unknown Tongue, let it be by two, or at the most by three, and that by course; and let one interpret. But if there be no interpreter, let him keep silence in the Church; and let him speak to himself, and to God"* (I Cor. 14:27-28).

The *sixth* situation when it is not proper to speak in tongues is where two or three messages have already been given. Paul gave instructions concerning this under the Anointing of the Holy Spirit. Some boast that in *their* church ten, twelve, or even more messages are given in a service. This isn't proper.

Paul speaks here about the normal worship service where the Spirit of the Lord moves upon one who possesses the Gift of Divers Tongues, and that person delivers a message with someone interpreting afterward. This is only to be done *in order*.

There may be times when a small group comes together to praise the Lord and worship in a more informal manner. Here, there may be variation. But in a *public* worship service there are limitations, and order must be maintained.

Everything should be done properly, led by the Holy Spirit. Due to the potential (both positive and negative) in the matter of speaking in tongues, it is very important that all be done *"decently and in order."*

GIFTS WITHOUT THE BAPTISM

The question is sometimes asked, can an individual have the Gifts of the Spirit without being baptized with the Holy Spirit? Many assume that it is *not* possible to have these gifts without the baptism, but Old Testament Saints hadn't received the baptism with the Holy Spirit as we know it today, yet several of the gifts were operable in their lives. It is, in fact, possible to have seven of the nine Gifts of the Spirit *without* being baptized with the Holy Spirit with the evidence of speaking in other tongues; the two gifts unavailable in this instance being the Gift of Tongues and Interpretation of Tongues.

The other gifts have obviously been operable in the lives of individuals who had not experienced the baptism with the Holy Spirit — according to Acts 2:4. It should be noted, however, that even though it is *possible* to have the seven gifts without being baptized with the Holy Spirit, we seldom *see* them in operation among those who don't believe or practice the baptism with the Holy Spirit.

The Holy Spirit is the Power Giver, and the Giver of these gifts. The Apostle Paul said that there are many gifts, but they are by one Spirit. There are thousands of preachers of the Gospel who do not believe in the baptism with the Holy Spirit as experienced in Acts 2, 8, 9, 10, and 19. It is possible for these preachers to have some of the gifts operable in their lives but this rarely occurs.

OTHER GIFTS AND MANIFESTATIONS

In addition to the nine Gifts of the Holy Spirit listed in I Corinthians 12:14, there are several other gifts and manifestations of the Holy Spirit that work in and through Believers. Some of these are indicated in Romans 12:6-9: *"Having then gifts differing according to the grace that is given to us, whether Prophecy, let us Prophesy according to the proportion of Faith; Or Ministry, let us wait on our Ministering: or he that teaches, on teaching; Or he who exhorts, on exhortation: he who gives, let him do it with simplicity; he who rules, with diligence; he who shows mercy, with cheerfulness. Let love be without dissimulation. Abhor that which is evil; cleave to that which is good."*

Included in this Passage are Prophecy, Ministry, teaching, exhortation, giving, and ruling (or administration). Prophecy has been discussed previously. Ministry includes service by deacons. The word for deacon (Greek-*diakonos*) means *"serve"* (minister to needs), and this has to do with a wide spectrum of services. The Church is to have deacons, divinely chosen and led, Spirit-filled, and empowered for service.

There are, within the Body of Christ, those who are anointed for teaching. Some demonstrate a great gift for mercy, relieving misery and distress. Others give comfort (Greek-*paraklesis*, meaning one who is called to one's side to give encouragement and assistance). A special ministry of giving is the privilege of some. They have God-given resources to share with others and are used in this area in a special way. These are all Spirit-endowed and directed services.

Related to some of the above is *"helps."* Reference to this is made in I Corinthians 12:27-28: *"Now you are the Body of Christ, and members in particular. And God has set some in the Church, first Apostles, secondarily Prophets, thirdly Teachers, after that Miracles, then Gifts of Healings, Helps, Governments."*

SELF-HELP STUDY NOTES

SELF-HELP STUDY NOTES

The word *"Helps"* (Greek-*antilepsis*) concerns the rendering of assistance. These, together with other qualities and manifestations, are from the Holy Spirit. There is great variety within the Gifts and Manifestations of the Holy Spirit as found in the Body of Christ for the benefit and uplifting of the Church.

Spiritual Gifts are, essentially, unique attributes given by the Holy Spirit to members of the Body for use within the Body. These are given according to God's Grace and the Body's needs. Every member (Believer) can and should have one or more Spiritual Gifts and be a vital, contributing part of a local Body of Believers. Everyone should help to meet needs within that Body, as well as needs within the community where the Body ministers. Each Believer should strive to discover his (or her) particular Spiritual Gifts and develop and use them for the greater Glory of God.

The Church, both the local and the *"universal"* Body, is wonderfully provided with everything needed to be the glorious, victorious Church that God intended.

PURPOSE OF THE GIFTS

FOR THE CHURCH — God intended that the Gifts of the Holy Spirit should accomplish definite purposes. The Gifts of the Spirit are never toys, or playthings, but God's Lovegifts to the Church. This is of vital importance, and any attempt to use them for selfish or frivolous purposes is a tragic mistake. Unfortunately, they are used in this manner at times.

The use of the Spiritual Gifts is often misunderstood, and even their basic significance is confused by many. They are not to be exhibited out of character or out of place. Of course, the Devil is *delighted* to see them perverted. He wants people to (out of ignorance or for *any* reason) misuse the Gifts of the Spirit. When this is done, the Name of the Lord Jesus Christ is reproached, and the Work of God is hindered. But just because some people debase the gifts (for whatever motives), there is no logic in rejecting the whole matter of the Holy Spirit baptism and the Spiritual Gifts. Unfortunately, some do this.

I would reiterate at this point: there are counterfeits to anything — including the Gifts of the Holy Spirit. One should not deny or reject the entire move of God, however, because of some distortion. As a parallel, just because there are hypocrites within the Church and some abuses of Salvation, it would be ridiculous to reject Salvation and fellowship on this basis.

EDIFICATION — The question may be asked, *"What are the overall purposes of God, and what specific purposes did He have in mind when He ordained these Spiritual Gifts?"* In answer, the *paramount* reason for the Gifts of the Spirit is to edify and build up the Church. By doing so, it can better serve as the functioning Body of Christ on this Earth.

This reason is given in the Twelfth Chapter of I Corinthians: *"For as the Body is one, and has many members, and all the members of that one Body, being many, are one Body: so also is Christ. For by one Spirit are we all baptized into one Body, whether we be Jews or Gentiles, whether we be bond or free; and have been all made to drink into one Spirit. For the body is not one member, but many"* (I Cor. 12:12-14).

Provision is made for the Church to be a *functioning* Body. Some reach the erroneous conclusion that because God saves us, everything should be up to Him. For some, the only responsibility of the Child of God is to win souls. While we do not minimize the significance of soul winning, the responsibility of Christians goes far beyond this. The Church is to be built up, strengthened, edified; and it should function in wondrous and glorious ways.

There are millions in the world with needs. There are any number who need deliverance — and then the touch of God in their hearts and lives. There are many Christians who do not know how to apply the Word of God to their lives and their problems.

We, as mature Christians, ought to have the Gifts of the Spirit, or at least *some* of them, operating within our lives so we can help those in need. We have great responsibilities. *"Unto whomsoever much is given, of him shall be much required"* (Lk. 12:48).

Many things are available through the Lord Jesus Christ and the provisions He has made. However, where healing or deliverance is needed — in fact where *any* need exists — it is up to Christians to serve as *His* Hands extend to the oppressed. Jesus is now at the Right Hand of the Father making intercession for the Saints. He can't *physically* lay His Hands on the suffering to heal them. But Christians stand in His place in the ministry, armed with the provisions the Lord has provided them to meet the needs.

The first thing the Devil wants us to believe is that we aren't *worthy* to be involved in ministering and meeting the needs of the downtrodden. Individuals feel, all too often, that God may use *special* persons, but that He won't use *them*. And this is exactly what the Devil wants Christians to think.

An individual may be a weak Christian, bogged down with problems and faults, staggering under the weight of his personal burdens, but rest assured that God's Grace is sufficient. If you are saved by the Blood of Christ, you're a member of the Body of Christ. You have been given the mighty Name of Jesus Christ as your weapon and your responsibility. We are not personally worthy by anything we have done, but we are worthy in what Jesus has done. He has done it all.

You can enter into the Throne room of Grace anytime you desire — through the shed Blood of Christ. You can lay hands on the sick, and they

SELF-HELP STUDY NOTES

SELF-HELP STUDY NOTES

shall recover. You can cast out devils. You can pray for things to happen, and they *will* happen.

If you are saved by grace, you are not a sinner. This doesn't mean you're immune to sin, but you are a Child of God and a new creation. Jesus Christ is your elder brother. God is your Heavenly Father, and the Holy Spirit is here to be your eternal Comforter and Companion. Old things are passed away, all things are become new and we are raised up together to sit in heavenly places in Christ Jesus (Eph. 2:6).

Never picture yourself as a poor ineffectual, spiritual weakling. Christians are Blood-bought, Blood-washed Children of God. They have been set free through the Redemptive Work of Jesus Christ at Calvary and have become an essential part of the Church of the Almighty God. The Gifts of the Spirit are given to us to demonstrate the Power of Christ on Earth and to go forth victoriously in that power.

Now, through His Children, the preaching of the Gospel is everywhere, the sick are being prayed for and healed, and Saints are being rescued from the bondage of sin and shame. People are being delivered from the powers of darkness because the Holy Spirit is being brought forth in Christian services. Today, by means of supernatural gifts, Christ is manifesting Himself through the Holy Spirit in every part of the Earth. The Church has indeed become the Body of Christ — doing His Works, ministering His Love, and extending His Compassion to the needy.

In a very real sense, the Church is actually His Eyes, His Ears, His Feet, and His Hands — carrying on His Work on Earth. The Gifts of the Spirit are given to the Body of Christ to manifest Jesus to the world, to evangelize the lost, and to empower the Church in these latter days.

We believe the Word of God totally, and we believe that the baptism with the Holy Spirit (with the evidence of speaking in tongues as God gives utterance) is for the Christian world today. We believe that God heals and delivers the unsaved and sets the captive free. We believe that He answers prayer, and that Jesus Christ is coming back soon.

God is working in lives today. I personally feel Him working in my own life everyday, and I try constantly to draw closer to Him. Many are joining in a renewed commitment to the things of God and His Great Commission. We must get the Word out to a fallen world. It is imperative that *all* of God's Word be received. We are not to add to, or take from, the Scriptures.

Paul said, *"But he who Prophesies speaks unto men to Edification, and Exhortation, and Comfort. Even so ye, forasmuch as you are zealous of Spiritual Gifts, seek that you may excel to the Edifying of the Church. How is it then, Brethren? When you come together, every one of you has a Psalm, has a Doctrine, has a Tongue, has a Revelation, has an Interpretation. Let all things be done unto edifying"* (I Cor. 14:3, 12, 26).

SELF-HELP STUDY NOTES

The Gifts of the Spirit are not given to puff ourselves up, but to edify the Church. And for that reason, limitations are placed on the gifts. They are not given to be used indiscriminately, but only to accomplish God's purposes. The Fourteenth Chapter of I Corinthians gives instructions as to propriety in the service. There is to be order so the greatest possible edification will result. And while Paul emphasizes edification, Spiritual Gifts are equally necessary in our personal efforts to minister to those in need.

DELIVERANCE — The next Purpose of the Gifts of the Spirit is deliverance. The Devil has placed all kinds of bondage upon people. This can manifest itself as physical, mental, or spiritual sickness. Whatever the category, the treatment is deliverance through the Gifts of the Spirit.

PERFECTING THE CHURCH — Closely associated with the edifying of the Church is God's eternal goal of *perfecting* the Church. Certainly, the Body will never become perfect within the concept of Christ's Perfection, but we should ever strive to move closer to that goal. The Gifts of the Spirit are manifested through chosen individuals — Apostles, Prophets, Evangelists, Pastors, Teachers — in order that the Church might be perfected (Eph. 4:11-13).

Even though people are devout Christians, there is always the possibility they might be deceived. God's People need the leadership of God-appointed men who can discern between true and false. Paul put it this way in Ephesians 4:14:

"That we henceforth be no more children, tossed to and fro, and carried about with every wind of doctrine, by the sleight of men, and cunning craftiness, whereby they lie in wait to deceive."

Because this is an age of deception, the Church needs the Gifts of the Spirit more than ever before. Satan is doing everything in his power to deceive *"even the elect."* It is not surprising that many people are being led astray. Unfortunately, many Christians are being seduced along with the unwary. Anything may look plausible and desirable *on the surface*, but being filled with the Holy Spirit and armed with Gifts of the Spirit, one will be enabled to discriminate between the genuine and the false. Ultimately, everything must be based on Scripture.

Basically, the Gifts of the Spirit are given as they are needed for a particular circumstance. Many people say that the Gifts of the Spirit are not needed today because the Holy Bible has been compiled. Certainly, nothing can take the place of God's Word, but we *also* need the operation of the Gifts of the Spirit.

We are told in I Corinthians 12:1-4, *"Now concerning Spiritual Gifts, Brethren, I would not have you ignorant. You know that you were Gentiles, carried away unto these dumb idols, even as you were led. Wherefore I give you to understand, that no man speaking by the Spirit*

SELF-HELP STUDY NOTES

of God calls Jesus accursed: and that no man can say that Jesus is the Lord, but by the Holy Spirit. Now there are diversities of Gifts, but the same Spirit."

The Holy Spirit is thus the Author of *all* the gifts. He is the One who gives the Gifts of Healings, the Word of Knowledge, the Word of Wisdom, the Gift of Faith, Discerning of spirits, and the others. Paul went on to add, *"And there are differences of Administrations, but the same Lord"* (I Cor. 12:5). These gifts work in different ways, for the perfecting of the Church, but the same Lord is behind them all.

"And there are diversities of Operations, but it is the same God which works all in all" (I Cor. 12:6). Three times in these brief Verses, Paul states that it is by the same Spirit, the same Lord, and the same God. Then he adds: *"But the manifestation of the Spirit is given to every man to profit withal"* (I Cor. 12:7).

Everybody is to profit. The Church as a whole is to profit (and be edified) by these Manifestations of the Spirit. In the Eighth Verse of I Corinthians 12, Paul starts listing the Gifts of the Spirit. There are individuals who operate in all nine gifts, and are used by ministering in many ways. More often, however, individuals function in specific areas.

One person may have a ministry concentrated principally in the Gifts of Healings while another may be more routinely involved in the Working of Miracles. And, of course, the other gifts all play their parts in the lives of individuals. But often there is one particular gift that predominates in a ministry.

Needs of all kinds exist in the lives of people everywhere. The Power, Manifestations, and Gifts of the Holy Spirit are on dynamic display as many of these urgent and pressing needs are met.

The Church of the Lord Jesus Christ is being built up and perfected through the marvelous and mighty Manifestations of the Holy Spirit.

ANTICIPATIONS

It is interesting to note that discerning Bible scholars of the Nineteenth Century were aware that the lack of Spiritual Gifts within the Church was not caused by God, but rather by carelessness within the Church. These scholars looked forward to, and even predicted, a great last-day outpouring of the Holy Spirit — and with it a reappearance of the Gifts of the Spirit.

Michael Baxter, founder of the great Christian Herald, wrote as early as 1866 that there would come an increased Faith to work miracles. He declared that an unparalleled boldness in preaching the Gospel would characterize the still-to-come Pentecostal outpouring of the Spirit of God. He also pointed out that the various ministries and gifts within the Church were for the perfecting of the Saints and for the gathering and completing of the perfect Church.

He said these had not yet been attained and, therefore, the gifts could not altogether have ceased or been withdrawn. He contended that there would yet be a mighty move of the Spirit of God. At the turn of the century, Michael Baxter's tremendous prediction (or prophecy) was fulfilled. At the beginning of this century, there was a great Pentecostal outpouring with new manifestations of the Gifts of the Spirit. Great things were happening, with greater things yet to come.

In the book *New Zealand's Greatest Rival*, a brother remarked to Smith Wigglesworth — one of the greatest men of Faith who ever lived — that he was tempted to envy Wigglesworth his great successes. Smith Wigglesworth answered him, *"Young man, it should be the other way around. I feel like envying you."*

Wigglesworth went on to say that he had experienced three great visions. He said that the first two had already come to pass, but that the third was yet to be fulfilled. He said he would most likely pass on to his reward before this happened, while the younger man would no doubt live to participate in it. He stated further that he couldn't tell God's secrets, but he asked the young man to remember what he had said.

It is apparent that Brother Wigglesworth's vision involved a great outpouring of the mighty Holy Spirit coming in an unprecedented way during the last days, just prior to the Lord's Return to snatch away His Church.

In a sermon shortly before his death, Dr. Charles S. Price stated, *"Yesterday we sang Showers of Blessings, but now we are awaiting the deluge. It is coming and nothing can stop it."*

Like every precious outpouring, this glorious experience — which is about to burst onto the world scene — will not be the product of an established church or system. Multiplied thousands, hungry for God and spiritually alert, will respond to the blessings and Spiritual Growth God has reserved for them. We are seeing more people saved today than ever before — miraculously, wondrously, and gloriously converted — which is the greatest miracle of all.

But we are also seeing hundreds baptized with the Holy Spirit, speaking with other tongues as the Spirit of the Lord gives the utterance. The hearts and lives of multitudes from all denominations are moving into the realm of the Spirit. All this is bringing new joy, excitement, and blessings to many.

The joy of the Lord is present, people are happy in their worship of the Lord, and they are becoming acquainted with Jesus Christ. There are those standing on the sidelines, scoffing religious leaders in opposition, but they are powerless to stop the mighty move of the Holy Spirit. Rather, they are missing the blessings God has for them. People are searching for a

SELF-HELP STUDY NOTES

SELF-HELP STUDY NOTES

vital, exciting relationship with God. They don't want a dead church.

We are not advocating fanaticism in a service. However, unusual things may sometimes occur under the leading and the Anointing of the Holy Spirit. What is happening is a beautiful flow of the Spirit of God into the hearts and lives of people.

The atmosphere of worship and praise now found in many services makes one aware that the Lord is very near. There are many individual churches exhibiting this today, and it is exactly what the Church of Jesus Christ in general needs — the flow of the Spirit. It is available for us today through the wonderful Holy Spirit of God.

APPENDIX 'A'

BIBLE REFERENCES PERTAINING TO THE BAPTISM WITH THE HOLY SPIRIT

Promised by Old Testament Prophets
  Isaiah 28:11
  Ezekiel 36:27
  Joel 2:28

Spirit Came UPON Select Few as Recorded in Old Testament
  Numbers 11:25, Numbers 24:2,
  Judges 3:10, Judges 6:34, Judges 14:6,
  I Samuel 10:10, I Samuel 16:13, I Samuel 19:20

New Testament — After Outpouring Upon All Flesh Believers FILLED
  Acts 2:4, Acts 8:15-17, Acts 10:44-48,
  Acts 19:5-6, Ephesians 5:18

John The Baptist
  Matthew 3:11, Luke 3:16

Jesus Promises
  John 7:37-39, John 14:16-17, John 15:26,
  John 16:7

Jesus Charges to Receive
  Luke 24:49, John 7:39, Acts 1:4-5

The Initial Outpouring
  Acts 2:1-4

Believers Received (Filled)
  Acts 2:4 They tarried (waited) blessing the Lord – Luke 24:53
  Acts 8:14-17 Laying on of hands
  Acts 9:17 Laying on of hands
  Acts 10:44-48 While word was preached, He fell upon them
  Acts 19:1-6 Laying on of hands

Prophetic Fulfillment for These Last Days — Upon All Flesh
  Joel 2:28-29, Acts 2:16-18

Believers' Benefits
  Power — Acts 1:8, Luke 24:49
  Refreshing — Isaiah 28:11-12, John 7:37-39
  Teacher — I John 2:27, John 14:26
  Guide into truth — John 16:7

SELF-HELP STUDY NOTES

SELF-HELP STUDY NOTES

To witness of and reveal Christ the Word — John 15:26, John 16:14, II Corinthians 3:18

Comforter, Inner strength — John 14:16-17 and 26-27, John 15:26, John 16:7

Power to witness (authority) — Acts 1:8

Gifts resident with the Holy Spirit (Spirit-given abilities) — I Cor. 12:4-11

Fruits product of Spirit — Galatians 5:22-23

Quickening Spirit — Romans 8:11

APPENDIX 'B'

HOW TO RECEIVE THE BAPTISM WITH THE HOLY SPIRIT

SELF-HELP STUDY NOTES

AN ENCOUNTER WITH GOD

Every detail of the incident is etched in my memory. It's a startling experience to be awakened abruptly out of a sound sleep by the Spirit of God; yet, that's exactly what happened to me one morning in 1970.

It was about 2 A.M. At first I just remained in bed, basking in the sweet Presence of God. The feeling was so overwhelming that I was unconsciously weeping. And then — I sensed that God was trying to speak to my heart. I stole from bed and went to my prayer room, not an unusual act in itself, yet somehow this time it seemed . . . different.

Once in my personal prayer closet, I started to pace the floor, praying; as I did, God's Presence became even more overwhelming. I remember slumping to the floor with the feeling that my heart would burst within my chest. Much as we all like to envision ourselves as someday living in the continual Presence of God, I truly wonder if a mere mortal could survive prolonged proximity to the infinite Holiness to the Most High God.

Before too long, God began to speak to my heart very specifically. The message would change my life and ministry. Among other things He revealed these facts:

He would pour out His Spirit upon the United States, Canada, and the world;

Multiplied thousands would receive the baptism with the Holy Spirit;

I was to set aside at least one service in every crusade to be devoted *exclusively* to bringing about the baptism with the Holy Spirit for those who had been seeking this experience in their lives; and,

He told me I would see *hundreds* receive the baptism in individual services.

I remained in my prayer room until almost dawn and my one overwhelming memory of the incident is a great feeling of unworthiness. I spent some time pointing out to the Lord that there were many men far more qualified than I to bring about such a result. While agreeing to *attempt* the mission, I *"argued"* with God that I was really inadequate for the task.

His answer? I must *obey* the instructions He had delivered because this was *His* Message and *His* Mission, and I was nothing more than the instrument chosen to bring about *His* Result.

SELF-HELP STUDY NOTES

OUR FIRST HOLY SPIRIT SERVICE

How well I remember that meeting in Canton, Ohio. I had announced previously that the Sunday afternoon service was to be a *"Holy Spirit"* service, but I was unprepared for what took place.

Over the years, I had prayed for many people and had seen many receive the Holy Spirit baptism. My system was to *persist* in praying and counseling with individuals *until* they received. But how was I to do this with the *hundreds* who came forward at my invitation? It was a literal impossibility. If I had even *briefly* ministered to each of the individuals seeking the baptism, my schedule would have been thrown off for weeks ahead.

I was disappointed, I was upset. I did the best I could in an unreasonable situation and, seeing very little fruit from my efforts, I returned to my motel room with a heavy and frustrated heart.

Picture the disappointment and chagrin filling my soul. I was so depressed that I began to question whether God actually *had* spoken to my heart in that dramatic pre-dawn confrontation. Was this something I had dredged up to inflate my own ego? Who was I to imagine myself worthy of acting as God's instrument in bringing His wonderful baptism to *masses* of people at one time? Obviously, I had proven to myself — and to God — that my capabilities and methods just weren't suitable for a mass production situation. I wept before God as I reviewed these facts and asked where I had erred. No immediate answer was forthcoming.

Our next scheduled meeting was a Full Gospel Businessman's breakfast in Toledo, Ohio. As I prepared to address those assembled, I was impressed of God that I was to speak on the baptism with the Holy Spirit. At the conclusion of my talk, I again invited those seeking the infilling to come forward, and it was obvious that God had used this meeting to show me *His* mass production technique.

It was at this meeting that God revealed to me the basic method I have followed ever since. I want to pass on this method to assist you in receiving the baptism with the Holy Spirit if you haven't as yet experienced this life-changing encounter with God, or to enable you to assist others who are seeking this great transformation if you already have.

On that memorable morning, a large number came forward and scores of them immediately received the baptism. My ministry hasn't been the same since that day. I have subsequently seen innumerable throngs receive the precious infilling. Today in crusades, we *expect* to see anywhere from 200 to 600 souls instantly, gloriously, and miraculously filled with God's Holy Spirit. This happens routinely at our Sunday afternoon Holy Spirit Impact Rallies.

NOT AN OPTIONAL EXPERIENCE

SELF-HELP STUDY NOTES

The Holy Spirit is not a denomination, a movement, or a church. It is a life-transforming experience meant to be received by *every* individual who has turned his life over to the Lord and accepted Jesus' Sacrifice for his or her sins.

The great truth, that this is not an optional experience but something intended for every Christian, came to me while I was preaching a sermon on the Holy Spirit. Although I do not recall the thrust of the sermon I preached that night, I remember the sudden awareness that I must proclaim to everyone that the baptism with the Holy Spirit is not a voluntary or elective move on the part of the Christian — it is an *obligation* within God's Plan for His Children.

Are those Christians who neglect or refuse to seek the baptism going to lose their Salvation and be cast into hell? I'm sure they aren't. But God's Word commanded us to seek and receive this life-changing experience. Those who fail to heed this injunction from God are going to spend their Christian walk hobbled by restraints. These *won't* hinder the Christian who has *accepted* all that God has prepared for them.

Jesus (in Acts 1:4) *commanded* His Disciples to remain in Jerusalem until they should receive the promise of the Father and be baptized with the Holy Spirit. The specific word used is *"commanded."* That's strong language. There's no suggestion of option or decision here, and we are quoting directly from the Word of God.

This was the revelation that came to me suddenly the day I was preaching on the Holy Spirit. The baptism with the Holy Spirit is a must, an imperative, and circumstance and condition *commanded* by our Lord and Saviour, Jesus Christ.

The life of the committed Christian is not easy. Knowing we are the shock troops in a continuing battle against Satan and all his wicked henchmen, our Lord prescribed a procedure which would prepare us to *adequately* stand against the powers of darkness. Without the indwelling Presence of God's Holy Spirit to augment our poor worldly powers, we are going to be ineffectual at best, and perhaps soundly defeated at worst. Is it any wonder then that our all-knowing Saviour made this an imperative rather than an optional item of equipment in our Christian armament?

SUBSEQUENT TO SALVATION

I am well aware that it is commonly taught among many denominations that every individual *"receives"* the Holy Spirit at the moment of conversion. Theologically and Scripturally this is correct. It is impossible for a

SELF-HELP STUDY NOTES

Child of God to receive *anything* from God unless the Holy Spirit be a co-participant in that which is received.

However, there is a very real and definite difference between being born *of* the Spirit, and being baptized *with* the Spirit. A person is not *baptized* with the Holy Spirit at the moment he is saved. The baptism with the Holy Spirit is an experience completely separate from Salvation; it can only come *after* Salvation; it must be consciously *sought* by the Believer (Lk. 11:13).

I believe the basic cause for the weariness and Spiritual lethargy within the Christian church today is that the majority of Christians have been taught that conversion is an experience complete within itself and, once experienced, leaves nothing further to be received or sought after. Unfortunately, this doctrine, if accepted, produces seriously hobbled Christians and, all too often, churches made up in their entirety of intellectual, do-nothing, accomplishing-nothing congregations.

Notice, as you read through your Bible, how many times the word *"fire"* and *"power"* are used in conjunction with the Holy Spirit. Why is this? Because God's Holy Spirit is the firepower factor in the life of a Christian. Without the Holy Spirit dwelling within us, we are shells with little substance, cannons with no ammunition, engines with no fuel. Oh, to be sure, we go through the *motions* of Christianity, but where are the *results*?

Look about you. Almost without exception the movers and shakers within the Christian world today are those who have *not* hesitated but have come forward to accept God's glorious infilling in the Holy Spirit. It is the Spirit-baptized Christian who stands in the breach and *defies* the powers of Satan to move forward against God's Church.

And... knowing this to be true, I will herewith lay out the specific method, given to me by God, by which means I believe *every* Christian can come to know the quickening of the Spirit which comes only through the baptism with the Holy Spirit.

1. IT IS OUR BELIEF THAT EVERY RECIPIENT OF THE HOLY SPIRIT (ACCORDING TO THE WORD OF GOD) SPEAKS IN OTHER TONGUES AT THE SAME TIME OF RECEIVING THE HOLY SPIRIT. THERE ARE NO EXCEPTIONS.

Acts 2:4 says, *"And began to speak with other tongues as the Spirit gave them utterance."*

Acts 10 says that Cornelius and his household *spoke with tongues* and prophesied.

In Acts 19, it says the Apostles of John (when the Apostle Paul prayed for them to receive the Holy Spirit), *spoke with tongues* and prophesied as they were filled.

We, therefore, teach that every single recipient of the Holy Spirit speaks in other tongues (as the Spirit gives the utterance), when they are filled with the Holy Spirit.

2. THERE IS ONE, AND ONLY ONE, PREREQUISITE TO THE BAPTISM WITH THE HOLY SPIRIT — AND THAT IS SALVATION.

Many individuals and many denominations have conjured up and formalized any number of requirements which must be met before the saved person can aspire to the baptism. In all honesty, there is one and only one requirement within God's set of rules, and this is that the individual must be saved.

Read Acts 19:2 and 8:14-17. Both incidents clearly describe the condition of the Believers who had not yet received the baptism with the Holy Spirit. They were saved Believers. They had not gone through any rituals or met any lists of preconditions. They were merely saved Believers. Knowing this, the Apostles prayed for them for the reception of the Holy Spirit and they received just that! Clearly, this is confirmation in God's Word that Salvation is the only prior condition which *must* be met before the individual may become a candidate for the baptism.

Where then do all the lists of prerequisites come from? Unfortunately, all too often they come, directly or indirectly, via the intervention of Satan. Satan, more than any Christian, is well aware that the Holy Spirit is the *source* of the effective Christian's power. Of all the things in this world that Satan doesn't want, more Spirit-filled Christians would no doubt lead his list. He will, therefore, put any stumbling block in the path of a Christian, and do anything within his power to convince a wavering Christian that the Holy Spirit baptism is not *for* that Christian.

He will tell you you're *unworthy*. He will tell you that you must first work out your own solutions in the areas in which you aren't yet victorious. He will point out your remaining faults. What about your temper? What about envy? What about your battle to overcome cigarettes (or alcohol, or whatever)? Problem after problem will be brought to mind as failing after failing becomes grist for his mill.

But the *truth* of the matter is that nowhere in God's Word are we cautioned to do certain things before God and ask for the infilling with His mighty Holy Spirit. All these *false* preconditions are manufactured by Satan, not God.

Shocking as it may be to some Christians, I have seen *many* Christians baptized with the Holy Spirit while they still smoked cigarettes or had uncontrollable tempers or while they still worked to fight down improper

SELF-HELP STUDY NOTES

SELF-HELP STUDY NOTES

sexual drives. And isn't it logical that once they experienced the baptism, they were able to *overcome* these wayward impulses through the help of the Holy Spirit!

How like God it is, recognizing our earthly weakness, to send us the Comforter and the Strengthener while we are still *imperfect*, rather than demanding that we clean up our abode all by ourselves.

This, of course, is why Satan does everything at his command to prevent us from seeking and receiving God's help. I am sure Satan is capable of understanding Greek, and he surely knows that the Name of the Holy Spirit in the original Greek is *Paraclete*. Paraclete is translated as *"one called alongside to help."* What a beautiful way of expressing the role of the Holy Spirit! *None* of us is capable of *completely* cleaning up his life on his own. Probably, none of us is capable of *completely* cleaning up his life even *with* the help of the Holy Spirit. But how much closer we come when we have that wonderful help given to us by our loving Father.

This is why it behooves the father of lies to set up a list of obstacles to *prevent* us from seeking God's help in our lives. The more things we have to do *before* we seek God's help, the more time Satan has to work his devilment in our lives and in the lives of those we might have influenced. Isn't it logical to realize that *any* prerequisites work to the benefit of Satan and *not* for the good of the besieged Christian? Any Christian, no matter how well motivated and no matter the degree of commitment, is *not* helping his Christian brother when he complies or condones a list of *"musts"* which have to be met before the assailed member can hope to receive the help of the Comforter.

The baptism with the Holy Spirit is truly a *"come as you are party."* Recognize the methods of the enemy and refuse to accept his lies. It is God's Word, not Satan's word, that we should trust. The Lord will baptize you with the Holy Spirit even though you have weaknesses and flaws within your character and life. If you are sincere before the Lord and you recognize and *reject* these shortcomings, He will account to you your *recognition* of them, and baptize you with His Spirit.

Once you have God's Spirit working within your life — once you are plugged into God's Great Power Source — how much more favorable the prognosis for overcoming these faults. On your own, it's going to be an uphill battle. *With* God's great Comforter, it might still be a battle, but how much better the chances of victory and how much easier the contest.

Satan knows this, and this is why he promotes all the false requirements *before* you can aspire to God's next great step after Salvation. When he (or a fellow Christian) tells you that you must do this, that, or something else *first* before you seek God's baptism, reject that word. God's Word contains only *one* prerequisite — that you be saved.

3. INSTANT BAPTISM.

Another myth connected with the baptism with the Holy Spirit is that we must *"tarry before God"* for some indeterminate period before we can expect to actually be filled. Again, this is not true.

No doubt, the basis for this is that the Disciples were commanded to *wait* in Jerusalem before departing to spread the Gospel. The point missed here is that they were told to wait for the promise of the Father *before departing*. This was to be the beginning of a completely new phase of God's relationship with man. Tremendously important accomplishments were to be required of the Disciples. Unimaginable persecutions awaited them, and there was a whole *world* of unsaved waiting to hear the Word which only they could deliver. Jesus knew, human nature being what it is, that it would be only natural for the Disciples to strike out immediately on their missions. Instead He cautioned them that they were *not* to attempt their ministries *before* they had received the irreplaceable help of the Comforter.

Unfortunately, this had been twisted to mean that a waiting period is part and parcel of the Holy Spirit baptism. This simply is not true. Although both Acts 1:4 and Luke 24:49 recount this admonition from the Lord to the Disciples, other Scriptures clearly indicate there is *no* tarrying period involved.

In the Eighth Chapter of Acts, the incident is recounted where Peter and John came from Jerusalem and prayed for the Believers in Samaria. These were saved Christians who had not as yet received the baptism with the Holy Spirit. And what happened? They were *immediately* filled when John and Peter prayed for them and laid on hands.

Again in Acts 9, when Ananias came to Paul and laid on hands and prayed for him, Paul was *filled on the spot* with the Holy Spirit. Later, in Acts 10, while Peter was preaching a great Salvation message to the kinsmen and friends of Cornelius, *"While Peter **yet spoke these words,** the Holy Spirit fell on all them which heard the Word"* (Acts 10:44).

In Acts 19:1-6, an incident is recounted where Paul came across a group of Christians who were baptized Believers but who had not heard of the baptism with the Holy Spirit. Paul explained the baptism to them, and *immediately* they were filled with the Holy Spirit. Each of these incidents involves *instant* baptism with absolutely no suggestion of tarrying.

Now please don't misunderstand. It is wonderful to tarry before God. Quite frankly, I don't think a day goes by when I *don't* tarry before the Lord awaiting direction as to what He would have me do with one or more situations. I truly believe this is a major component of the Spiritual Strength within my life. But the fact remains, tarrying as a precondition to receiving the baptism with the Holy Spirit is *not* discernable as a viable

**SELF-HELP
STUDY NOTES**

SELF-HELP STUDY NOTES

Scriptural doctrine. All those mentioned in each of the above Scriptures received the baptism immediately. This would certainly tend to indicate to me that we don't *have* to spend a tarrying time as we seek out God's baptism in His Holy Spirit.

This doctrine is no doubt rooted, partially at least, in our all-too-human tendency to think we can *earn* the things we seek from God. Perhaps it is tied up with the doctrine of *"doing penance."* In truth, though, God does not run a redemption center where we come to pick up trinkets once we have saved enough *"Brownie points."*

Acts 2:38 clearly describes an occasion when Peter points out that the assembled would receive the *Gift* of the Holy Spirit. A gift is something entirely different from wages. We earn wages, but we *receive* gifts without expending labor for them.

Every Christian knows that Salvation is a gift, unmerited and freely given to the undeserving through the generosity of God. Yet knowing this, some try to make the baptism with the Holy Spirit (also defined Scripturally as a Gift) something to be earned. This is not consistent or reasonable within theology or Scripture.

The only major difference between the Gift of Salvation and the Gift of the Holy Spirit is that Salvation is God's Gift to the world, while the Holy Spirit is God's Gift to His Children. What do I mean as I say this, time after time, to congregations all over the world? Simply this: The wallower in the world (the sinner) may receive God's Gift of Salvation. Anyone, no matter the depth of his sins, may receive Salvation freely and without prerequisites. But God's Gift of the Holy Spirit is reserved for His own Children, those who have come *out* of the world through accepting Salvation. Only *then* do they become eligible to receive the Holy Spirit.

Beyond this, though, there are *no* prior conditions which must be met before we can aspire to receiving the Holy Spirit. As Paul said in Ephesians 2:9, *"It is not by works, lest any man should boast . . . it is the Gift of God."* Paul spoke specifically of Salvation when he said this, but the conclusions are the same. The baptism with the Holy Spirit *is* a Gift of God, and as such it may be received instantly.

4. TWO HINDRANCES CAN KEEP YOU FROM BEING BAPTIZED WITH THE HOLY SPIRIT.

There *are* two factors which can throw up a wall preventing the believing Christian from receiving the baptism with the Holy Spirit. The first of these is *unbelief.*

The person who comes forward to receive the Holy Spirit, while harboring doubts in his heart, can go away unfilled. Personal reservations as to the validity of the experience will almost surely prevent the seeker from receiving it. If you aren't sure something's real, you aren't going to pursue and realize the end result.

Satan, of course, uses this doubt to prevent many from receiving the Holy Spirit. And this, of course, is an important truth for every Christian to face. Satan *will* send doubts, but it is up to the individual Christian to *reject* them and stand on Scripture *claiming* what God has promised.

This again comes under the broad coverage of confession, good or bad. If we stand on our Christian position, throw the lie back in Satan's teeth, *claim* God's Word and God's eternal commitment to standing behind His every Word, we don't *have* to entertain Satan's lies.

Once we have done this, the problem of doubt is removed once and for all from our pursuit of the baptism with the Holy Spirit. Unfortunately, the second interfering factor is not as easy to banish from the equation. This is the matter of *yielding*.

Yielding is inextricably wound up with our all-too human need for individuality. We are taught from childhood to *"stand on our own two feet,"* to *"make our own way,"* and *"not to be beholden to others."* This is good advice within the worldly realm and will, in most cases, stand up in good stead when dealing with other humans.

Unfortunately, this human tendency becomes so ingrained that we find it difficult, when confronted with the necessity of yielding our will to that of God, to give up our lifelong search for *"independence."* God doesn't *want* us independent of Him. He is the loving Father who wants us to *turn* to Him with our every need. We are therefore torn by conflicting forces. On one hand our lifelong training says, *"Keep control of every facet of your life."* The other side of us, however, says, *"Give in and throw yourself on the Mercy of God."*

At the moment of seeking the baptism with the Holy Spirit, we all feel a strange pressure growing within ourselves, a bubbling up of a force demanding expression. So what are we to do? Are we to *"keep control of ourselves"* as we have always been taught, or are we to capriciously throw ourselves down a new path which leads to who-knows-where?

This is the moment when the problem of *"yielding"* is most dramatically brought to the fore. The business of speaking in other tongues isn't something that can be easily and logically explained within the perimeters of our overly sophisticated and scientifically oriented world. Perhaps this is the very reason God has set things up in this way.

Paul explains in I Corinthians 3:19 that God's standards and the world's standards are in conflict when the areas of wisdom and foolishness are concerned. God laughs at the things mankind values as great wisdom. Conversely, mankind in its smugness, laughs at those who *believe* the simple

SELF-HELP STUDY NOTES

SELF-HELP STUDY NOTES

unvarnished Word of God.

What could be more natural, then, than for God to choose something which could be basically *"embarrassing"* (and capable of being scoffed at by the world) as the benchmark of submission to His will? On the surface, what could seem *less* logical than uttering words we don't understand?

Yet that is exactly what God has chosen as *His* documentation of *our* willingness to yield the moment-to-moment control of our lives to Him. *Are* we willing to stand up and make ourselves *"fools for Christ"* as Paul was (I Cor. 4:10)? Of course, once across that great divide and recipients of the Holy Spirit, *"old things are suddenly passed away"* and that (which moments before *appeared* foolishness) suddenly becomes a bubbling forth of *"Living Waters"* — a praise song from the innermost foundations of our being.

Jesus documented the validity of all this when He spoke of *"rivers of living water"* springing up *"out of the belly."* Many things in the Bible are symbolic and *"belly"* certainly points to the very center of our Spiritual and worldly life. Where else then should we expect to feel these first stirrings of a *new* language crying out to be released and freed to praise the God who saved us?

Now let's make this abundantly clear. Once *over* this hurdle and into the great Holy Spirit brotherhood, it all makes perfect and immaculate sense. But before stepping across that line, it can be frightening and it can be confusing. When we, for the first time in our lives feel a compulsion to open our mouths and speak forth supposedly unintelligible phrases or sounds, the first rational inclination is to clamp our mouths shut so no one else will suspect there's something wrong with us. That, of course, is *precisely* the wrong reaction.

Sometime ago in a service in Florida, an incident illustrated this situation perfectly. Toward the end of the service, we had invited those seeking the baptism to come forward and we had prayed for them. A goodly number received, but one rather forlorn woman approached me at the end of the service and asked for personal prayer to receive the Holy Spirit.

"Sister," I asked, *"why didn't you come forward with the others during the service when we had a general call for this purpose?"*

"Oh, I did," she said.

"And you heard the instructions I gave to the group?"

"Oh, yes."

"Did you feel a stirring inside you, a welling up of unknown phrases or sounds crying to be brought forth?"

"Oh yes, I did, Brother Swaggart," she said, *"In fact it took every ounce of my strength to keep from just blurting it all out."*

Naturally, God's Purposes are brought forth with difficulty when our *worldly* self marshals up our free will to *thwart* the impulses put there for God.

I placed my hand on this dear, confused soul and explained to her that she must stop *fighting* God's leadings. Immediately she burst forth in tongues, gloriously receiving the Gift of the Holy Spirit.

Well, Hallelujah! The problem of course is that all too many Christians simply don't know how to *yield*. We are beset on all sides by worldly considerations. What will the neighbors think? What will the family think? What do *I* think? On the surface, speaking in tongues just doesn't seem to make sense. But what does the Word of God say? Worldly wisdom is foolishness to God and Godly logic is foolishness to the world. Sometimes in our Christian walk there are times when we have to *"let go and let God."* We have to take a giant Faith step forward into the unknown — trusting God for the result before we can *document* the result based on experience.

Our Lord and Saviour said, in John 20:29, that they are blessed who believe *without* previous proof! This is exactly the situation when God prompts us to open our mouths and *voice* the stirrings within us. Truly it is a situation of stepping out on Faith.

The very moment a Believer asks the Lord Jesus to fill him with the Holy Spirit (and he or she is sincere in heart), God's promises will *work. Down inside there will be words or phrases or "sounds" that will start to form and seek expression. This is the Holy Spirit "giving the utterance."*

Now this is an important point I want to emphasize: *That is as far as the Holy Spirit will go!*

From this point on, it is up to the Believer. This is the point where *you* must take over and do *your* part. It is up to *you* to part your lips, expel your breath, and *voice* the sounds crying out for expression within you.

It will no doubt sound unlike anything you have ever heard before. It will no doubt sound different from what you *expected* it to sound like. Satan will no doubt intrude and say, *"But surely this isn't the way it should sound."*

Ignore Satan and ignore your own natural skepticism. This *is* the Holy Spirit giving the utterance. Just open your mouth and start to speak out and, at that precise moment, you will have received the baptism with the Holy Spirit.

5. THE HOLY SPIRIT WILL NOT SPEAK FOR YOU.

Many Christians seeking the baptism believe, erroneously, that there is some type of coercion or possession involved in speaking in tongues. They believe that some strange trance descends on the baptized Christian and he *must* bring forth the message stirring inside him, whether he wants to or not. This simply is *not* the case.

SELF-HELP STUDY NOTES

SELF-HELP STUDY NOTES

A Spirit-filled Christian retains full control of all his faculties at all times. God's Holy Spirit is the ultimate example of propriety, courtesy, and restraint. The Holy Spirit does not impose, He *suggests*. No leading of the Spirit will ever cause any Christian to do anything improper. By the same token, the Holy Spirit will never *force* anyone to speak in tongues. Always — this is under the control of the individual.

Of course, the question then arises, *"But if it is up to me to speak in tongues, then it will be me speaking in tongues and not the Lord."*

Yes, this is true. But here again, who reaps the *benefit* of your speaking in tongues? The Lord's situation and the Lord's plans will proceed apace whether you speak in tongues or not. *Your* plans and situation, on the other hand, will be *dramatically* affected by your speaking in tongues. Let's look to Scripture to demonstrate what I am saying.

Acts 2:4 says, *"And they were all filled with the Holy Spirit, and began to speak with other tongues."* Now notice that the pronoun *"they"* appears once, but only because the second writing of it would be redundant. The *complete* Passage might read, *"And they were all filled with the Holy Spirit, and they began to speak with other tongues."*

Notice that this Passage does *not* say, "They were filled with the Holy Spirit, and the *Holy Spirit started to speak through them."* It is quite clear. *They* were filled — and *they* spoke with tongues.

The important, almost crucial, point to remember is that the Spirit gives the utterance (plants the *"message"* within the Believer), *but the Believer does the speaking!* There is no place in the Bible where a single word expresses the thought that the Holy Spirit either speaks in tongues, *or forces anyone else to do so.*

In Acts 10:46 it says, *"For they heard **them** speak with tongues."* Notice, they heard *them*, the people, speak in tongues, not the Holy Spirit. And again in Acts 19:6, *"And **they** spoke with tongues, and prophesied."*

I believe this may well be the greatest single hindrance to the receiving of the Holy Spirit by Christians. They have somehow come to believe that God will speak in tongues *through* them (like some kind of spiritual radio set); or He will take control of their tongue; or He will put them into some type of *"possession"* or trance. Possession is the domain of the Devil. God respects our free will (even when it sometimes gets us into trouble).

God does *not* overwhelm us with His Power and *"take over"* our normal functions. I believe that there are thousands, perhaps millions, of Christians who are ready, willing, and able to receive the baptism with the Holy Spirit but who are frustrated in their quest because they just don't realize that they are the ones who must open their mouths and *express* the utterance formed inside them by the Holy Spirit.

Have *you* been seeking the baptism? How many times have you sensed the Presence of God? You *want* to be baptized with the Holy Spirit. You've sensed God living in your life. His Presence has flooded and overflowed you. Deep down inside there were stirrings of words you didn't recognize as English or any other language you've ever heard.

But did you take the positive step of opening your mouth and *"speaking out"* these sounds? Probably not. Why not? Maybe you were frightened. *But more likely you waited for some miraculous "expulsion" of these words without your help.* Unfortunately, this is not going to happen.

When this next happens, just relax and speak out the words (not in English or any other language you have learned) that you hear or sense down inside of you.

The Holy Spirit is the One giving the utterance. *You* are the one who will do the speaking. To be perfectly frank, I believe most *every* Christian is ready at this very moment to receive the baptism with the Holy Spirit. The only thing holding up the whole glorious process is the reluctance (or lack of awareness) to go ahead and speak out what's bubbling up inside of you! God has given the promise. The Lord Jesus is the Baptizer. He wants you to have this experience. The only thing remaining is for you to step out on Faith and receive.

6. YOU WILL SPEAK IN TONGUES.

We have already stated that tongues are a positive sign and an internal component of the baptism with the Holy Spirit. But a few more words should be said in this regard.

The duration, *"quality,"* and expertise of *"your"* particular gift of tongues can vary dramatically from what you *thought* it should be. Some preachers and teachers even go so far as to teach that you must speak for some specific period before that you can be assured that you *have* been filled. This is not so.

Sometime ago a fine Christian brother came to me in an ecstatic mood. When I asked why he was so *"high"* he told me that the Lord had filled him with the Holy Spirit. In the course of the conversation, he mentioned that his tongues consisted of just one single word. (Would this make it a tongue?)

I was somewhat disturbed. I had never heard of it happening quite like this. I have spent the major part of my life in the great Pentecostal way, but I have never heard of someone receiving the baptism with just one *word*. I frowned and decided to caution him that perhaps he hadn't truly received.

Before I could speak, I felt a great forewarning fill my heart. Words seemed to come to mind. *"I am the One who baptizes and I am the One who decides how the baptism will come. Just join him in praising the Lord for it."*

SELF-HELP STUDY NOTES

SELF-HELP STUDY NOTES

I choked back the promptings generated by my years of Pentecostal training and tradition and thanked God for his receiving. He was literally almost delirious with joy.

Sometime later we met again. He smiled and said, *"Brother Swaggart, I got tired of repeating just the one word. Today tongues flow forth like a river from my heart."*

What would have happened if I had blurted out what I intended to say? I might have thrown a stumbling block into his path that would have *disastrously* impeded his walk with God. Thank God, I *did* listen to that still, small Holy Spirit prompting and *refrained* from expressing the misgivings that seemed perfectly proper within the context of my worldly experiences. How much, at *any* point in our Christian experience, we *still* have to learn!

All too often our preconceived (and often predigested and secondhand) ideas are *not* Scriptural. Of course, we enjoy hearing people flowing forth with beautiful, rolling renditions in tongues. We enjoy so much hearing those who can speak out in tongues for some extended period. But there is nothing in Scripture that states that this is the way it *must* be. At the time of receiving the Holy Spirit, the tongues given may be long and flowing, or they may consist of nothing more than a few gasping, stuttering syllables. This is no reflection on the validity of the experience, nor is it a mandate for the good Christians present to pass judgment on the validity of the experience. Almost without exception, those who *do* start out haltingly receive much greater facility as time goes by.

For those who have recently received the baptism and who are *"disappointed"* in the *"quality"* of their particular tongue, I would say this: Do *not* be disappointed or question the validity of the experience. Any preconceived notions on exactly what tongues *"should"* be can get you into trouble. Let me give an example:

Some years ago one of my dear friends was saved from a life of gross sin and iniquity. God performed a miracle of Redemption within his heart and life. A few months later, he received the mighty baptism with the Holy Spirit. *When* he received the tongues he was to speak, it was unlike anything I had ever heard before in my whole Christian experience. Although it may sound strange, more than anything else in the world it sounded like a burst of machine gun fire.

In my heart of hearts, I harbored secret doubts as to whether this was truly *"speaking in tongues."* Was it a sham? Had he in his desire for the baptism *manufactured* a strange tongue to comfort himself with?

I worried so about the matter that I went before the Lord with it. Should I counsel with him and explore this matter further?

Immediately some questions popped into my mind. *"Is he faithful?" "Is his life now clean?"* The answer, of course, was that his life was exemplary and there was no hint that he was not a good, committed Christian. After this I felt the assurance of the Lord that he had, indeed, received the baptism with the Holy Spirit, and it was nothing I should concern myself with further. I dropped the whole matter.

I thought no more about it for almost twenty years. And then an incident brought it to mind rather dramatically.

I was at home on this particular evening during one of those rare times between crusades when I could just sit and relax with a magazine or the paper with the evening news on in the background.

If I recall correctly, Walter Cronkite was speaking. Half immersed in my reading, I was vaguely aware of his stating that they would transfer to the United Nations where the newest member nation was being invested into the organization.

I only subconsciously noted the scene as the new representative came onto the screen with his flowing robes and his odd, round hat; but as soon as he opened his mouth to speak, I sat bolt upright. My flesh tingles with Holy Spirit Power as I recall the incident.

The words that came forth from his mouth were *exactly* the same as those of my friend's prayer language which I had heard so skeptically on that long-past day. The detached outburst of *"speech"* caused me to freeze in rapt attention as the paper fell from my hand. Tears began to roll down my cheeks as the Spirit of God brought the whole incident back to me so vividly.

Words framed themselves in my mind. *"Do you recall when you asked me whether your friend's gift was real? Here now, after a period of time, is your confirmation of the legitimacy of his tongues. If there were any remaining doubts, you can rest assured."* How good God is — and how different His time frame is from the impatient, harried pace we set for ourselves here on Earth.

There are all kinds of tongues. If all the languages of the Earth were to be catalogued and transcribed, I suppose the libraries of the world couldn't hold the volumes. It is up to God as to which kind of tongue we will receive at the time of the Holy Spirit baptism. We make a mistake when we preconceive just what this tongue should be like. When you receive *"your"* tongue, if it isn't exactly the flowing, melodious expression you've *decided* it should be, don't despair. It is from God. It is in His Plan. Just give Him the Praise and the Glory.

And a final word on this matter of tongues. I am often asked why God has chosen tongues as the specific sign of the baptism with the Holy Spirit. Of course I don't know precisely, and some suggestion of a reason lies in the matter of the difference in worldly wisdom and Godly wisdom, as mentioned. But another illustration seems appropriate here.

SELF-HELP STUDY NOTES

SELF-HELP STUDY NOTES

Walking into a darkened room, we reach to a spot on the wall and flip a tiny switch which floods the room with light. Someone who didn't understand electricity might ask us how the *switch* works to provide illumination for the room.

The answer is that the switch doesn't provide illumination for the room. The switch is only an insignificant cog in a huge and powerful force involving power grids, dynamos, and industrial might. The switch, though, is an outward *manifestation* of the great force we tap into, and an essential component *for* tapping into that mighty force.

The role of speaking in tongues is analogous to that light switch. As I said before, I don't know why God specifically chose the matter of speaking in tongues as His sign of the Holy Spirit baptism. But I know Scripturally that he did, and I know that *willingness* to reach up and flip the switch (or open our mouths and blurt out the pressure within us), is the action that taps into a distant powerhouse.

The Power of God, of course, makes any earthly dynamo seem puny by comparison. The lifesaving illumination dispensed by the Holy Spirit makes our poor incandescent bulb insignificant in comparison. The *power* available to those who hold the keys to the kingdom would melt down the mightiest power station in the wink of an eye. Why then hesitate to utilize the God-given *"switch"* which gives us access to this power for our Christian life?

Surely, the person who stumbles around in the darkness while a light switch stands on the wall next to him will be considered foolish. Why then shun the equally valid means of access to a greater power — simply because we don't know whether or not it is *"logical"* within the definitions of worldly wisdom?

7. YE SHALL RECEIVE THE GIFT OF THE HOLY SPIRIT.

One of the greatest mistakes Christians can make, when it comes to the matter of Holy Spirit baptism, lies in going before God with a *"hope so"* attitude. God's promises never contain *"maybes."* We should never, therefore, stand to claim them with a *"perhaps"* attitude.

I recall years ago talking to a Christian brother who recounted to me all the approaches he had used in *"trying"* to receive the baptism. He had fasted for days, he had prayed for hours on end. And despite years of such an approach, he *still* hadn't been filled with the Holy Spirit.

When I told him that his problem lay in the fact that he was going before God with a *"maybe"* attitude, he was absolutely stricken. As he thought about what I said, you could see recognition dawning on his face. He nodded, *"Of course, Brother Swaggart,"* he finally said, *"I've been doing just about everything except getting on with the business of receiving!"*

Without question, this is what we, as Children of God, should be doing. We should be *"getting on with the business of receiving."* When we were children, and it was Christmas morning or our birthday, as we sprang out of bed we didn't embark on some involved and complicated ritual — we just walked out of our bedrooms and *received* our gifts.

The baptism with the Holy Spirit, as we discussed earlier, is a *Gift from God!* It is ours for the claiming — with no ritual, no precondition, no *"ifs,"* *"ands,"* or *"buts."* God has it in His Hand and it is extended in our direction. The only thing remaining is for us to extend *our* hands to receive it. Nothing complicated, nothing mysterious, just a matter of saying, *"Thank you, Father, I accept."*

The time has come, therefore, for you to step forth and receive the great and mighty baptism with the Holy Spirit. No matter how many times you've been prayed for, no matter what hindrances you have *apparently* felt as you have sought this condition for your life, the time is *now* and the Gift is proffered for your acceptance.

Do not go to God with a *"hope so"* attitude. Whether in your local church tonight, or in your private prayer closet right now, step forth *believing* His Promises. God never lies. He said this was for you and for your children throughout the ages. Step forth and accept it without further ado.

8. PRAISE GOD IT'S YOURS.

You now have the complete method given to me by our Father to *ensure* reception of the Holy Spirit by *every* Christian seeking it. Over the years, I've received countless letters from people telling me they've received the Holy Spirit in their automobiles, in their beds in the middle of the night, in churches and in countless other places and times. No story about receiving the Holy Spirit is capable of surprising me anymore because it seems obvious that God is not restrained by any format when it comes to delivering this gift.

The fact of the matter is, whether or not you have at the present moment received the Gift of the Holy Spirit, the promise *is* to you. Don't let Satan tell you otherwise and don't let anyone tell you it isn't for Catholics or Episcopalians or Lutherans or whatever. As a Child of God, it is for you and the Word of God says it is.

Of course, when you receive this great gift you will immediately become a Pentecostal. What does this mean? Only that you have participated in the Pentecostal experience just as Peter and the Disciples did on that *first* Pentecost (and which *millions* have shared since). It does *not* mean that you just rush out and join some particular denomination, but it does mean you are going to find yourself in the fire-breathing, power-laden,

SELF-HELP STUDY NOTES

SELF-HELP STUDY NOTES

not-afraid-to-witness Christian you've always dreamed of being.

The great Pentecostal experience is a pan-denominational experience. I don't know of a single denomination which doesn't include within its membership a considerable number of Spirit-filled Believers. Our Lord paid a terrible price at Calvary that we might have the opportunity to receive the Holy Spirit. Before Jesus came, the Holy Spirit would, on rare occasions, fall upon certain individuals God had set aside for special missions.

After the death on the Cross, however (by making it possible for *any* man to be saved), *any* man could become a clean vessel for the residence of God's Spirit. Ephesians 2:22 tells us, in fact, this is the *reason* for Salvation — so we *can* become the habitation of God, *through the Spirit!*

Many Believers do not realize it, but this is the *basic* reason why God saves your soul, so that He may inhabit Himself within your life. He wants to baptize you into His Holy Spirit so that He may, little by little, make you into His Image. There is no way for this to come about *except* through the indwelling of the Holy Spirit.

And one final caution on this matter. If you have read the above and believed it and followed the procedure outlined, you *will* receive the infilling of the Holy Spirit. Do *not*, at that time or afterward, let Satan work to take this away from you. You may or may not feel a euphoria; you may or may not feel a complete reversal in your life when this happens. Different people react differently. The point is, your experience will be *your* experience even if it is different from that of *your* neighbor or your friend. It is still, nevertheless, valid.

It is Satan's constant method to attack us when we are weakest. A week, or two, or three, down the line — when you aren't feeling on top of the world — a small insidious voice will creep in and say, *"But are you sure that was what it was?"*

Stand against that voice and rebuke it in Jesus' Name. The father of lies is attacking you and trying to steal God's greatest Gift to His Children.

Now, armed with the great and mighty baptism with the Holy Spirit, praise God for what He has given you. *Then* take your place among the army God is choosing up for these perilous end times. Peter said it almost 2,000 years ago:

"And it shall come to pass in the last days, saith God, **I will** *pour out of My Spirit upon all flesh. For the promise is unto* **you** *and to* **your children**, *and to all who are afar off, even as many as the Lord our God shall call."*
Amen.